GH00707689

Wakefield Press

Awakening
FOUR LIVES IN ART

Eileen Chanin and Steven Miller are Sydney-based authors. Eileen Chanin is a historian at the University of New South Wales, and is currently the Menzies Fellow at the Menzies Centre for Australian Studies, King's College London. Steven Miller heads the National Art Archive at the Art Gallery of New South Wales Sydney. Their last book, *Degenerates and Perverts: The 1939 Herald Exhibition of French and British Contemporary Art* (2005), received the NSW Premier's Australian History Award. They also co-authored *The Art and Life of Weaver Hawkins* (1995). Eileen Chanin's other books include *Limbang Rebellion: 7 Days in December* 1962 (2013) and *Book Life, The Life and Times of David Scott Mitchell* (2011). Steven Miller's *Dogs in Australian Art* was published by Wakefield Press in 2012.

'Dora Ohlfsen's medals in their subtle, low relief, of necessity restrained as to light and shade, vibrate with an intense spirit of life as do some of those amongst the most famous medals of our Renaissance'
Rivista di Roma

'She built a record catalogue that became the envy of the commercial moguls of the gramophone world, whose initial scorn turned into grudging admiration and then furtive and finally open imitation. They learnt that there was one thing you could not do to Louise Dyer, and that was to ignore her'
The Times

'So far as paintings in oil and water-colours are concerned, it would not be easy to give a fairer impression of contemporary English talent than Clarice Zander's exhibition'
London Evening Standard

'Since her arrival in New York four years ago, Mary Cecil Allen has lectured on modern painting at institutions throughout the country and in addition has written two books on art which give an analysis of the creative principle expressed in the modern movement. In her landscapes and figure pieces America is reflected as seen by Australian eyes.'
American Art Digest

Awakening

FOUR LIVES IN ART

Eileen Chanin and Steven Miller

Wakefield
Press

Wakefield Press
16 Rose Street
Mile End
South Australia 5031
www.wakefieldpress.com.au

First published 2015

Cover designed by Liz Nicholson, designBITE
Edited by Penelope Curtin
Text designed and typeset by Wakefield Press
Printed in Australia by Ligare Pty Ltd

National Library of Australia Cataloguing-in-Publication entry

Creator: Chanin, Eileen, author.
Title: Awakening: four lives in art / Eileen Chanin and Steven Miller.
ISBN: 978 1 74305 365 2 (paperback).
Notes: Includes bibliographical references and index.
Subjects: Ohlfsen, Dora, 1867–1948.
                    Hanson-Dyer, Louise, 1884–1962.
                    Zander, Alleyne Clarice, 1893–1958.
                    Allen, Mary Cecil, 1893–1962.
                    Women sculptors – Australia – Biography.
                    Art patrons – Australia – Biography.
                    Artists – Australia – Biography.
Other Creators/
Contributors: Miller, Steven, 1962–   , author.
Dewey Number: 700.92

Publication of this book was assisted
by the Commonwealth Government
through the Australia Council,
its arts funding and advisory body.

CONTENTS

INTRODUCTION

Four women are the subject of this book. Born in Australia between 1869 and 1893, they made their reputations around the world: Dora Ohlfsen in Rome, Louise Dyer in Paris, Clarice Zander in London and Mary Cecil Allen in New York. Trained as artists, they achieved prominence in the early decades of the twentieth century.

Our interest in these women developed when we were working on an earlier book, *Degenerates and Perverts*. This considered the 1939 Herald Exhibition, a milestone in Australia's cultural coming-of-age. In it we examined the themes and ambiguities shaping the early modern period. We challenged the received view of modernism in inter-war Australia, presenting a picture of multiple, interweaving modernisms in contrast to the view of modernism in the arts as the succession of one avant-garde movement after another. We continue that examination by looking at the lives of these four women, our aim being to understand what, if anything, makes the Australian experience of the 'new' and the 'modern' distinctive.

As biography, this book does not aim to be exhaustive. It focuses on the period between the close of the nineteenth century up to the outbreak of the Second World War. The women were from colonial Victoria and were working from the early years of Federation, a time when women emerged with a sense of their own place in the world of artistic endeavour.

They were significantly shaped by conditions in Australia during the second half of the nineteenth century. Lady Casey, a contemporary who knew them all, noted in her book *An Australian Story* that women of their time 'were affected by the windy climate and sense of space in the same way that the larrikins were: they were spirited, independent, capable of improvisation'.[1] These qualities enabled them to meet the challenges of their era and become pioneers in their chosen fields.

Successful in their lifetimes, today these four are largely unknown, and it is our view that their remarkable lives and achievements deserve recognition. Although all four women are mentioned in anthologies and are now the subject of postgraduate research, only Louise Dyer has received in-depth attention, from Jim Davidson in his account *Lyrebird Rising: Louise Hanson-Dyer of Oiseau Lyre, 1884–1962* (1994). With the exception of Louise Dyer, much of the work they made also no longer survives. It has suffered the fate that Germaine Greer described in *The Obstacle Race* (1979), having been lost or assimilated by their better known male contemporaries.[2] Sculptures by Dora Ohlfsen in public collections, which for years languished in storage, are now lost. American and Australian collectors bought Mary Cecil Allen's work, yet today the whereabouts of most of these works is largely unknown.

These stories are more than an account of four disparate lives. They throw new light on the milieu in which these women lived and show the difference they made to it. They worked at a pivotal time, with the newly federated nation eager to assert a position in the world. Women also claimed their place in the new dawn of the nation. All four were awake to the true nature of art and regarded artistic achievement as central to Australia's 'birth' into the twentieth century and beyond. Dora Ohlfsen's sculpture *The Awakening of Australian Art* expressed this. In it, art and Australia are embodied as an Antipodean Venus in the centre of a sun, from which energy radiates. To them, more was needed than rousing images that glorified Australia's urban and rural landscapes, as painted by the men of the Heidelberg School. Australia needed proper systems to support and enable its young culture to flourish and each in their own way worked to establish this.

A number of key themes emerge with their stories. All four benefited from developments that brought about change for women in Australia. The new roles women assumed and the opportunities they created for themselves is a central theme. Each championed women's rights and played their part in breaking down barriers to women in the arts, which they achieved in different and sometimes competing fashions. Their stories highlight the ambiguity that is part of lived experience and challenge the neat schemas of both feminist and art history.

National identity, as it was being defined at the time, is another thread that runs through their lives. Dame Nellie Melba, Australia's first international superstar, was a role model. A close friend of both Dora (to whom she sent a photograph of herself, inscribed 'from your rival') and Louise, Melba believed that 'art is not national. It is international'.[3] Melba rejected local parochialism, commenting that 'while we encourage the best at home', Australians had to be reminded 'to welcome the best from abroad'.[4] Proud of their Australian origins, all four shared Melba's international outlook. Art was their ticket to escape from confining conventions, their means to join a diaspora of ability that knew no national boundaries.

This was in keeping with the optimistic assertiveness that marked Australian Federation in 1901. Over time however the national mood altered, such that by the nation's Sesquicentenary in 1938, horizons had narrowed under a preoccupation with protectionism and the establishment of a national history. Yet these four women retained the confidence and belief in progress that had stamped their childhood. The political rhetoric of the day made much of the fact that Australia was a 'new society', not as culturally rich as Europe, but more advanced politically and socially. Newness was apparent everywhere: Melbourne had sprung up within living memory. Cultural institutes – state galleries and museums, universities and libraries – were founded in a move to counter the brash materialism that many believed boom-time conditions were creating.

From their parents, all four learned the importance of activism and service. Novelist Henry Handel Richardson, a contemporary, spoke about how life at her restless father's side engendered a taste for change and improvement.[5] And such was the legacy of these four women. Arriving from Germany, Dora's engineer father built important public infrastructure, while Mary's developed medical standards in Victoria. Louise's father, also a doctor, entered politics and was elected to the Legislative Assembly, where he promoted progressive reform.

Resilience and resourcefulness were necessary qualities for surviving the boom and bust cycle that characterised Australian life during the depressions of the 1890s and late 1920s, with economic uncertainty also mirrored in the cultural sphere. Ambitious projects like extending the Melbourne Public Library and erecting the National Art Gallery of New South Wales were begun amidst expansionist rhetoric, but were left unfinished. For sixty years, the imposing sandstone façade of the Sydney gallery disguised an incomplete building behind. All four women contributed to the growth of institutions like these and played a critical role in developing infrastructure and supporting systems in the arts.

The First World War was the defining point for their generation. Over 300,000 Australian troops were sent overseas, with half of them wounded and nearly a fifth killed. Louise's brother fell at Bapaume in France and was buried there. Clarice's husband recovered from his physical wounds, but returned home lost in depression and alcoholism.

The war highlighted divisions in Australian society; it also created opportunities. These four women believed that art had a key role to play in both imagining and creating a new world order. 'The only language which is the same to all peoples', Mary told the press, is 'the language of art. Art is the greatest ambassador in the world'.[6] She supported the efforts of Russian-born Nicholas Roerich to achieve a 'Pax Cultura', or peace through culture. Louise similarly aimed to foster a spirit of international music by her cultural activities bridging Europe and Australia. All four were internationalists at a time when agencies of international cooperation were beginning to grow. Their histories, above all, are about belief in the power of art and its capacity to develop understanding and enrich lives.

Part 1

THE ARTIST
DORA OHLFSEN (1869–1948)

Opportunities, 1869–1902

Australian achievement was the subject of Sir Redmond Barry's speech given on New Year's Day 1869 in Ballarat, a town then barely twenty years old. Barry spoke with pride of the country's colonists, who were often criticised for being a people 'engrossed in the pursuit of wealth', but who had recently spent £70,000 on building a library in Melbourne. Ballarat's fine Italianate library – designed by Christian Ohlfsen-Bagge – was a similar achievement, Barry told the four hundred gathered that morning. He believed that each person there had an obligation to make the most of 'the opportunities which prosperity creates'.[1] Ohlfsen-Bagge, a refugee from unsettled Europe, had a profound sense of the opportunities afforded him by his new home and of his duty to repay these. His daughter Dora inherited both her father's creativity and sense of duty. As was later noted, 'she possessed in advance blood which determines character'.[2]

Christian Hermann Ohlfsen-Bagge, of Norwegian lineage, was born in the village of Grabionne in East Prussia (now modern Poland).[3] He migrated to Australia in the wake of the European revolutions of 1848–9. His prospects in the Australian colonies, with engineering and surveying qualifications, were promising. In the mid-nineteenth century Australia was marketed as 'an El Dorado and an Arcadia combined . . . where every striving man who rears a race of industrious children, may sit under the shadow of his own vine and his own fig tree'.[4] Christian was among the many German-speaking migrants who headed for Adelaide in 1849, where – just the year before – Australia's

Photograph of Dora Ohlfsen from *The Triad*, 10 September 1921.

first foreign-language newspaper had been launched: *Die Deutsche Post*.

Migrating at the same time was Hamburg-born Frederick Sinnett. With similar training in surveying and engineering, the two became business partners in Adelaide. When Sinnett moved to Victoria he remained in contact with Christian, encouraging him to join the Victorian Institute for the Advancement of Science, which he chaired. Sinnett's career, like Christian's, was distinguished. He published the first critical essays on Australian art in the 1856 *Journal of Australasia*.[5] He also launched Melbourne *Punch* and wrote an important account of Victoria for the 1862 International Exhibition in London.

A slender thread of archival records allows us to track Christian over his early years in Australia. From the middle of 1851 goldfield after goldfield was discovered in Victoria. Like many other young men in South Australia, Christian took off in the hope of making a fortune, with the Victorian census of 1856 listing him prospecting around Bendigo (plate 2). In 1857 he married Kate Harrison, daughter of the Victorian squatter Captain John Harrison and a descendant of the convict George Howe, the first government printer. Dora took pride in this ancestry, saying that 'on that showing I should be a good Australian'.[6]

Settling in Melbourne after their marriage, Christian entered into a partnership with the Swiss immigrant architect Alfred Kursteiner, before moving to Ballarat in the early 1860s with three young daughters.[7] Here he was employed as engineer to the Borough of Ballarat East, designing the library and the important Gong Gong Reservoir. With three older sisters – Minnie, Emaline and Florence Kate – Dora was born on 28 August 1869 and registered on the birth certificate as Adela Dora Ohlfsen-Bagge. Her mother had earlier lost two girls and one boy in childbirth and Dora was named Adela in memory of the daughter who had died almost a year before. She never used the name in later life.

In Ballarat, Christian was part of a circle of professional men who were building infrastructure and nurturing cultural life in the town. This 'big, rich, bustling, go-ahead township' attracted a stream of enterprising settlers from the larger urban centres, including, in 1867, the poet Adam Lindsay Gordon.[8] Gordon found Ballarat's population to be surprisingly international. Christian and his wife were among the one hundred residents of 'Scandinavian stock' who attended a dinner in 1869 to celebrate the marriage of the Crown Prince of Denmark to the Crown Princess of Sweden and Norway. On a visit in July 1871 Anthony Trollope was astonished by the development of the city: 'it is not only its youth . . . but that a town so well built, so well ordered, endowed with present advantages so great in the way of schools, hospitals, libraries, hotels, public gardens, and the like, should have sprung up so quickly with no internal advantages of its own other than gold'.[9]

Dora spent the first fourteen years of her life in this environment. She was shaped by Ballarat's pioneering spirit and retained a continuing affection for the city. In later life she completed a series of sculptures celebrating the pioneers of Ballarat. She left when her father, aged almost sixty, moved the family to Sydney in 1883 in order to take up a senior position in the Department of Public Works. Their new home at 4 Mona Terrace, Darling Point, overlooking Sydney Harbour, became, as the *Sydney Morning Herald* noted, 'a centre of hospitality in the 'Eighties'.[10]

In July of 1884 Dora, a month before her sixteenth birthday, enrolled at Sydney Girls High School, which had been established a year earlier. Her fellow students who went on to achieve distinction in letters and the arts included

Classroom photograph of Sydney Girls' High School at the time Dora Ohlfsen attended the school from the *Australian Town and Country Journal*, 25 February 1903.

the novelist and poet, Louise Mack, and Ethel Turner, of *Seven Little Australians* fame. Classmate Lilith Norman recalled that the school suited 'a lively, alert, intelligent girl . . . for whom a little French and drawing, the dates of the kings of England . . . were not enough'.[11] As a pioneer in women's education, the school broke away from the 'accomplishments' curriculum, which discounted girls as future makers of culture.[12] Sydney University had opened itself to women in 1882 and the school focused on preparing its students for university entry.

Dora and her fellow students were reminded of how much had been accomplished by the Australian colonies in less than a century and how women had been integral to these pioneering achievements. A sense of national pride was fostered in the girls, along with the ambition to extend and surpass these achievements. During the 1880s the Australian colonies enjoyed enviable prosperity. With talk of Federation, all were aware they were building a unique history because, in Barton's words spoken on the occasion of Federation, 'for the first time in history there is a continent for a nation and a nation for a continent'.[13]

Dora showed talent at school for music and languages. Her father was ambitious and encouraged his daughters to be likewise. Music, in particular, was an important part of family life at Mona Terrace, where the young Melba was a guest.[14] Dora and her sisters received musical training that took them beyond amateur competency. Her elder sister Florence Kate was an accomplished pianist and the younger Rita became one of the first women to give a recital on the Sydney Town Hall organ. An uncle, a graduate of the Berlin Conservatorium, taught voice and keyboard in Brisbane, Sydney and Hobart.

Dora studied piano privately with Austrian-born prodigy Max Vogrich and with Henri Kowalski, 'the prince of the pianoforte in Australia'.[15] Inspired by the current theories of synesthesia in art, which proposed that sense experiences could be transposed and with music experienced through colour, Kowalski enthused his students with the expressive possibilities of their art: 'by the nature of a chord, more or less discordant or more or less soft, the many effects of painting could be produced and found in music'.[16] Described as 'all fire, energy and spirit', he had an enormous impact upon

Dora.[17] She was distinguished among his students as one who played more like an accomplished professional than a pupil, and with 'very great executive brilliance'.[18]

Upon leaving school, she focused intensely on her musical studies and began to give recitals. She performed before the Governor and the Countess of Jersey at Centennial Hall on 16 May 1892.[19] Like all promising musicians, however, she aspired to the opportunities afforded by European study. At the age of twenty-three – the same age her father had embarked from Hamburg for Australia – Dora decided to follow her own dream. Berlin was the natural choice of a place to study. Theodor Kullak's *Neue Akademie der Tonkunst* was one of Europe's foremost music schools, specialising in piano.[20] Dora, who spoke German, had an aunt living in the city and her uncle had told her of the rich musical life there, where he had been a promising student.[21] Dora sailed for Germany in December 1892. Standing at 5 foot 8 inches, she was described as 'a tall, willowy girl . . . with a very distinguished manner, beautiful dark eyes and hair and a brilliant complexion'.[22] Ahead of her awaited rigorous training, which would take its toll on her.

The standard of training at Kullak's was very high. Along with the conservatory at Stuttgart, it was considered to be the most prestigious place to study the keyboard in Europe. Liszt believed that Kullak's pupils were the 'best schooled of any'.[23] Dora had private lessons with Moritz Moszkowski, viewed as the most skilful composer for the piano after Chopin, and performer Emma Koch. Such teachers attracted talented musicians from all over Europe to the school. Studying at the same time was the brilliant Josef Hofman, who was accepted by Anton Rubinstein as his only private pupil after falling out with Moszkowski. It is likely that Dora found the technical abilities of her fellow pupils daunting, as did American pianist Amy Fay, who said: 'It gave me a severe nervous headache just to hear them'.[24] When Fay's teacher 'used to sit down in his impatient way and play a few bars, and then tell me to do it just so, I used always to feel as if some one wished me to copy a streak of forked lightning with the end of a wetted match'.[25] Dora became just another one – in her own words – among '10,000 young pianists in that city, each dreaming of a great career'.[26]

Novelist Henry Handel Richardson, who had been taken by her mother to Leipzig, found her musical studies both mentally and physically taxing. Being 'hammered on the great anvil, shaped, tempered and toughened' meant that many musical students broke down under the pressure.[27] Australian poet Christopher Brennan travelled to Germany at the same time as Dora, possibly on the same boat.[28] He studied Classics at the University of Berlin and eventually married the eldest of two girls in the household where he was staying. His German sister-in-law suffered severe mental illness due to the stress of her musical studies.

Australians studying in Germany also found Prussian society rigidly conformist by comparison with society back home, and living conditions, particularly in Berlin, were spartan. Fay voiced their discomfort: 'only the newest homes have gas and water-works, or even the ordinary conveniences that *every* house has with us . . . the Germans are fifty years behind us . . . they have parts of meals five times a day, but never a complete one. They give me two boiled eggs for supper, so I manage to live, but oh!'[29]

Dora Ohlfsen, *Nellie Melba* 1919, copper medallion, 4.0 x 9.8 cm. *Collection of the Ballarat Art Gallery.*
Gift of the artist in memory of her father Christian Hermann Ohlfsen-Bagge, c. 1922.
The whereabouts of Ohlfsen's other portraits of Melba are currently unknown.

Despite all these privations, Dora found the cultural life enriching and was fired by her 'one ambition in life, to become a musician'.[30] A constant round of concerts and operas, with virtuosi like Rubinstein giving special recitals for students, kept her inspired and committed. Some ensembles, such as the celebrated Hallé orchestra from Manchester, she had already heard in Sydney. She made friendships in the musical world that were to last her for life, such as with the Italian baritone Mattia Battistini. Her own connections from Australia also proved useful. She introduced Melba to the impresario Jules Sachs, who was eager to engage Melba for a round of concerts.[31]

After three years of intensive study Dora completed her training and performed for the Kaiser. As she was about to embark on a performing career, she developed neuritis in the arm. She told a reporter that she suffered a 'breakdown . . . the outcome of overwork'.[32] Neuritis was a term that gained considerable currency around this time, as did neuralgia, and it was not uncommon for either to be given as an excuse for abandoning a planned artistic path. In Louise Mack's novel *Girls Together*, Caroline, a writer who leaves Australia for Paris, explained that her life changed because she 'had neuralgia and couldn't write'.[33] Dora's family however believed that her troubles stemmed from inadequate earlier training in Australia. Pianist Amy Fay, who went on to have a distinguished career, recognised that 'it is a great disadvantage to begin studying after one is grown up. One ought to be learning while the hand is forming'.[34]

Dora gave her physical condition, brought on by overwork, and 'too little money' as the reasons for her breakdown. Her father, who had been supporting her studies, could no longer draw an income from investments. The depression of the 1890s forced change upon many, as the experiences of other Australian artists overseas demonstrate. When family fortunes were lost, many women took up another occupation besides their art to make a living.[35] These developments affected Dora profoundly. She confided that they:

> made me so changed that I was not the same girl any more. I was so ambitious before, I just lived for my ambition . . . The shock of that one blow never left me, and it seemed impossible for me to be ever sure of realising anything else as long as I lived.[36]

Unsure of her future, she travelled to the Gulf of Finland to recuperate with friends.[37] It was probably at this time that she met Elena von Kügelgen, who became her lifelong partner. Born in St Petersburg in 1869, Elena's family came from the part of the Baltic region that today comprises Estonia and Latvia, but which during the late eighteenth century had become a province of Imperial Russia; it had a population of 125,000 who were predominantly German-speaking. The Baltic German influence was considerable in Russia, 'they pervaded every walk of life . . . the embodiment of efficiency and culture'.[38] Elena's family was well connected, with one uncle a physician to the Tzar and another the editor of the influential Petersburger German newspaper.[39] The family also boasted several prominent artists, two of them former court painters.[40]

Elena, like many others from St Petersburg who were associated with the court, often holidayed on the Gulf of Finland. In fact, her brother was ADC to Grand Duke George Mikhailovich, who had a villa there. For Dora, these connections must have made the prospect of starting a new life in the Russian capital exciting. Her aunt Alma, with whom she had stayed in Berlin, also introduced her to the Russian bridge engineer Stanislav Kerbedz, vice-president of the Siberian Railway. The railway linked the Russian empire for the first time, spanning the Asian and European coasts. Kerbedz's appointment to the board responsible for administration was confirmed by Tzar Nicholas II, who chaired the railway's Construction Committee.

Even with these highly placed connections, Dora had to forge a new life for herself. She was resourceful, recalling, 'I think I did everything under the sun. I taught, I coached students for the Conservatorium, I did journalistic work for the American Consul-General, I did anything that offered'.[41] Her association with Kerbedz was advantageous, as it gave her access to the administrative elite and, through them, to the Crown. She was engaged by the American Ambassador as a researcher.[42] At the time, Englishman William Steveni (who spent twenty-seven years in Russia) considered the best-informed individuals in the city, next to the diplomatic corps, to be the small group of English and foreign writers who 'got busy' searching for news items all over the city, Dora among them (plate 3).

She quickly gained familiarity with Russian events, writing articles on Russian music, theatre and drama for newspapers in America. They were published under the name of the Ambassador. She also wrote a study of the development of Russian music for a further series of articles:

> To enable me to do this the editor of the only Liberal paper then allowed in Russia placed the whole of his library at my disposal. Later the editor of the chief Conservative paper gave me the same privilege, so I had the use of two fine libraries to help me in my researches, which were extended to the history of the Russian theatre and drama and other educational movements.[43]

Music proved an important link between her former life in Berlin and her new and exciting time in St Petersburg. Her friend the Italian baritone Battistini was feted by the Romanov court, returning to St Petersburg for twenty-three seasons. Josef Hofman, a fellow student from Kullak's, received critical acclaim for his concerts during 1896. She was thrilled to meet the composer Glazunov, whom she described as 'tall, solemn, pale, who does not walk but moves'.[44] St Petersburg's cosmopolitan make-up reflected the ethnic diversity of the empire, and included many descendants of those whom Peter the Great had drawn from Italy, Denmark, France and England. Also by this time, Russia – the 'Kingdom of Shadows' – was opening up to the world. This was apparent with the building of the Trans-Siberian Railway and by the fashionable trend in the West for *le style Russe*.

Dora was eyewitness to this 'Silver Age' of Russian culture, which saw extraordinary development across the arts. Russian culture flowered through a rediscovery of its past. The Alexander III Museum of Russian Art, now the Russian Museum, opened in 1898, marking the progress which Russian art had made in fashioning its own style. Its curator was Grand Duke George. The 1900 Russian Pavilion at the Paris World Fair, with a handicrafts section designed by Alexandr Golovin and Konstantin Korovin, was one of a number of international displays prompting the widespread adoption and imitation of Russian style.

Many of the influential artists of the time congregated around the journal

Mir Iskusstva (The World of Art), published between 1899 and 1904 and edited by Sergei Diaghilev. Women were well represented among this group and Dora found their achievements inspiring. She described Russian women as 'the most fascinating in the world, and the most emancipated in their inner life. Even when they are quite children, there is no book they may not read and no subject they may not discuss freely'.[45] Higher education had opened up to women in St Petersburg from the late 1890s and educational opportunities were taken up with alacrity. Conscious of the extremes which marked Russian society, many women had become radicalised during the process, participating in social reform or in the revolutionary movements. As one foreign observer noted, 'women have given to . . . the revolutionary associations a very strong contingent. When courage, passion and self-abnegation have been requisite, they have often surpassed their brethren'.[46]

Dora's time in St Petersburg was crucial, since it was here that she embarked on her artistic career. She claimed that she began sculptural studies at the behest of 'voices which she believed to be those of spirits', an admission indicating her receptiveness to the heady mixture of spiritualism and theosophy fashionable in Russian society at the time.[47] While she 'dabbled in psychic and occult phenomena' during her stay in Russia, she had probably been exposed to the new spiritualities in Australia.[48] The brother of Frederick Sinnett, her father's friend and early business partner, was a prominent supporter of theosophy.[49] The movement, with its evolutionary focus, had a particular resonance for Australians. With colonies barely a century old and with marked evidence of progress made – and being made – Australians had a keen progressive sense. Theosophy's appeal lay in its emphasis on building a new civilisation and a better future. Underpinning theosophical teaching was a belief that the world exists for the purpose of evolving the spirit and that social systems should be constructed to further this end. Artists particularly were attracted by the Theosophical Society's objective of forming a Universal Brotherhood of Humanity.

It is not surprising that theosophy found fertile soil in Russia, where a deep respect for spirituality and mysticism already existed. Dora's time in Russia coincided with a period of reaction against realism and naturalism across the arts. Rather than imitating the visible world, artists sought instead to express the inner life, by suggestion and evocation. This anti-rationalist focus became known as symbolism, named after *les symbolistes*, a group of French writers, and flourished in the arts between 1885 and 1910. In 1886, the poet Jean Moréas wrote that art should aim to clothe ideas in sensual forms and to resolve the dichotomy between the material and spiritual worlds. Dmitry Merezhovsky, who popularised French Symbolism in Russia, wrote in his book of poetry *Symbols* (1892) – quoting Goethe – that all art must be symbolic. He defined the three basic elements of the new art as mystic content, symbols and a broadening of artistic impressionability, a theory that resonated with theosophical principles. Symbolism was a broad philosophical movement that impressed an outlook across the arts, rather than dictating a particular style.

One of the most widely read thinkers of the time was Friedrich Nietzsche, whose ideas on Apollonian and Dionysian dichotomy, eternal recurrence, the Superman and the 'Will to Power', influenced Russian artists and poets – as well as the anarchists working to overthrow the established political order.[50] Tapping into Nietzsche's analysis of the irrational Dionysian impulse, symbolists reworked the stories of Oedipus and the Death of Orpheus, while a revival of interest in Greek culture also led some to critique traditional morality and to reappraise homosexuality. Magnus Hirschfeld, an author Dora later regarded highly, established the Berlin Scientific-Humanitarian Committee in 1897, arguably the first gay activist group.[51] Dora's art, correspondence and comments to the press indicate that these contemporary philosophical and artistic currents all influenced her.

Dora's interest in sculpture, and more particularly medallions, probably dates from her six years in Russia. It is not unlikely that she was encouraged by Grand Duke George himself, who had the largest collection of glyptic art in Russia and who wrote a number of standard texts on the art of medals. What survived of his collection was sold after the revolution to the Smithsonian Institution in America. He may have even been 'the nobleman' she said encouraged her to study art formally. The royal family took note of her work, buying a few examples from the Imperial Bazaar.[52]

Dora gave as the reason for her move to Italy her desire to further her art

11

studies. However, working for the American Consul-General in 'the rather delicate task of getting "copy" for him' gave her a realistic sense of the fragile political situation in Russia.[53] By the end of 1901 even the Australian press was lamenting a government that censored private correspondence and controlled the press: 'the result is a prolonged darkness, in which even strong men might well lose their nerve'.[54] Dora had witnessed the unprecedented growth of St Petersburg, with the city becoming the world's fifth largest metropolis. Yet for more than sixty per cent of the population, metropolitan life meant soup kitchen queues, cramped flophouses and unrelenting toil. These conditions were fertile soil for the democratic principles advanced by the Decembrists and their followers. Urban riots increased as the new century approached. Strikes and street protests were brutally put down, adding to the tensions between officials and workers. Dora recalled, 'One lived under espionage everywhere, and did not dare even to utter the word "Emperor" in the street. It may have been quite harmless, but then you were under suspicion if overheard because, who knew, you might be talking in cipher and actually preaching sedition'. Her sympathies lay with 'the young university students [who] were most interesting, and were almost all members of societies plotting against the Government'.[55]

By 1902 it was clear that she would have to leave Russia. With her interest in sculpture, Italy was a natural choice.[56] Moreover, for many Russian intellectuals at the turn of the twentieth century Italy represented an ideal. A romantic phenomenon of 'longing for Italy' (*toska po Italii*) characterised the period, with artists like Nikolai Gogol spending extended periods working in Rome.[57] Even the Decembrists invoked Republican Rome in their reformist agenda for Russia's autocracy. Symbolist poets wrote of Moscow as the 'Third Rome'. When Dora and Elena moved to Rome they too could say, with the symbolist poet Valerii Briusov:

> Not as a stranger did I come
> To the Roman Forum – to this country of graves,
> But as if to a familiar world.[58]

Rome, 1902–1920

Dora arrived in Rome at a time when the city was undergoing rapid and radical change.[59] The couple found a large studio with an apartment attached at 72 via San Nicola da Tolentino (plate 1). This was on the high ground to the east of the city, not far from the Central Railway Station and a stone's throw from the Piazza Barberini with its famous Triton fountain. Opposite her apartment block was the handsome church of San Nicola. Her plan was to study painting, but she quickly realised that 'sculpture attracted me most, and I worked at that'.[60]

Near her studio, the baroque jewel box of Santa Maria della Vittoria housed Bernini's theatrical depiction of St Teresa in ecstasy. Close by, in Santa Maria degli Angeli, the church that Michelangelo built in the remains of the Diocletian baths, stood the giant figure of Saint Bruno by the French sculptor Jean Houdon. Westward stood the Villa Medici, with its concourse of garden statuary and masterworks by Bernini inside. Along the Via Salaria, in the Villa Albani (sold in 1868 to Prince Torlonia and opened to the public) was a bronze of Apollo Sauroktonos, considered by art historian Winckelmann to be the Praxiteles statue described by Pliny, and arguably the most beautiful bronze in the world. Further afield, the Vatican and Ludovisi collections contained numerous sculptural masterpieces from antiquity, including *Aphrodite rising from the sea* – found in 1887 – which Dora believed to be 'the divinest expression of Greek art at its highest'.[61]

The streets around her studio housed hotels and studios and swarmed with foreigners, both tourists and residents. Visiting Australian painter Louise Riggall gives a picture of Dora's neighbourhood. Riggall travelled to Rome with three companions in 1905, settling in a *pensione* opposite Dora's studio. Riggall recorded her impressions in her diary: foreigners are everywhere; swarms of noisy Germans pass them; priests scuttle away from the women like 'black beetles'; the Italians appear picturesque, carrying everything on their heads, women labouring alongside men. Linking up with three other women, Louise and her companions have dinner one night in a nearby studio. On rugs and cushions, around a table decorated with pink almond blossom, they roast chestnuts on the gas and 'play the Bohemian'. They christen one of their new companions 'The Lady of all Nations', because 'she belonged to so many nationalities and spoke nearly every language under the sun'.[62] It is not implausible that this was a description of the Russian-born, Baltic German, Spanish-speaking von Kügelgen, who was fluent in six languages – or indeed of Dora herself.

Photograph of Piazza Barberini, Rome, c. 1900, showing the entrance to Dora Ohlfsen's street on the left. *National Art Archive, Art Gallery of New South Wales*

Riggall's journal captures something of the fluid cosmopolitan community amongst which Dora lived in Rome. This community created a flourishing trade in painting, sculpture and antiques, with little having changed in terms of how art was made and sold since the English sculptor John Flaxman had been part of Rome's sophisticated artistic community in the late eighteenth century. He provides a picture of artists and collectors from all over the world being drawn to Rome in the hope of garnering a share of the commissions available or finding collectors' bargains. Artists working in this environment were reliant on patrons and mentors to advance their careers. While Flaxman found this demanding and more competitive than he was prepared to entertain, Dora was not deterred.

New sculptors learned and gained work from the studios of more established artists, while the studio was an essential base from which to sell work. Flaxman found that Canova's studio was a meeting place for many foreign visitors and where less prominent sculptors might obtain commissions. Dora's building was occupied by American celebrity sculptor Franklin Simmons, who had become rich from his portrait busts of visiting Americans.[63] Up until his death in 1913, Simmons's studio, like Canova's, was a destination for the art-minded visitor to Rome. Whether Dora benefited from this in terms of sales is unknown, but it would be unusual if she had not. While newspaper reports describe work in bronze, lead and marble made by her, one of the difficulties with Dora's history is that much of her work has not survived. Whether transported beyond Italy or remaining there as unknown artistry, these works have not been traced since.[64]

The Australian press reported that Dora was a student of the French Academy, yet the Academy was only open to male French citizens at this time, which means that she probably attended the less formal evening drawing classes there.[65] Although scholarship winners at the various Roman academies were discouraged from taking private students, many did so to supplement their income.[66] Female artists like Dora not only benefited from their teaching but also from their connections. The French Academy was an important cultural centre in Rome – its celebrations in 1903 marking a hundred years of residence at the Villa Medici were opened by the King – and Dora probably met her earliest patrons and subjects there, many of whom were from Italian aristocratic circles.

The artists she cited as teachers included the French sculptor Camille Alaphilippe, in Rome on the Prix de Rome between 1898 and 1902, and the Valencia-born realist painter Manuel Benedito-Vives, on a bursary at the Spanish Royal Academy in Rome between 1899 and 1904. She also said that she took lessons with Paul Landowski, who won the Prix de Rome for sculpture in 1900 and would become later renowned for his statue of Christ the Redeemer (1931) above Rio de Janiero. Of greatest influence was the engraver Pierre Dautel, in Rome between 1903 and 1905, also on the Prix de Rome. Having trained at the École des Beaux-arts in Paris, he was known for medallion work, favouring intimate expression over monumental statuary. He was responsible for reviving medallion art at the turn of the century and his work was often compared with that of the Renaissance artist Pisanello.

Aspiring to work in all scales, across different materials, Dora was nonetheless realistic. She followed Dautel by specialising in medal art and quickly achieved success. The years between 1903, when she first exhibited in the annual exhibition of the *Società Amatori*, and 1909, when she became the first Australian to be included in Forrer's international *Biographical Dictionary of Medallists*, were extremely productive.[67] The annual exhibitions of the *Società Amatori* were a yearly highlight of the Roman art calendar and only those artists invited by the central committee could exhibit. Dora showed medallions, bas-reliefs in bronze and sculptures in 1903, 1906 and 1907, and a painted portrait in 1908.[68]

Much of this work has not survived. In her first group of exhibited work she included a portrait of Elena, which was later reproduced in the popular cultural journal *Rivista di Roma*.[69] A medallion of a mother and child, now in the collection of the Art Gallery of New South Wales, was exhibited in 1907 amongst a group of 'studies of children' (plate 5).[70] The Australian press followed her progress, noting that she 'has exhibited every year since she entered upon her new career'.[71]

Other portraits completed in these years included many musicians, among them Mattia Battistini and the Ukrainian soprano Salomea Krusceniski, who was popular in Italy, where she settled from 1903. Dora modelled both in 1906. Dora and Elena kept up their Russian connections, along with their musical ones. The social pages reported their presence at a grand reception given by the Russian Ambassador, where Elena, who was a celebrated beauty, was singled out as 'ravishing in a beautiful black dress'.[72] Dora and Elena clearly made an attractive couple, their sense of style and diversity of interests, combined with an element of bohemianism, gave them access to a wide range of potential patrons. At this time Elena was working at the Spanish Academy, possibly modelling.

At the beginning of 1907 *L'Italie* gave an account of a salon at Dora's studio, which illustrated the connections she had made with celebrities like Donna Nicolleta Grazioli, the Countess de Lutzow and Princess Maria Rospigoliosi, formerly the American heiress Marie Reid Pankhurst.[73] Many of Dora's patrons were from the Italian nobility, at a time when the patronage of living artists had become fashionable through the activities of the art-minded Queen Margherita. Church commissions came from Cardinal O'Connell of Boston and Josef Alteneisel, Prince-Bishop of Brixen in the Tyrol.

In the following year, the *Rivista di Roma* included a feature article on her by Arturo Jahn Rusconi, an art historian and critic who published widely, from monographs on Botticelli and Michelangelo, to museum handbooks. In 1907 he had singled out Dora's work in the annual exhibition of the *Società Amatori*, writing of her:

> delightful bas-reliefs in bronze, portraits and various compositions, executed with tremendous grace and subtlety of spirit. This year, as well as some portrait medals and plaquettes finely worked up, she has exhibited a very beautiful plaque, *Autumn*, which together with refined taste also demonstrates mastery of sculptural modelling.[74]

Rusconi went further in the *Rivista di Roma* article and claimed that Dora's 'medals in their subtle, low relief, of necessity restrained as to light and shade, vibrate with an intense spirit of life as do some of those amongst the most famous medals of our Renaissance'.[75]

Rusconi's article reproduced the 1907 medal *The Awakening of Australian Art*, a work with which Dora achieved international recognition. She exhibited it in a centenary exhibition organised by the city of Paris at the Petit Palais. The French Government acquired the piece, the first work of Dora's to enter a public collection. For her, this was the realisation of an ambition first conceived when she had read the Ukrainian-born painter Marie Bashkirtseff, whose journal described the struggle of women artists.[76] As Dora explained to a journalist:

> when I was walking through the Petit Palais with some friends, we came to one of her [Bashkirtseff's] pictures. It was really the thought

of how young she was, and of what she accomplished in so short a time before her death, that inspired me more than her work. I walked on quickly away from all the others, and I said to myself, 'Oh, if I could only have my works exhibited there'. Six months later the letter came asking me to send an exhibit.[77]

The front of *The Awakening of Australian Art* shows a naked woman standing in profile. Australia is personified as the New Dawn or Venus rising from the sea. She stands on land with native Australian vegetation, the stylised rays of a rising sun behind her. The motif of the rising sun had been used from 1902

Dora Ohlfsen, *The Awakening of Australian Art* 1907. Photograph of the plaster cast of the medal.
National Art Archive, Art Gallery of New South Wales, Sydney.

as a badge by the Australian army and became symbolic of the Anzacs after the First World War. It was also a common decorative feature in *Art Nouveau* graphics. The reverse of the medal shows a lone horseman watching over a flock of grazing sheep on a wide plain. One Australian critic noted that this type of scene would normally form the subject of a large canvas, but that Dora had managed to convey in miniature 'the whole soul and spirit of wide spaces, of marvellous solitude and of newness and freedom' (plate 4).[78]

Dora's modelling on this medallion is looser and bolder than her earlier work. She admired the eclectic work of Rodin's assistant Bourdelle. His style combined the naturalism that inspired British artists of the 'New Sculpture' movement with a simple, more abstract approach. British artists reacting against the neoclassicism of late nineteenth-century sculpture sought to replace an 'inanimate idealism', as one contemporary critic noted, 'with a sturdy realism . . . striving for actuality, character and individuality'.[79] Dora's work shows that she shared some of these concerns, even though her sources of inspiration were clearly continental rather than English. She had seen the work of Rodin and Bourdelle in France: they were less interested than their British counterparts with anatomical naturalism, emphasising the rhythmic and expressive qualities in sculpture and making an inventive use of space. Australian opinion, however, placed Dora's art narrowly within a familiar British context. The *Argus* likened her nude 'Australia' to Bertram Mackennal's *Circe*.[80]

Comparison with Mackennal was undoubtedly intended as a compliment to Dora. In 1908 Mackennal was a well-established figure, having secured the commemorative medals commission for the London Olympics and shortly after becoming an associate of the Royal Academy. It is interesting to speculate about what she made of this comparison. She envied his success, joking later with the Director of the National Art Gallery of New South Wales, 'I am not Mackennal, at whose feet Australia pours mines of liquid gold'.[81] Yet she came to believe that she was his successor as Australia's foremost sculptor, writing in 1932 that sculpture for the Victorian War Memorial should be entrusted to her, as 'I know I am the only Australian sculptor eligible for this work, Mackennal being dead'.[82]

Dora's figure of Australia lacks the demure reticence normally expected of the female nude in art. She is all 'sinuous and energetic', as one review noted, 'her hair streaming in the wind, the light of dawn falling upon her face'.[83] The naked female form was a recurrent image in Dora's art, represented allegorically and figuratively as Spring, Dawn, Passion, Salome and other subjects, although her representations of this subject differed from those of her male contemporaries.[84] All Dora's nudes are recognisable individuals, not a type of eroticised femininity.[85] For Dora the naked female body also had a deeply personal symbolism: it was an image of the artist freed from European conventions. She explained to a journalist:

> A new country gives great gifts to her daughters . . . the air must account for it – the feeling of newness and vitality and power. Australians have [this] splendid heritage, the nervous energy that inspires them with the desire to get everything out of life. We are untrammelled by traditions. We may begin where we please, and yet, unabashed, hold out our hands for fame, gold, and power.[86]

Dora's understanding of Australia's position in the world anticipated many of the themes taken up by 'vitalist' artists in the years between the wars. From Nietzsche Dora had learned an appreciation for 'the energised life-affirming body', which holds sway over the intellect and reason.[87] Yet at the same time she subverted conventional Nietzschean ideology by feminising the figure of Dionysius in her statue of him, unlike Nietzsche who cast Dionysius as the personification of masculine energy (plate 14). The Australian vitalists Rayner Hoff and Norman Lindsay depicted the sexualised energy that drives creation in terms of masculine virility. Despite claims about the complementary importance of the feminine, this thinking relegated women to the traditional role of nurturers and supporters in the creative process.

The Awakening of Australian Art was featured in a presentation of Australian women's art at the Franco-British exhibition in London during 1908. It was singled out for its expressive qualities and Dora was presented with an award, alongside Thea Proctor and New Zealander Frances Hodgkins.[88] The medal was then offered to the trustees of the National Gallery of New South Wales, but

Dora Ohlfsen *Le septième voile* 1911, present whereabouts unknown.
National Art Archive, Art Gallery of New South Wales, Sydney.

21

it was rejected by them.[89] It would have been an unusual acquisition since very few works by Australian sculptors were in the collection, apart from Theodora Cowan's memorial marble busts of two founders of the gallery. At the time the gallery was awaiting the delivery of a commissioned bas-relief panel for the façade of the building from the English-born Countess Feodora Gleichen. She represented a benchmark for women sculptors: she was successful, attracting commissions from around the world, yet her background gave her advantages open to few others. A grand-niece of Queen Victoria, Feodora lived in St James's Palace, where she and her sister Helena were encouraged by their sculptor father 'to go ahead as if we had been boys'.[90] However, even with these advantages, working as a professional sculptor was not easy for Gleichen since women's work was routinely assumed to be inferior. Restricted opportunities in art training also hampered them from fully developing their talents. For most of the nineteenth century women were barred from the major art schools, and the facilities available to them were of lower standard than those open to men. Art schools for women focused on portraiture and still life painting, subjects regarded as suitable to women's natures and abilities.

Sculpture was seen as a masculine art, requiring physical force and dirty procedures that entailed working with skilled trades, knowledge of which was considered beyond the experience of most women.[91] Between 1908 and 1914 only five solo exhibitions by woman sculptors were staged in London. Sarah Bernhardt appears to have been the first, with Feodora Gleichen following in 1907. Paradoxically, living in Italy, a country so often characterised as patriarchal, had advantages for women sculptors, particularly foreign ones. Gleichen came to Rome, attracted by its collections, the availability of materials and the cheaper cost of living. The pace of life was slower than in London or Paris, but it was still cosmopolitan. 'If you stay long enough in Rome you meet everybody you have ever heard of. All the world comes here sooner or later' said American writer and Roman resident Maud Howe Elliott.[92] As foreigners in Italy, women like Gleichen and Dora enjoyed an independence difficult to achieve elsewhere, with Italians largely indifferent to the activities of the *stranieri*. As one expatriate wrote, 'this attitude on the part of Italians makes living among them very easy and gives to some people who have suffered from bigotries and narrow-mindedness . . . a spiritual freedom which is to be had nowhere else in the world'.[93]

Conditions for Italian women, however, were different. The sanctity of the family constrained their activities, at least in the public sphere. An article written in 1899 by Italian poet and philosopher Dora Melegari for the *Contemporary Review* concluded that 'the number of women murdered annually for love, jealousy, or vengeance is grimly significant . . . In the land of the sun the psychology of woman is still dependent upon that of man'.[94] Yet Italians were not immune from the changes marking the times, and an Italian feminist movement was emerging.[95] Dora Ohlfsen watched the slow but gradual emancipation of Italian women: 'Italian men are learning to respect them', she said, 'instead of regarding them as beautiful and fragile toys. The ideas of the young girl are also changing'.[96] Supportive of fledgling Italian feminism, she attended the Roman congress of the International Woman Suffrage Alliance in 1923.

In the reporting of her European achievements, *The Awakening of Australian Art* was repeatedly singled out. One reviewer noted: 'The figure suggests youthful resolution, and eagerness to pursue the thorny path of high ambition'.[97] The image was charged with a symbolism that was deeply personal: at the age of thirty-eight Dora was well launched in her career and realising her dreams. Articles profiling her achievement began to appear in the Australian press. She achieved a coup in 1909 when the swashbuckling poet Gabriele d'Annunzio was persuaded to sit for her. As the press noted, to Dora fell 'the honour of executing the only portrait of him (up to that time) in existence' (plate 6).[98] That same year the National Art Gallery of New South Wales purchased a cast of *The Awakening* through Sir Joseph Carruthers, a former New South Wales premier and a long-serving trustee of the gallery. This was the first of Dora's works to be acquired by a public gallery in Australia.

This was a full-sized cast of the medal made from the plaster model. Although she wanted them to buy the model for £200, with the right to reproduce medals in various sizes from it, they opted for a cheaper cast. From Dora's surviving medals it is clear that she used a number of processes in making them. The most traditional – used for the portrait of d'Annunzio – was to cut the design on a soft block or a die, working from a model in wax. The die was then hardened and placed in a hydraulic press and the medal struck from this. For other medals like *The Awakening of Australian Art* she appears to have used a reducing machine, which allowed her to model the design in soft wax or modelling clay. From the model a plaster cast was taken in the negative and from this, a positive casting in iron or bronze. This large metal model was then placed in a reducing machine and copied in a reduced size mechanically, probably on demand and often by a Parisian company which specialised in the process. Most of her plaster casts have subsequently been lost.

In 1912 Dora returned to Australia after a twenty-year absence. Her father had died in 1908. Both her mother and her sister Rita were ill, with Rita dying only a few months after Dora's return. She barely recognised Sydney: the city's growth, she noted, 'has overwhelmed me'.[99] Innovation in flight, cinematography, urbanisation, rail and motor transport had transformed everyday life. Australia had become a federation while she was away and its population had almost doubled. Women had been given the vote ahead of many parts of the world and important welfare programmes, such as the old age pension, had been introduced. Culturally, the country was also much altered. Symphony orchestras and conservatoriums had been founded, along with new universities in Queensland, Tasmania and West Australia. The arts were receiving attention as never before.

Dora's reputation preceded her arrival. The Royal Art Society of New South Wales featured a special presentation of her work in its annual show. Her twenty works were described as 'a collection of fine medallions and statuettes such as are not often shown here'.[100] Other reviews remarked on the 'many subjects and such varied treatment' they displayed.[101] Her works traced her stylistic development over the previous seven years, evolving from decorative *fin-de-siècle* memorials, such as the portrait of Krusceniski, to symbolist panels, and to more consciously modern works with bold designs and pared-down details. A quarter of the show was purchased by the National Art Gallery of New South Wales and the *Sydney Morning Herald* devoted a feature article to her medallions.[102]

Dora's return home was for family rather than professional reasons, yet she encountered such interest in her work that she set up a studio-salon on

May Moore, Photograph of Dora Ohlfsen 1913. *National Art Archive, Art Gallery of New South Wales, Sydney.*

a Roman model in Bathurst Street, where she exhibited works, conducted portrait sittings and entertained.[103] Like much of her Roman work that has disappeared, work that she made in Australia has also been lost. Press reports recorded that she 'recently executed in Sydney commemorative panel portraits of the Chief Justices of New South Wales for the new law courts'.[104] The whereabouts of these panels is unknown, as is a commission for the Melbourne Athenaeum and medallions of Shakespeare and Goethe for the Little Theatre in Sydney. Surviving works include a plaster relief medallion of Sir Edmund Barton, a bronze medallion of the New South Wales Premier W.A. Holman and portraits of many of the city's most prominent citizens (plate 8).[105]

The building of the National Art Gallery of New South Wales marked how far Australian society had advanced since Dora's departure, with prosperity providing leisure and money for cultural pursuits. The neoclassical sandstone building in Sydney's Domain had been completed in early 1909, the practical embodiment of an awakened Australian art. Its façade was adorned with blank sculptural recesses intended to illustrate the six epochs of art. First to be

The final stone of the pediment of the National Art Gallery of New South Wales is put in place, 24 March 1902. *National Art Archive, Art Gallery of New South Wales, Sydney.*

installed was a bas-relief representing Greek art, by the Englishman Percival Ball. Next were works by English sculptors, Gilbert Bayes, a foremost exponent of New Sculpture, and Feodora Gleichen, depicting Assyrian and Egyptian art. Three panels remained to be filled and the trustees were considering their choices. Dora became a candidate: the next panel was intended for the depiction of Roman art.[106]

The bas-relief panels on the façade of the gallery were not the only areas of opportunity for sculptors in 1912. A programme for the ornamentation of the gallery entailed work for the front portico and free-standing sculpture. Dora sent in a portfolio of sketches to the trustees. These have not survived. In August 1913 they wrote that her sketches 'for a bas-relief panel, proposed to be placed in the exterior wall of the entrance portico of the gallery building and two panel portraits have been approved'. She was commissioned to complete a full-size panel in plaster for £350 and a duplicate of it, for safety's sake, for an extra £25. The panel was to be 24 feet 10 inches long by 3 feet 7 inches wide and when finished would be cast in bronze and placed immediately above the entrance door to the gallery (plate 11). Two portrait roundels, also cast in bronze, would eventually sit on either side of this rectangular frieze. Dora's fee for this commission was on par with what Bayes and Gleichen – artists at the apex of sculpture in the British world – had been paid. Dora was to supervise the bronze casting at her Paris foundry of Siot-Decauville. Sculptors working abroad like Dora were valued for their practical knowledge of the entire process of design and fabrication, with very little casting done at this time in Australia.

Dora's visit to Australia was well timed. Development in the major cities and in the emerging capital of Canberra, whose foundation stone was laid in 1913, held out promise of opportunities for sculptors. Commissions were even beginning to come from private patrons, with the politician Henry Gullett announcing in September 1913 that he would personally fund a Shakespeare Memorial to celebrate the Tercentenary of the Bard's death in 1916.[107] The Federal Art Advisory Board had been established, with the Director of the National Art Gallery of New South Wales, Gother Mann, a member. Dora's connections with Mann went back a long way. Mann had been Chief Engineer with the Public Works Department, which her father managed. She wrote to him in October, asking to be kept in mind for the decoration of Old Canberra House. This was the headquarters of the Federal Capital Advisory Committee and was being constructed while she was in the country. 'Being an Australian myself', she ended her letter, 'I should naturally wish that if possible some work of mine should have a place on any edifice of so much interest to all Australians'.[108]

She was full of ideas for new work and told reporters that she was planning a worldwide tour of her medallions, statues and a series of pastel studies of 'Australian types', which she had just completed. After sixteen months in Australia she had a container load of clay models carefully packed to send back to Europe for eventual casting in Paris. 'Several', she told reporters, 'have already been sent to Paris and finished, and are now on their way back; but those I have just finished I am taking with me'.[109] This was a risky undertaking as clay models could easily be destroyed or become lost in transit. In fact, the bronzes which she worked on in Australia and which were 'on their way back' were lost in 1914 just as the war broke out.[110]

Dora Ohlfsen, *Head of Australia* 1917, plaster cast, 66.0 cm (high), present whereabouts unknown.
Photograph from the National Art Archive, Art Gallery of New South Wales, Sydney.

When Dora returned to Rome she focused on her Sydney commission, renting a supplementary studio space in which to build the model. In late July 1914 war was declared in Europe, although Italy initially identified itself as neutral and refused to commit troops. In December of that year she heard from the Sydney trustees of their satisfaction with her progress. She had sent them designs for a long bronze panel depicting a chariot race, as they had specified. On either side of the panel, portrait roundels of Michelangelo and Da Vinci were planned. These subjects were chosen by the Gallery Board as 'classic in nature, to harmonise with the architectural features of the building'.[111] They suggested that she take as a model for the central panel the chariot race from Ben Hur.[112] At the time she was not familiar with this popular silent movie of 1907.[113]

She reported regularly to Mann on the panel, which the trustees noted was already significantly improved on the early sketches. When they asked her to amend some aspects of the design, they explained 'this is an important panel and the Board are desirous that it should be entirely successful'.[114] In September 1915, four months after Italy joined the Triple Entente and declared war on Austria-Hungary, she visited her foundry in Paris to discuss casting and obtain quotes. While there, she also arranged the casting of a large plaster medallion from Sydney of the New South Wales Premier, William Holman. She had exhibited this at the Salon des artistes Française in the previous year and she noted to Mann: 'I have had a great success with it'.[115] Towards the end of 1916 members of the Venice Biennale Jury visited her studio and saw the National Art Gallery of New South Wales panel, along with other commissions.

Progress on the commission became increasingly difficult for Dora. The estimate to cast her panel was exorbitant. She also began to find fault with the brief. She wrote to the trustees in November 1916 recommending that the portrait roundels be replaced by decorative sculpture because 'those two enormous heads in relief will kill the importance of the principal panel'. In her judgement, replacing the portraits of Michelangelo and Da Vinci with allegorical figures was aesthetically superior, as the portraits were an anachronism that neither 'go with the epoch nor the Grecian style of the facade'.[116]

Dora's experience with this commission was typical of the difficulties sculptors faced. A sculptor's raw materials were costly and the financial compensation for work was relatively meagre. A commission to design a work, first cast in plaster, was no guarantee that it would be realised in permanent form. Commissioned sculpture was often circumscribed by financial constraints and subject to decisions made by committees, thereby denying to sculptors the element of self-expression they believed to be integral to a work of art. While she was battling with the Sydney trustees, her colleague Giovanni Prini was designing a relief panel for the 1911 International Exhibition in Rome. He titled his image of an athlete leading a rearing horse through a tempestuous current, *The artist and the artistic battle*.[117] Prini's battle, like Dora's, was with the Board that had commissioned his work and Dora's frustration at the Sydney trustees' interference with her artistic judgement is evident in a letter to Gother Mann. She testily asked 'how many photographs did Countess Gleichen send out of that amateur abortion of hers which adorns the walls of the art gallery?'[118]

Melbourne sculptor Margaret Baskerville illustrates some of the challenges Dora faced looking for commissions for major work. Baskerville, Ballarat-born like Dora, was nine years older. She had spent two years in Europe from 1904, but it is not known if their paths crossed in Rome, although Dora may have known that Baskerville's work had been singled out by Rodin when he saw it at London's Royal College of Art in 1905. Upon returning to Australia, Baskerville became studio assistant to sculptor 'Charlie' Douglas Richardson, marrying in 1914, after which they became an artistically successful pair. In 1929 Baskerville was the subject of the first monograph published in Australia on a sculptor.[119] Baskerville undertook many commissions and was hailed, like Cowan and Dora, as 'the only woman sculptor in Australia'. Still, Baskerkerville paid a creative price for the patronage she gained. Critic Blamire Young wrote that sculptors 'were obliged to supply what the small community wanted . . . This accounts in a great measure for the class of work Miss Baskerville produced. It explains the over-emphasis of the sentimental side of things, the buxom babies, the flower-decked maidens and the well behaved soldiers'.[120]

Dora's forthrightness, along with her unwavering commitment to her own artistic vision, probably cost her the Sydney commission. Photographs of the plaster cast survive and show a furious chariot race, with two naked riders in the foreground and another pair receding and approaching. The modelling is bold; the panel has an extraordinary cohesion and would have made a most dynamic impression on the gallery's exterior. Even eighteen years later, the Melbourne *Herald* considered 'the panel . . . is superior to so very much we already have in Australia'.[121]

Dora's work cannot be judged on the photographs of the plaster cast alone, as the Sydney trustees did. They believed the subtleties of her work would be lost when translated into a monumental scale.[122] She sensed this and showed the photographs to Sir George Hill, future Director of the British Museum in London and an expert in Renaissance medals. He realised that Dora had exaggerated details so that the panel would retain an impression of movement, especially when seen from a great height, as was intended. He also correctly saw that she had modelled the horses on antique Greek prototypes. Dora noted that:

> he did not give a single adverse criticism on the composition or the drawing as anatomy. I asked him if he thought the anatomy too visible in general. He said 'No, that is your way of seeing movement and when an artist is given a commission that artist is paid for his manner of working and his manner of seeing things'.[123]

Stylistically, Dora's chariot race shows that she was moving away from the expressive naturalism of Rodin and Bourdelle. By 1914, the influence of New Sculpture was waning, even in Britain. Dora had been tremendously impressed by the Serbian pavilion at the 1911 International Exhibition in Rome, which featured the expressive works of sculptor Ivan Meštrović. She told a niece 'the greatest sculptor in the world is Mestrovich [sic] the Serbian artist. He was extremely and naturally primitive when he exhibited for the first time in 1911, a huge show. He really was primitive. He went through an Egyptian stage and is now 500 BC Greek'.[124] This period of Greek art was also the inspiration for her chariot race.

While working in Italy on the Sydney commission, Dora battled with the increasing restrictions imposed because of the war. She wrote home: 'In Rome one only thinks and talks war'.[125] She and Elena joined the many other women nursing with the Red Cross, first assisting during the Avezzano earthquake of 1915, which killed over 30,000 people. She also worked as a volunteer in the Italian Auxiliary Hospital, which was situated opposite her studio.[126]

In September of 1919, a few months after the Treaty of Versailles, the trustees of the New South Wales Gallery cancelled Dora's commission, giving a shortage of funds as the reason. She wrote to Premier Holman questioning the decision, as she knew that the trustees were spending thousands of pounds on finalising two large equestrian statues by Gilbert Bayes for the front of the gallery.[127] She suggested that if finances were tight, her plaster panel be painted to resemble bronze and put in place until the cost of casting came down. This would also allow the trustees to judge its success. She cited the Victor Emmanuel monument in Rome, where the disruption of war had necessitated the installation of plaster friezes for seven years. At the same time she made contact with foundries and devised a way that her panel could be cast at less than pre-war prices. The trustees were unmoved. Chairman Sir John Sulman wrote dismissively to Mann: 'Miss Ohlfsen is a woman, and although she has no case, can cause mischief'.[128]

Rescuing the future 1920–1939

The cancellation of her Sydney commission was the great disappointment of Dora's career as a sculptor. She told the London agent for the National Art Gallery of New South Wales: 'I cannot tell you how amazed I am, nor how incomprehensible it all seems to me nor how unexpected'. She had devoted two years to the project. Integral to her disappointment was her realisation that this cancellation would result in 'very great damage to me as an artist since it will deter the possibility of any other work in Australia'.[129]

Despite this setback, the war years had nonetheless been productive for Dora as an artist. She had made, amongst other work, bronze medallions of George Mounsey, the first Secretary of the British Embassy in Rome,

Dora Ohlfsen, *Tosti di Valminuta* 1916, marble bust, present whereabouts unknown. *National Art Archive, Art Gallery of New South Wales, Sydney.*

and of Nellie Melba, along with an equestrian model of Archduke Eugene, commander of the Austro-Hungarian forces in the Tyrol and a cousin of the Austrian Emperor. A bust of Duke Tosti di Valminuta was commissioned by officers from the duke's regiment. With his administrative quarters around the corner from Dora's studio, he became a close friend and patron.

In Australia, she is best known, however, for a work called 'the Anzac medal' (plates 9–10). Regarded among her finest works, it is one of the first pieces of commemorative sculptural art dedicated to the Anzacs. It is often dated to the end of the war, but archival records show that it was modelled in October 1916. Dora intended it as the first of a series, writing to Mann in January of 1917 that she was making a series of medals 'on my own account' to commemorate the war: 'One for "Anzac" which is finished, one for the Italians, one for the artists of the French Academy (Villa Medici) in Rome and one for the Russian Cavalry'.[130] She later added a medal commemorating the

American Air Force, with an allegorical design on one side and a quote from President Wilson on the reverse (plates 9–10).[131]

Only the Anzac Medal has survived. One side features the figure of Australia crowning a dead son with laurel. The obverse shows an Anzac, with gun cocked in silhouette. Dora noted 'I have made "Australia" and her son very young – representing as they do the youngest country and the youngest army'.[132] The figure of Australia was modelled on twenty-one-year-old Alexandra Simpson, whom Dora had represented before in *The Awakening*. She was chosen as 'a type most clearly approaching that of the Australian girl at her best'.[133] Simpson was born in China, the daughter of the British High Commissioner, and had worked, like Elena von Kügelgen, as a Red Cross nurse on the Italian front.

Dora went to London in July 1919 to promote the medal, negotiating to sell it under the British War Charities Act in aid of permanently disabled Australians and New Zealanders. A committee to manage the funds was established, which included Sir Charles Wade as chairman and generals Birdwood, Monash and Talbot Hobbs. The Prince of Wales accepted the first medal struck. Profits from sales were given to the Australian Branch of the British Red Cross Society. While in London Dora also made a number of portrait studies.[134]

Most of the fundraising medallions memorialising the Dardanelles campaign were produced in 1915. Later material commemorated 'Our heroes' or 'Our boys at the front', with the exception of items produced for Anzac Day itself, first marked in April 1916. Although produced in large numbers, none was as large as Dora's medallion or of particular artistic worth. Some – like the 'Dead Man's Penny' – were presented in memory of service. Dora's medal was eventually adapted for the post-war effort, amended from her original 1916 conception to include the inscription '1914–18' on the medal. The Australian press wrote that the medal was a tangible expression of Dora's patriotism, despite the fact that she had lived for a quarter of a century overseas.

Unlike other medals, hers does not glorify war. She was critical of war, writing to a niece 'how men love war! If they did not there would be no wars'.[135] Sentiment about the war was not uniform within Australia. The

Dora Ohlfsen, *Mrs Grey* 1917, pastel on paper, present whereabouts unknown.
National Art Archive, Art Gallery of New South Wales, Sydney.

war had created polarising divisions over conscription, independence from Britain, income tax, price control and even the operating hours of public bars. Australian women, being fully enfranchised, felt a particular responsibility, and growing numbers pressed for international peace. The Sisterhood of International Peace was formed in Melbourne in March 1915 by thirty women, amongst them stenographer Eleanor Moore and Jessie Strong, a pastor's wife. By August of that year there were close to two hundred members and it grew to become part of an international movement. In January 1916 an International Committee of Women for Permanent Peace was established in The Hague.

Calls for disarmament gathered momentum through the 1920s and signatures were collected worldwide, with over 100,000 Australians demanding world disarmament.

Dora shared the aspirations of women working for peace. She completed a series of floral paintings symbolising the flowering of peace after the horrors of war. More controversially, she modelled a portrait of Donald Grant, only recently released from prison. As the Sydney leader of the Industrial Workers of the World, Grant had campaigned against conscription and for action against the war and capitalism. He was arrested on a contentious charge of arson and incitement to sedition. Four years later he was released when a Royal Commission judged that he had been wrongly imprisoned.

Dora again returned to Australia in August of 1920 and stayed for almost a year. Aged fifty-one, she returned to promote her Anzac medal and possibly to revive her Sydney commission. She held two solo exhibitions. One, a collection of medallions displayed in the main court of the National Art Gallery of New South Wales, may have been arranged to appease her for the loss of the commission. The other included twenty pastels, three statuettes, eight medals and plaquettes and fourteen portrait medallions, shown in her studio at the Albert Building, under the patronage of Dame Margaret Davidson, wife of the Governor.[136] A number of the works she exhibited recorded the Italian war experience.[137]

Dora visited Melbourne, where she gave a lecture, 'Futuristic art in its relation to Bolshevism', and sketched the celebrated Sir John Monash.[138] She also visited her birth town of Ballarat, presenting the Ballarat Art Gallery with a number of her works, including a bronze medallion of General Pipino Garibaldi, a grandson of the famous Giuseppe. He had been born in Melbourne during his father's refuge there and for that reason was known in Italy as 'the famous Australian'.[139]

On the face of things, her return was successful; in reality, she was frustrated. The recent war provided opportunities for memorialising, both with new buildings and monuments and through commemorative collecting. She was involved in little of this. The council of Mornington Peninsula incorporated a large version of her Anzac medal into their war memorial, dedicated in 1925. When they quibbled about the cost, Dora allowed them to use it without charge.[140] She offered the Australian War Memorial, not yet housed in Canberra, portrait medallions of generals Monash and Birdwood, both by now friends of hers.[141] Committee member Web Gilbert, who had just sold a work to the National Art Gallery of New South Wales for forty guineas, thought her price of fifty guineas for both works too high and suggested fifteen.[142] C.E.W. Bean, also a member of the committee, argued that 'a medallion is not a very interesting form of a portrait' and doubted (incorrectly) 'if they can be portraits from the originals'. In Italy the medallion had a recognised pedigree, from the coins and medallions of ancient Rome, to their revival by artists of the Italian Renaissance, and into the present. In Australia the medal, on account of its size, was routinely discounted as a less vital communicator than painting.

Over 1400 memorials were erected in Australia after the First World War. The most significant of these was the Shrine of Remembrance in Melbourne. It was the largest in Australia and reportedly the costliest in the British Empire. The competition for the design of the shrine was launched in March 1922. It was open to British subjects residing in Australia and – importantly for Dora – all Australian citizens, even those residing permanently overseas. The competition was conducted in two stages. First, six sketches were selected from eighty-three designs submitted by architects and sculptors, with a final selection then made from the six. From her correspondence, it seems that Dora was one of the eighty-three who submitted a design. When announced on 13 December 1923, the award was won by Melbourne war veterans and architects, Philip B. Hudson and James H. Wardrop.

Plans for the sculptural decoration of the shrine were ambitious. Monumental buttress sculpture was intended for the exterior corners of the building, symbolising Peace and Goodwill, Justice, Sacrifice and Patriotism, along with carved tympana. Inside there were to be twelve high-relief friezes in sandstone, recording the various branches of the Armed Forces, and eight free-standing sentinels guarding the inner shrine, carved from marble, illustrating the virtues of Love, Charity, Courage, Integrity, Strength, Faith, Honour and Brotherhood.

Dora was considered as a possible sculptor for some of the statuary.[143] Monash loyally recommended her, as he told her he would do. He was the driving force behind the project, pushing it through, despite opposition from Keith Murdoch at the *Herald and Weekly Times* and alternative plans for memorial hospitals and victory arches. Monash was qualified as an engineer and took personal charge of construction.

However, Englishman Paul Montford was favoured by the architect Philip Hudson. In July 1928 Hudson told the sub-committee formed to manage the sculptural decoration of the shrine that in his considered opinion, Paul Montford was the greatest Architectural Sculptor of the age. Montford was commissioned to do the buttress groups and tympana.

When Montford began work he immediately positioned himself to take control of all decoration on the shrine, noting that 'had he been entrusted with the whole of the sculpture of the Memorial he would have been in a position to bring capable sculptors from England to carry out the work'.[144] Alderman Stapley said that he had been questioned about Montford not being an Australian or a soldier, explaining that the public wanted to see Australians working on the monument. With this in mind, Hudson visited Eva Benson at her studio in Sydney, and Montford asked another Sydney sculptor, Lyndon Dadswell, to come to Melbourne. The twenty-year-old Dadswell was eventually chosen to work on the inner friezes.

In March of 1930 the committee turned its attention to the symbolic sentinel sculptures for the inner shrine. Dora was one of the eight sculptors invited to submit sketches, the others being Bertram Mackennal, George Lambert, Harold Parker, W.L. Bowles, Frank Lynch, W. Wallace Anderson and Eva Benson. Dora was invited to take as her subject *Charity*. When Lambert died in May of 1930, Dadswell was asked to take over his figure of *Courage*. Then, after Mackennal, Parker and Lynch had rejected the commission, Arthur Murch was asked to do Mackennal's figure of *Strength*, Daphne Mayo, Parker's figure of *Integrity* and Frank Lynch's figure of *Honour*. This left Dora to design sculptures representing *Charity* and *Love*. She sent in plaster models for both. She did not hide her disappointment, telling a niece, 'Sir John procured for me this crumb "*Charity*" – not even two statues out of the eight, although I was asked to send in more than one model'.

Other sculptors also completed more than one figure, so that by February of 1931 there were thirteen models from which to choose. Seven were eventually rejected, although Dora's two sculptures survived the first cull.[145] Bernard Hall and John Longstaff were then brought in to pass artistic judgement on *Strength* by Montford, *Brotherhood* by Anderson, *Courage* by Dadswell, *Integrity* by Mayo and Dora's *Charity* and *Love*. They told the committee that they 'were able to recommend, unconditionally, only two of the six models submitted, viz: *Strength* by Mr Paul Montford and *Integrity* by Miss Mayo'.[146] They noted that Dora's *Love* 'possessed undoubted merit', but that she should be asked to modify her design so as to bring it 'more into harmony with the stand and style of the recommended works'.[147]

Working on her frieze for the National Art Gallery of New South Wales Dora had encountered excessive interference from the commissioners of the work, but this was the first time she had been asked to match her creative vision to that of other artists and pre-ordered display plinths. It seems that she lost interest in the project from this time. A visitor to her Roman studio saw her unmodified model for *Charity* and was impressed by the 'the Madonna-like gesture of protection and the grace of the draperies'.[148] With Monash's death in 1931, three years before the shrine was completed, plans for its interior sculpture were abandoned.

The Victorian war memorial is representative of the fate of most of Dora's monumental works. They rarely made it beyond the plaster cast or, if completed, are now lost. She is remembered today as a medallist, despite having worked on large sculptural works in bronze and marble. Reports of her studio frequently mention such work.[149] Her bronze bust of Duke di Valminuta is known only because of a surviving photograph of the plaster cast. The South African Parliament commissioned her to make a statue of politician William Percy Whitford-Turner, which, according to Dora, would have proceeded 'if this cursed war had not intervened'.[150] A convent in New Zealand approached her about the decoration of their chapel, but hesitated because of customs duties.[151] She was further disappointed over an equestrian portrait of Monash. Plans were made to erect this in the vicinity of the shrine and he had posed for her in 1919 and 1922 with the statue in mind, also sending her photographs of himself on horseback.[152]

The period from the end of the First World War to the beginning of the next was for Dora, as for most of those living in Italy, a time of change, excitement, confusion and disappointment. The years following the first war had been the darkest in Italian history since unification. War had ruined the economy. The currency was devalued and inflation was out of control. As the cost of living kept rising, riots broke out. Economic tensions exacerbated social disharmony. Communists looked as though they would grind the country to a halt and topple the old order. Dora and Elena were reminded of the brittle situation in Russia they had escaped twenty years earlier. At first they thought of moving to Australia or relocating to London. As early as 1919 Dora confided to Gother Mann, 'I shall not be living much longer in Rome. Certainly the coming winter will be my last'.[153]

The first fascist squads were made up of disaffected, unemployed young men, angry with Italy's post-war humiliation at the hands of its professed allies and angrier still with the internal enemies whom they believed were destroying their country. These squads were welcomed by landowners and industrialists, who were directly threatened by working-class militancy. For the church they were a bulwark against the godless tide of communism. Artists too believed that fascism could be a means of defending civilised values.[154] Australian artist Stella Bowen observed that her artist friends supported fascism under the conviction that it would provide the patronage and social stability essential for their survival: 'As creators of something entirely without material usefulness they have sought the protection of the Strong man, in the hope that he would calm the only waters in which they have, with difficulty, learnt to swim'.[155]

Still in Rome in October 1922, Dora was among the crowds who lined the streets to welcome Mussolini and his followers as they entered the city. She told the press: 'We had been hearing about the threatened "March on Rome" of the *fascisti* without paying much attention, but everybody began to sit up and notice when 30,000 men marched into Naples and held a convention there on October 24th'. She described Mussolini's March on Rome as 'the most extraordinary sight. From early morning they poured into Rome singing their different songs, the principal of which is called "Giovenezza" (Youth), illustrative of their movement, which is essentially a young man's movement – the golden youth of the nation'.[156]

Mussolini, she added, was being 'described as a cross between Beethoven and Napoleon I'. Not long after the March on Rome she was able to judge for herself, when the owners of the bauxite mine, Predil, commissioned a portrait of him to be placed at the entrance to their mines. She visited 'Il Duce' five times and made detailed studies of him as he worked in his apartment at the Palazzo Chigi. She found him, as others did, 'a great dynamic force. He is a creation of the times and he has great personal magnetism' (plate 18).[157]

Her old friend Tosti di Valminuta was promoted by Mussolini to Undersecretary for the Department of Foreign Affairs. Through his patronage Dora was entrusted with the design for a war memorial at the naval base at Formia near Naples. She worked on it without payment. The central figure of the 30-foot-high monument represents Italian youth – the 'golden youth of our nation' – typified as a young soldier leaping forward to offer himself in sacrifice. The monument is entitled *Sacrifice* and Dora intended to evoke in plastic form Leopardi's verse from his poem 'To Italy': 'O my country, the life thou gavest me I now return to thee'. On one side of the large supporting pedestal is a female figure, who faces inward, holding a palm of victory in the left hand and a laurel branch in the right, over the names of fallen soldiers. The arms of the young soldier are intentionally disproportionate for expressive impact, with the figure designed to be seen at a distance against the skyline (plates 15–16). This exaggeration was a common feature of the work of Meštrović and French sculptor Paul Landowski.

The Formia memorial, with its central figure representing beauty, youth, strength and sacrifice, anticipates much of the monumental fascist sculpture of the late 1920s and 1930s. Dora's choice of bronze and marble for her monument, the decorative band of fasci at the top of the support and her coupling of masculine sacrifice with feminine nurturing fits well with the fascist agenda for sculpture, in its promotion of the myth of *Italianiatà*. Vitalist notions popular at the time probably also influenced the work. Dora had always been interested in physical culture, teaching a younger sister its 'rigorous laws' on her first return to Australia.[158] Interest in 'body culture' was a feature of the 1920s, with both communists and fascists emphasising physical fitness as a key to national regeneration.[159] The recent war had occasioned much comment about the fine physical qualities of Antipodean soldiers and at this time Dora made sculpture which the Australian press read as embodying these qualities. The press described her *Australian Apollo*, modelled on a young Anzac, as 'the product of those far-away dominions to which the British Empire owed so much during the Great War'.[160]

Fascist boy scouts salute the flag at the dedication of the Formia memorial.
National Art Archive, Art Gallery of New South Wales, Sydney.

The memorial at Formia was dedicated on 18 July 1926 in the presence of the Admiral of the Italian fleet, the Archbishop of Gaeta and a number of war veterans (plate 17). She was deeply moved when 'the peasant women and children came down from the hills to search for the names of their dead on the base of the statue, and to strew flowers upon its steps'.[161] She received the

Freedom of the City for the memorial, writing proudly to a friend that she was the only Empire artist to receive this honour, 'for it is not a complimentary honour but a legal one and conferred on me by unanimous vote of the population'. With her first large work erected, she considered, 'I am young as a sculptor'.[162] She was fifty-seven years old.

The Formia memorial highlighted some of the ambiguities Dora was now facing as a long-term expatriate artist. She was in the unique position of having completed a war memorial for a country where the design of monuments was normally a jealously preserved right of the Italian-born.[163] Mussolini was reported to have said to her: 'you may now be considered an Italian sculptress'.[164] Although there is evidence that she continued to be considered an Australian artist living abroad, little work came her way from Australia.[165] The letters she wrote to her family suggest that she was feeling that dislocation or 'emptiness' that Nathaniel Hawthorne observed among many long-term expatriate artists living in Rome.[166] Each year as the wattle bloomed outside her apartment she was overcome with homesickness.[167]

Yet as the 1920s progressed, prospects brightened, particularly for artists. Ambitious building works undertaken by the fascists, along with large international exhibitions like the Venice Biennale and Rome Quadriennale, gave art a new prominence. Living in Rome felt like being 'in the very hub of world happenings'.[168] Dora wrote:

> there are three huge exhibitions going on at present . . . That's one thing they do well here. They give their own artists work – and another thing is that there are practically no unemployed here. Work is *made* for people. Rebuilding and renovating everywhere.[169]

Dora was caught up in the project of the new Italy. She began exhibiting in the vibrant *mostre sindacali*, or trade union exhibitions, which characterised Italian art under fascism (plate 13).[170]

An influential journal of the time was *Valori Plastici*, edited by Mario Broglio in Rome. It promoted artists like Carlo Carrà, Giorgio de Chirico and Giorgio Morandi, who were moving away from the expressionist work popular before the First World War to firm contours and the balance of classical sculpture.

As the 1920s progressed, and the fascists tightened their grip upon Italian life and culture, many artists lost their initial enthusiasm for the movement. Some sculptors, like Arturo Martini, resisted the harnessing of their art to fascist ideals and, instead of drawing upon the language of classicism, borrowed from the vernacular styles of the Italian peninsula, including the Etruscan and the Romanesque, working in simple porous stone and clay.

Dora looked for new sources of institutional patronage away from the state and began making work for the church, taking up the art of fresco painting. In contrast to the muscular athletes and boxers that increasingly characterised Italian sculpture under fascism, she made modern encaustic icons – blending pigments with beeswax – of popular saints like St Francis of Assisi and St Anthony of Padua, surrounding them with native Australian animals and plants. Her unusual, highly feminised statue of the Good Shepherd drew upon the early Christian paradigms that blurred the distinction of sex in the earliest images of Christ (plate 12). Stella Bowen thought that artists who flirted with fascism failed to reckon with 'the Strong Man's hatred of their liberal and independent spirit'.[171] Dora was realistic about working as a sculptor under fascism. Like Arturo Martini, sculpture for her was a profession that sometimes entailed serving 'the devil as much as the Eternal Father . . . just as Canova did for Napoleon when he conquered Italy and the same as Beethoven with his symphony . . . The sculptor is like a shoemaker who makes shoes for those who order them'.[172] Notwithstanding, her activities during the twenty years of the fascist *ventennio* eventually made it impossible for her to achieve the recognition she desired in Australia as well as in her adopted country.

Back in Australia she sought the patronage of the recently retired Attorney-General, Sir Robert Garran, now that Monash was dead. Dora probably knew Garran through her father. Garran's father had migrated to Adelaide and was a journalist for the *Austral Examiner* when Dora's father was working in that city. The two travelled to the Victorian goldfields at the same time and later to Sydney. Garran and Dora's friendship was consolidated when Garran visited Rome. He was among the Australians, like mutual friends James and Louise Dyer, whom Dora guided around Rome during their visits to the city. They appreciated her knowledge of the city and her connections. Garran found that 'all doors opened to her – even in the Vatican'.[173]

By 1932, retired in Canberra and promoting artistic life there, Garran corresponded with Dora about several sculptural proposals. He recommended her work to the executive of the Returned Soldiers League when they were considering building a memorial in Canberra. Special value was placed on monumental sculpture, which was seen as the proof of a sculptor's worth. Dora was enthusiastic but wary, telling Garran, 'I have the most glorious idea you can conceive of for the Canberra War Memorial but do not dare to tell you . . . These are very hard times for me and I simply have not got the money to go to Australia unless it is for something definite'.[174] Furthermore, there was an emotional price to pay for anticipating commissioned work. Uncertainty was worse than lack of funds, she told Garran: 'supposing I *had* the money available (it is not a question of a mere steamer ticket) and went to Australia and after a heart-breaking fight did not get the work I would be so smashingly disappointed that I would be quite capable of killing myself!'

As before, nothing came of these plans. Garran wrote of her disappointment: 'It was her heart's desire to be commissioned for an important work of sculpture in Australia, and she visited Australia more than once, but did not receive in her own country the recognition she had won in Europe'.[175]

Louise B.M. Dyer
1932

Part 2

THE PATRON
LOUISE DYER (1884–1962)

Melbourne, 1884–1909

The discovery of gold in Victoria in the Roaring Fifties made the colony a mecca for adventurous spirits from all parts of the world. From 1851 gold fever transformed the small port town of Melbourne, barely twenty years old, into a metropolis unique for its age. Progress could be seen everywhere: 'rambling suburbs of new red-brick villas, financed by land banks and speculative builders and erected by the largest team of building workers ever assembled in Australia, sprang up along the route of the new cable-trams, to house more than ten thousand migrants arriving annually'.[1]

Dr Louis Lawrence Smith prospered in this climate. The son of a London impresario, with family connections across the theatrical and military worlds, he had the 'midas touch of enterprise'. Quick to spot opportunity, he was a medical doctor whose entrepreneurialism included running an anatomical museum and offering medical services by mail.[2] In defiance of those established Melbourne circles which excluded him for his 'raciness', he created his own society, centred on his opulent home in Collins Street, and quickly became a colonial celebrity.[3] He had a family of six children and when his wife died he remarried. His second wife, English-born Marion Jane 'Polly' Higgins, was twenty-four years his junior. They had four children. He delivered the first child from this marriage, Louise Berta Mosson Smith, on 19 July 1884.

Louise's childhood was played out against the backdrop of the 1880s, a time (as Nellie Melba remembered) of ebullient *joie de vivre*. Melbourne's increase in population and wealth saw the development of a new social order, with

Louise Dyer in 1932 as Lady Mayoress. *Photograph courtesy of Mr Rodney Davidson.*

Dr Louis Lawrence Smith and family, 1892. *Photograph courtesy of Mr & Mrs N Gengoult Smith*

Government House setting the example. The colony's governors entertained lavishly and prosperous families did likewise. Spacious gardens and homes, such as Colonel Sargood's Ripponlea, resounded with the gaiety of concerts, parties and balls. Musical performers flocked to Melbourne, as did opera companies doing the Empire circuit. The city kept pace with Europe. Gilbert and Sullivan's operetta *Patience* and Ibsen's provocative play *The Doll's House* were staged only a few months after their London premieres. International orchestras were engaged for festivals – during the six months run of the 1888 Centennial International Exhibition 244 concerts were given. Smith was chairman of the Exhibition Trustees, actively promoting Victoria and its products and representing the colony at intercolonial and international exhibitions, as in New Zealand and Amsterdam.

For almost twenty years Smith also held a seat in the Legislative Assembly, 'his political creed being ultra-Liberalism'.[4] His name became familiar to all Victorians when he privately funded a press campaign, whereby the postal fee was reduced from 4d to 2d. From 1886 he represented Mornington as a member of the short-lived Liberal Government formed by Graham Berry. Before Berry lost office, his government commissioned an inquiry into the state of education in the colony and sought recommendations on how to improve it. This was conducted by Charles Pearson, a far-sighted educationalist, who was the first headmaster of the Presbyterian Ladies College (PLC).

This school was founded in 1875 to promote 'the higher culture of women', as Pearson titled one of his lectures. Like Sydney Girls High School, it prepared girls for entrance to the University of Melbourne, which had opened to women in 1871. Pearson believed that women should not be barred from higher education or influential careers. College alumnae included Constance Ellis, the first Victorian woman to receive the degree of Doctor of Medicine, Flos Greig, the first woman to be admitted to the Victorian Bar, and Vida Goldstein, suffragette and the first woman to stand for election to federal parliament. PLC's most acclaimed alumna was Ellen Mitchell, later known as Nellie Melba.

Louise was enrolled at PLC from 1891, before her seventh birthday. Her force of character is already evident in the portrait Tom Roberts had painted of her three years earlier, commissioned to celebrate her recovery from a serious childhood illness (plate 20). By then Louise was accustomed to being at the centre of attention, as Roberts's painting suggests. A family photograph of Louise reading with her father indicates their close relationship.[5] Having lost his first daughter, he treasured Louise, the first child of his second marriage.

She accompanied him often, including as he campaigned for elections in Victoria. Louise was travelling abroad from the age of two, accompanying Smith to England when he supervised the Victoria Court at the opening of the Imperial Institute in 1893. At the age of four she was photographed sitting before a crowd of exhibitors from Victoria at the New Zealand Intercolonial Exhibition. In Chester, her mother's birthplace, she was photographed wearing Welsh dress, and in America she was photographed with her parents at Niagara Falls. Such experiences encouraged in the young Louise a global outlook and a strong sense of civic duty and ambition, as well as independence of mind.[6]

Louise Smith before the Victorian exhibitors at the Dunedin World's Fair in December 1889.
Photograph courtesy of Mr & Mrs N Gengoult Smith

These qualities also led her to feel keenly the constrictions of school, particularly during the two years when she was a boarder. PLC was a tight-knit community and many students, including Louise, made some of their most enduring friendships there. However, the privileged position the girls enjoyed could not cushion them from the financial crisis of 1893. After a decade of lavish spending, financed by British lenders, a swing of the pendulum brought a devastating collapse. There was a run on the banks; some suspended payments and others went into liquidation. When typhoid broke out in Melbourne, there was an exodus from the city. 'The worst effect of all, because it lasted for life', Ada Plante, a student at the time, recalled, 'was the loss of a sense of security, a dread that things were not as they seemed and that something terrible might happen at any moment'.[7]

Louise's father, dubbed '££ Smith' by the *Bulletin*, was not as severely hit as others. His interests, ranging across viniculture, model farming, racehorses and newspapers, were sufficiently diversified to reduce the effect of the depression. Maie Casey, a neighbour, remembered the high life continuing unabated in the doctor's household, and Smith himself as 'a dapper little man with a beard and a diamond ring'.[8] The Smiths lived among the colony of doctors in upper Collins Street, near the top of what was called the Eastern Hill. Dominating the crest of this street stood the Treasury Buildings and, alongside, Parliament House. A vast building completed in 1892, it epitomised many of the contradictions of Melbourne, where edifices were built on a more fragile footing than their grandeur suggested. The city's pretensions were noticed by Anthony Trollope, who observed 'no street in it is finished'. Little had changed twenty years on: another visitor described Collins Street as 'this bubble and collapse – of nothingness'.[9]

The collapse of the 1890s delivered a blow to the self-confidence of the colony. Victorians however were resilient. The approaching new century and plans for the Federation of Australia gave reason for optimism and also extended horizons beyond the colonial perspective. Federation was promoted as a means of economic and national progress by those native-born colonists who aspired to be 'one people with one flag, one cause and one destiny'.[10] Pledges of imperial loyalty were heard alongside calls to develop Australia, although how to do both was unclear, given the already over-stretched resources. As Casey recalls, 'the means of developing the Australian continent were argued endlessly with rising enthusiasm . . . My father's friends spoke of war, of the balance of power between nations . . . of the might of Britain but also of her distance from Australia, of human flight, of local events'.[11]

Younger men born in the colony formed the Australian Natives Association, with a women's group following shortly after. The association urged the necessity of retaining Australia's sons, many of whom had abandoned the country for South Africa after the financial collapse of 1893. It was argued that the continent's population had to expand beyond its four million if the nation was to grow. The need to import primary producers was emphasised, as they were seen as being indispensable to national prosperity. These challenges were viewed with optimism, and the newspapers and social commentary of the period give the clear impression that Victorians thought themselves equal to the task: 'Small though our population was in relation to the tasks to be done it did not occur . . . that there was any we could not do for ourselves'.[12] Such expansionist sentiments for Australia coloured the milieu in which Louise, born a child of the Empire, was raised, as the Exhibition Building, over which her father presided, was prepared for the Inaugural Ceremony of the Commonwealth.

Louise left PLC to focus on her study of music and language. French was highly valued in her home. Her father had trained for a year in Paris. His paternal grandmother was the daughter of a First Empire General, Baron Louis-Thomas Gengoult, who later became Sous-Préfect of Paris. Louise attended language classes at the Alliance Française from the age of eight. She received musical instruction from Adelaide Burkitt, teacher to the young Percy Grainger, and subsequently from Joseph Gillott.[13] At the age of thirteen she achieved the highest marks for piano and harmony in the junior examination of the Associated Board of London's Royal Academy of Music and Royal College of Music. In May 1898 she made her public debut, performing a nocturne by Chopin. In 1900, when she was aged sixteen, Leipzig-trained Eduard Scharf from the Melbourne Conservatorium awarded her the gold medal on behalf of the Associated Board of London for the highest marks obtained in Victoria for the senior examination in piano.[14]

Tragedy struck Louise in January 1902, when her younger sister Gladys, aged nine, was crushed by a boulder in a freak accident. Louise was deeply affected, and in her sorrow intensified her training. She took up the harp and began singing lessons with a former pupil of renowned *bel canto* teacher

Madame Marchesi. In 1905 she enrolled as a student at the conservatorium, an institution making news at the time because of the provocative views of the Director, George Marshall-Hall, on art and the role of artists in society. She was fortunate in her piano teacher at the conservatorium being Scharf. At the turn of the century musical training in Melbourne was criticised by leading musicians for being disorganised and uneven in quality, with many of the 33,000 individuals in training wasting their time and money.[15] Scharf was both practical and scholarly, requiring of his students technical facility as well as sound musicological knowledge to underpin intelligent and compelling performance. With him Louise escaped the common colonial plight of mediocre teachers flattering students to believe they were accomplished artists. With Scharf's training, Louise gained her licentiate in piano from London's Trinity College as well as in harmony and piano from the Associated Board.

At the age of twenty-one, she stood at 5 feet 4 inches, was blond and spoke with a mild lisp, pronouncing her 'r's as 'w's'. Her deep-set, intense blue eyes were her most compelling feature. Her sense of style also set her apart. Maie Casey noted that Louise 'had something of the shock and excitement of an Act of Nature, like an earthquake or an eclipse'.[16] Her manner was described as being somewhat breathless, her voice alternately high and husky. Seemingly coy, her lisp masked her sharp brain and business acumen.[17] A penetrating look and firmly rounded chin signalled a determination that, with her immense energy, would not be dissuaded. Those who knew her would remark that she had 'an intensely focused gaze . . . and instant, hawk-like decisiveness'.[18]

When her younger brother Louis went to study at Edinburgh University, Louise accompanied him. They arrived in London in 1907 with a letter of introduction from the Victorian Premier Sir Thomas Bent and were presented at Court. In Scotland between 1907 and 1908, Louise centred her studies on French, literature, the relatively new science of psychology and the piano. She studied with forty-one-year-old Philip Halstead, a leading pianist in Glasgow who had trained in Leipzig under Carl Reinecke and in Paris under Élie-Miriam Delaborde. Reinecke, close to Mendelssohn and Schumann, counted among his pupils Max Bruch, Arthur Sullivan and Edvard Grieg.[19]

An hour by train from Edinburgh, where Halstead also taught, Glasgow was the largest city in Scotland and after 1880 was Scotland's artistic capital. The city was famously engaged with music, as it was with industry and with life. It enjoyed a period of musical excellence from 1880 when musicians like Sullivan, Hans von Bülow and August Manns conducted there. It was home to the merged Scottish and Choral Union Orchestras, Scotland's leading instrumental ensemble under the direction of Frederic Cowen (1900–1910), who had conducted at and organised the musical festival that accompanied Melbourne's International Centennial Exhibition in 1888. The city also boasted the Glasgow Orpheus Choir and the Glasgow Grand Opera Company. The Orpheus Choir was shaped by Hugh S. Roberton into a world-famous choral

'Scoticus' cartoon of Sir Hugh Roberton from the *Scottish Field*, May 1936.

ensemble, drawing its members from Glasgow's workers. It was a musical phenomenon of international renown. The choir's freshness was a revelation to audiences and proof that music could be accessible to all and need not be an elitist pleasure.

Halstead taught at the Glasgow Athenaeum School of Music, now the Royal Scottish Academy of Music and Drama. The school prospectus for 1908 advertised a staff of fifty professors offering a complete musical curriculum, both theoretical and practical. Private tuition was available, with teachers offering instruction from 9 am until 10 pm. Henri Verbrugghen, future Director of Sydney's Conservatorium of Music, was professor of violin, chamber music, orchestra and opera.

The Athenaeum was located in Buchanan Street, the business centre of the city and, according to its Diamond Jubilee Souvenir of 1907, was replete with all modern improvements and conveniences, offering 'the advantages of a club and of an Educational Establishment'.[20] It was the first school of music to be established on a public basis in Britain's north and achieved a reputation for the ability of its teachers and for the training of its students. It had a powerful influence in raising the standard of musical taste and musical culture in Glasgow, with a student roll second only to London's Guildhall School.

Working with Halstead, who was a member of the Glasgow Society of Musicians, Louise saw the vitality of Glasgow's musical scene, the conviviality of its social life and the city's pride in its Conservatorium.[21] She could not fail to observe the importance of music in the community. She saw how musicians took leadership, being involved in fundraising benefits for the University Chair of History and the city's Wallace Monument.

Senior Athenaeum students could access the Euing collection, which included a library of 2500 volumes of early printed music, as well as 130 incunabula, collected by William Euing (1788–1874), a Glasgow insurance broker and bibliophile who wished to spread knowledge of music. His collection also contained manuscripts of medieval liturgical works and a set of part-books belonging to the seventeenth-century publisher John Playford. The published music included contemporary editions of works by Byrd, Purcell, Gibbons, Lully, Couperin, Frescobaldi and others, while among the theoretical works were rare items, such as Thomas Morley's *Plaine and easie introduction to practicall musicke* (1597) and Thomas Mace's *Musick's monument* (1676).[22]

In Glasgow, values instilled in Louise by L.L. Smith – belief in the arts and pride in artistic achievement and its benefits to the community – were reinforced. Glasgow was, as the music historians, Hugh and Kenneth Roberton saw it, a 'tightly enclosed, self-assertive community . . . idealistic and highly articulate'.[23] Louise was there during a restless period of questioning and revolution. Something of the *sang-froid* that Louise possessed came from Glasgow's enterprising spirit and can-do attitude.

This was her fifth trip abroad. She travelled with her brother to Ireland and crossed over to the continent, visiting Paris for the first time as an adult. It was a bracing time to be in Europe. Musical interest had swung to the largely unexplored storehouse of folk music, just as painters and sculptors had turned for inspiration to 'primitive art'. The new aesthetic of cubism was making an impact in the visual arts. While Louise was in Paris, George Braque made headlines with the rejection by the Salon d'Automne of all six of his cubist canvases. Outstanding personalities held the stage, among them Melba, Caruso, Paderewski and Pavlova, all not far from their prime. In Paris, Sarah Bernhardt appeared in *Camille* and Eleonora Duse in *The Doll's House*. In London at the same time, Kipling, Wells, Shaw, Barrie, and Conrad dominated English literature. Social change was in the air. At a rally of over quarter of a million people in Hyde Park, Mrs Pankhurst raised her voice over the hecklers to demand the vote for women.

In common with Dora Ohlfsen and other musicians trained in Australia and who had travelled to Europe for intensive study, Louise eventually abandoned plans for a professional career as a pianist. She told a journalist that 'her interpretive powers were of a high standard, but she lacked technique'.[24] She returned to Australia facing a future, aware that, as *Vanity Fair* put it, 'a girl no longer takes up an occupation or profession merely to pass the time until she is married, but resolutely sets herself to master its difficulties and gain, if possible, a high place therein, so that she may eventually become self-supporting and independent'.[25]

Marriage and patronage, 1910–1926

In 1910, a year after she returned to Melbourne, her father died. His loss was felt severely by the family and particularly by Louise, who had been a favourite. Moreover, his death forced change in the family's living circumstances. They were required to move to a smaller house, lower down in Collins Street, a reduction in circumstances that affected Louise.

Seventeen months later, she married Scotsman James Dyer, a widower twenty-five years her senior (plate 21). He had arrived in Australia three years before Louise's birth as the Australasian representative of Kirkaldy Linoleum. The company's motto – 'Strive without ceasing' – was a sentiment which Dyer took to heart, becoming became one of Melbourne's richest men. He was a founder of the influential Melbourne Scots organisation, an early member of the Royal Melbourne Golf Club and a generous subscriber to appeals. Not tall, and although balding, he was attractive; he dressed smartly, was well travelled and had a sharp Scottish wit. He had first met Louise when she was aged fourteen and they both shared a love of music, with Jimmy (as he was known to friends) singing tenor in the Royal Victoria Liedertafel. His devotion

Photograph of the wedding of Mr James and Louise Dyer published in *Punch*, 4 January 1912.
Image courtesy of the State Library of Victoria, Melbourne.

to music found expression in liberal gifts to further the development of the arts in Melbourne.

Louise set the tone of their marriage from the start. On their wedding day, as the press reported, the bride redeemed the ceremony from orthodox monotony.[26] Instead of the customary Wedding March by Wagner, she chose a choral version of 'The voice that breathed o'er Eden' to accompany the bridal procession. The reception was held in the banqueting hall of the Exhibition Building, decorated with the flags of all nations. 'John Amadio was the engaged artist', one guest recorded, 'and when he played his flute all the birds in the fernery woke up and sang'.[27] Guests received a copy of the wedding sonnets of Elizabeth Barrett Browning, bound in white brocade.

The Dyers set up home in a Queen Anne style house at Hawthorn Grove, near the Presbyterian Church, which Jimmy had helped to build. He was a match for Louise's firm will, financially astute and a kindly provider. Their home was hung with paintings which Jimmy, a keen collector, had amassed. They included works by Thea Proctor, John D. Moore, Janet Cumbrae-Stewart, Blamire Young, Septimus Power and James R. Jackson. He had a lyre carved above the fireplace in their living room, signalling how central music was to be in their married life. Like Louise's father, James Dyer was a self-made man; by this time he was developing his financial interests from an office in Flinders Lane. His wealth and friendships extended into levels of society previously beyond Louise's reach and as Mrs Dyer she moved effortlessly into Melbourne's high society.

Appointed to the committee of PLC's Collegians Association, she became active on the music sub-committee. Profits from an annual garden party held by her were used to fund a university scholarship. Melbourne was full of musical activity, although standards were variable. With professionalism in the musical world sharpening worldwide, Melba for one was alarmed by what she viewed as musical stagnation when she returned to the city in 1911. In Melbourne, music-making was dominated by well-intentioned and vigorous community groups. 'Melbourne?' exclaimed singer Frances Martineau to the press on her return to France, 'it is vast acres of humming shirt fronts'. Violinist Jascha Heifetz went further: 'It is useless talking about the future of music in Australia', he said, 'there's no future!'[28] Although Martineau dismissed Melbourne's community choirs, Louise appreciated from her Glasgow experience the value of community involvement in music. Over the next twenty years she would become one of the most forceful and practical promoters of musical professionalism in Australia, raising standards through performances, programming, educational activities and patronage.

At the beginning of 1914 Louise fell ill during the early stages of a pregnancy (plate 22). She was advised to undergo a hysterectomy, a decision that weighed heavily on the couple, along with the realisation that their plans for having a family would never eventuate. As with the death of her younger sister, work and music again blunted the edge of her sorrow. She raised funds for war orphans and for the Red Cross. A committee member of the Alliance Française since 1913, she also worked on an appeal for French war charities. As the war dragged on she became anxious for her brothers stationed in France. Harold, the younger, was wounded twice and Louis, to whom she was closest, fell at Bapaume, where he was buried.[29] Melba, stranded in Australia, was setting the standard for fundraising for the war effort. Louise knew Melba through PLC and through Jimmy. Melba's first concert engagement had been with the Liedertafel, in which Jimmy sang and over which he presided for ten years from 1918. Both he and Melba were recipients of the choir's honorary Golden Lyre. Melba raised over £100,000 for patriotic purposes and, upon selling a guinea flag for £2200, was dubbed the 'Empress of Pickpockets'.

In 1921 Louise was appointed president of the Alliance Française. The growing popularity of the association under her steerage saw the committee attempt more ambitious projects: lectures on French literature and performances of Molière plays were arranged. In 1923, when Louise offered to resign her presidency, the members refused her resignation. The ball she arranged for Bastille Day 1923 was a typical invention of her energy and imagination. She transformed the hall for the night on the theme of 'Les jardins de Versailles', covering the floor in stone, over which lawn was laid, and dotting it with fountains and orange groves. Professional musicians were hired to perform French baroque music in period costume. And Louise covered all the costs.

A move to a new home, Kinnoull in Toorak, with grounds overlooking the city, provided the opportunity for more ambitious fundraising, particularly after Louise succeeded Melba as president of the PLC Old Collegians Association. The college's celebration of its golden jubilee in 1925 was launched by Louise with a garden party at her home. The events she staged at Kinnoull were more than mere elegant socialising, with her home becoming the stage from which she promoted and supported artists, poets, composers and musicians. This role came naturally to her, she having been active from an early age at her father's 'salons' in the family home. She also inherited L.L. Smith's flair for publicity. Period costumes, elaborate staging, lavishly illustrated programmes by artists of the calibre of Thea Proctor and Blamire Young: everything was calculated to win the widest press possible for the artists and events she promoted (plate 29).

In August 1921 she and Jimmy launched the Victorian Branch of the British Music Society (BMS) with a foundational gift of £10,000. They also set up a music library for BMS members, the only music library available to non-professional musicians in Melbourne at the time. The society's objectives were to promote knowledge of British music, encourage Australian composers, assist Australian musicians studying and performing abroad and foster 'the spirit of International music'. The British Music Society had been established in 1918 in England by Arthur Eaglefield Hull and a branch of the society set up in Sydney the following year. The society drew support from those who were mindful of the necessity of music to national culture. It was thought that the society's activities, as with much musical activity, depended on 'lay-work which cannot be done by composers and artists for themselves'.[30] Visiting English composer William Gillies Whittaker, who stayed with the Dyers in 1923, believed that the BMS owed its success to Louise. In a concert of songs hosted in her home for over two hundred guests, he gave the first performance of 'Love's Coming', by the Australian poet John Shaw Neilson, whom Louise supported. Whittaker was overwhelmed by Louise's energy, enthusiasm and generosity. He noted that she was not only supporting the BMS, but also 'subsidising a string quartet (there is no permanent organisation of this kind in Melbourne), which is to be known as the British Music Society Quartet, and is to appear several times each season at their meetings, besides being available for other concerts'.[31]

There was a resurgence of interest in British music after the war, with emotions turning sharply against Germany. The post-war embargo upon goods imported from Germany was accompanied by a reduction in the promotion of German cultural products. Building on the popularity of Elgar, composers like Frederick Delius, Gustav Holst and Ralph Vaughan Williams were creating a new school of English music. They drew inspiration from French impressionism and particularly from the rich soil of English folk music. As Russian composers had revolted against the Germanic tradition in the nineteenth century, launching a musical renaissance based on their native folk and religious traditions, so a similar musical revival occurred in England after more than two hundred years of inertia.

In Australia Louise was a key promoter of this renewal. Her interest in the new generation of British composers, which included Australians, New Zealanders and Canadians, went beyond anti-German sentiment or even the patriotic attachment to England common to her generation. Her perspective was that of the musicologist – at this time the discipline of musicology was taking shape.[32] For her, music was a complex and diversified practice, in which historical, aesthetic, sociological and physical considerations intermingled. Her work in music research, publishing and recording make this abundantly clear.

In April 1925 the Alliance Française presented her with a silver medal on behalf of the parent society in Paris. Engraved with an open book bearing her name, this was unintentionally apt, for at the age of forty-one she was now contemplating what she hoped to achieve as her life's work. A visit to Europe the year before had helped to sharpen her focus. Her ambition was for something beyond the role of a wealthy salon hostess. The following years saw her commission new works, underwrite performances and explain and defend new forms of musical expression to the general public through performances and lectures. She continued to use her home as a centre for musical activity, with the BMS as the principal vehicle for her patronage.

Over twelve months from September 1925 she arranged the first performances in Melbourne of music by Henry Purcell, Peter Warlock, Gustav

Holst and Vaughan Williams. Australian premieres included two song cycles: Warlock's *The Curlew*, based on poems by Yeats, and Vaughan Williams's *On Wenlock Edge*. From that time she looked for venues that would give the widest exposure to her concerts. The Public Library, Museum and Art Gallery on Swanston Street was central to Melbourne's cultural life and Louise suggested to its trustees that chamber concerts be held there. The first of these was held in the Macarthur Gallery in conjunction with a recently instituted series of art lectures. Soprano Inez Hunter and contralto Freeda Northcote sang before artist Max Meldrum gave a lecture on sculpture.[33]

At this time the idea of a 'return to order' after the devastation of the recent war was having an impact on music as well as on art. The neoclassical works of composers like Prokofiev, Stravinsky and Albert Roussel evoked a world of balance and restraint. Louise had high regard for Roussel, who was hardly known in Australia (plate 25). She admired how he was able to draw upon the structural and formal vitality of older French music, particularly upon Baroque masters like Rameau, and create something new in a contemporary idiom. At Melbourne's Assembly Hall, she staged a concert of Roussel's Trio for piano, violin and cello, with young Melbourne musician Biddy Allen at the piano.

A concert she presented through the Alliance Française in May 1925 demonstrated the depth of her interest and knowledge of French music. The programme of over fourteen items swept through French musical history. Alberto Zelman's Symphony Orchestra – composed largely of amateurs and Zelman's own pupils – performed Rameau's orchestral suite *Les Indes Galantes* (1735), and music from three ballets by Lully. Interspersed throughout the programme were short lectures on thirteenth-century French composers Thibaut de Champagne, Adam de la Halle, Guillaume de Machaut, plus the 'Noel' tradition of 1550. Songs were included by the early eighteenth-century composer André Campra and Roussel and Berlioz. On the piano, Doris Hadden played Couperin, Rameau and Daquin; Harold Elvins played Debussy, Arthur Honegger, Georges Migot, Darius Milhaud and Poulenc. Much of this music was presented for the first time in Australia, with programme notes written by French-born critic and musicologist Michel Calvocoressi. Louise's selection reveals her interest in both early and contemporary music; it hints at the position she was to occupy at the forefront of both the early music revival and contemporary music.

Gustav Holst, like Roussel, had freed himself from an early romantic chromaticism by drawing upon folk traditions and the modal harmonies of the East. Roussel had travelled in southeast Asia, and Holst had become passionately interested in Hindu spirituality (plate 26). Taking inspiration from the East had been a feature of musical innovation since the late nineteenth century. As the music critic for Brisbane's *Courier* explained to readers:

> with the passing of time, progress and intellectual development demand wider artistic comprehension. The great masters of the race then take the beautiful and, to them, the unusual intervals and cadences of other races and make them their own. To the Western temperament, the music of the Far East appears grossly fantastic and barbaric until its national colour and sentiment are understood. Then, adopted because of its power to furnish new and characteristic material, it gives new beauty and life to the somewhat commonplace standards of long usage.[34]

The aim of many of the composers who turned to the East in the early twentieth century was to promote a new vision of humanity through art, to foster peace and mutual respect, aspirations frequently underpinned by spiritualist or theosophical beliefs. Russian painters and musicians reviving their folk traditions, or the new scales and modes imported from the East by Roussel and Holst, were all opening up 'mighty territories of mystery . . . to the music lover' and were viewed as part of the dawn of a new Golden Age.[35] Today the musical orientalism of the period is criticised for engaging with the East at a mere surface level, while the aspiration of creating a new fraternity of humanity through art is viewed as naive. At the time, however, these developments were seen as both progressive and sincere. In June 1925 Louise devoted an entire programme to Holst. This included his *Vedic Hymns* (1907–08) and the first performance in Australia of his orchestral work *The Planets* (1914–16), for which he is best known today. Louise presented this, scored for two pianos, only eighteen months after Holst had conducted the first complete performance.[36] Holst based his chamber opera *Savitri* (1908) on a tale from the *Mahabharata*. In 1926 Louise staged the opera as a benefit performance to augment the initial endowment she and Jimmy had made to the BMS. It was a risky choice. The one act opera is scored for three soloists, chorus and a chamber orchestra of twelve musicians. Considered by many to be Holst's first masterpiece, it was nearly thirteen years before a professional company would perform it. It was first staged in 1921 in London, produced by English baritone Clive Carey, who sang the bass part in Melbourne, with Bernard Heinze conducting.[37]

The story of the opera tells of Death calling for the husband of Savitri, eventually being defeated in his aim by her wit and intelligence. From the opening passages when Death sings offstage unaccompanied, the unfamiliar sparse, but intense, work made a great impression upon the audience. At its conclusion, 'there was that moment of breathless silence which is the greatest tribute that can be accorded. Then came the applause'.[38] The performance raised over £500 and established the Victorian Branch of the BMS on a firm footing, despite the parent body in Britain closing down not long after, in 1930. The Victorian branch exists today in Melbourne and so remains the only survivor of the movement to support British music that began in 1918.

Staging *Savitri* was an achievement, given both the limited resources and audience expectations in Melbourne. Alberto Zelman, for instance, was angered by how Melbourne audiences disturbed performances. He spoke out about the problems performers faced in Melbourne. Among them was the practice of knitting at concerts. 'Last night I attended an orchestral concert', he protested, 'and every time I looked towards the platform my attention was distracted by the continual movement of knitting needles'.[39]

Zelman, like Louise, worked assiduously to raise standards. Zelman was the son of an Italian musician who had come to Melbourne to conduct opera and who had remained (plate 24). His main instrument was the violin, but he quickly learnt that in Australia he was required to be an all-round musician. When a tenor soloist fell ill before a concert performance of Wagner's *Lohengrin*, Zelman sang his part, as well as conducting the orchestra. Zelman campaigned tirelessly for the establishment of a permanent orchestra.[40] Jimmy offered to put up £10,000 to underwrite one, if funds were matched by the public. Melbourne's City Council decided to launch an appeal, known as the Million Shilling Fund, headed by engineer and philanthropist Herbert Brookes. Conductor Bernard Heinze considered that £450,000 was needed.[41]

Both Louise and her husband knew Zelman well and worked closely with him. He was respected and liked by all who had dealings with him. Hardworking, optimistic and amiable, he shared the ambition of the Dyers to raise musical standards in Melbourne, when it served as Australia's federal capital, in order to enrich national life generally. They believed that music could be 'a popular recreation, but it would be a recreation in the literal sense of the word, bringing fresh strength and inspiration into the daily life of the community'.[42] Zelman, having just returned from conducting the Berlin Philharmonic, most clearly pictured the ambivalent situation of music in Melbourne at the time:

> Although it is very true that Melbourne is 'musically starved' it is a remarkable fact that there is probably no city in the Commonwealth where there can be such crowds and such enthusiasm over the indifferent fare that is often the best available. The musical sense of the people has not been starved to death; it has only been starved to an acute degree of hunger. . . . If any criticism of the musical appreciation of the public is justified, it is that, having been so long musically starved, it is willing to swallow almost anything with undiscriminating enthusiasm.[43]

In this climate it is not surprising that during the mid-1920s Louise was beginning to feel the limits of what she could achieve through her support of musical culture in Melbourne. Her drive is evident from the portrait W.B. McInnes painted of her in 1927. Constraints on her work in Australia came from practical obstacles, such as funding and training, as well as from broader cultural and technological developments. Zelman believed that 'all the crowds that throng the picture shows and provide the box office justification for cheap theatrical entertainments, are capturable for something better. They can be reached through their love of music'.[44] However, the wireless, the gramophone, and the picture shows were stealing audiences away from the live performance of music. As one wit exclaimed:

Our Gramophone
Oh! it nearly drives me crazy
When it starts to buzz and whirl,
And my brain grows dim and hazy,
And a brick I long to hurl
When Caruso sings 'La Donna'
In his fullest, clearest tone –
And McCormack murmurs 'Tiny hand'
On our expensive gramophone.[45]

Despite economic prosperity there were few government initiatives to match the generosity of the Dyers. His offer of £10,000 was never matched from the public purse. Significant public spending on music-making did not really happen until the Australian Broadcasting Commission established orchestras in the early 1930s. Without an organised system of government subsidies, concerts continued to be a financial gamble. Audiences were not assured and conductors could barely find the resources to pay musicians for

Melbourne makes a frantic effort to insist on the necessity for hearing more music.

Cartoon from *The Home*, 1 August 1927.

66

performances, let alone rehearsals. The cost for a concert with around seventy performers and only three rehearsals ranged from £400 to £550. Zelman appealed for public support. He hoped the public would provide an audience worth £150 pounds for each concert. 'Surely this is not a great deal to ask', he appealed, 'if this amount can be guaranteed per concert I undertake that the programme will be forthcoming'.[46]

A burgeoning sense of nationalism in the years between the wars was also having an impact upon Louise's efforts to promote new music. In the immediate aftermath of the war, German music had been branded unpatriotic and had been passed over in favour of other repertoire. As the 1920s progressed, even French and British music began to suffer from a narrow preoccupation with the affirmation of national identity through art. One critic argued that, 'Nationalism has been the greatest factor in musical history. It is not only of the utmost importance to the composer, but it also underlies all musical evolution and progress'.[47] Australian musicians, like Australian painters, wanted to free their art from the stupor of English pastoralism. This might involve the use of bush ballads or motifs taken from Indigenous music. For the theosophist Phyllis Campbell it involved creating masses of spiritually significant vibrations.[48] Musicologist Henry Tate even proposed the creation of alternative 'Australian scales' based on Australian bird calls. Louise was not indifferent to these aspirations, publishing the work of young Australian composers and supporting the performance of their work. However, like Melba, she had little time for a prescriptive nationalist agenda in the arts.

Louise's efforts were being noticed beyond Melbourne. In mid-1926 a Hungarian pianist who had studied under Bela Bartók wrote to her from Hanover. Having heard of her patronage, he looked to her for help to promote young composers. He inquired if she, as a champion of modern music, would stage concerts in Melbourne that were impossible to perform in Hungary. 'Our new music is now "out" with Bartók and Kodály but not many cities have this music on their concert stages'.[49] This was written at a time when Louise herself was realising that she could achieve little more in her own country.

Zelman's death in March of the following year brought her frustration into clearer focus. His friends believed that he had died from overwork. He was only ten years older than Louise and she was aware of what Zelman had sacrificed when he turned his back on opportunities abroad to devote himself to Australian musical advancement. Louise tried to console Zelman's widow, the soprano Maude Harrington who was a PLC Collegian and who deplored the waste of her husband's talent and ambition. The *Sun* expressed her sentiment:

> A community such as this can ill-spare its enthusiasts in the arts, and least of all those who are willing to throw their very soul into musical endeavour. Virtually every moment was consecrated by Alberto Zelman to music and in self-sacrificial zeal he laid down his life for a cause as literally as though he had been on a field of battle – and sometimes the fields of music are more war-like than Elysian.[50]

Mr. JAMES DYER.

Mr. James Dyer, of "Kinnoull," Toorak, Melbourne, patron of Music and the Arts, whose gift of £10,000 for the establishment of a permanent orchestra in Melbourne, stands as a gesture of a section towards the country of his adoption. The notable Dyer collection of pictures and antiques will be offered for sale in Melbourne early this month.

Louise and Jimmy sold their art collection through the recently opened New Gallery in Melbourne. Louise attended her last meeting with the Alliance Française in early April 1927, where her final task there had been to establish prizes for French in twenty schools across Melbourne and at Melbourne University. Shortly after, the Dyers left for London.

Cartoon from *The Home*, volume 8, number 3, 1 March 1927.

The Lyrebird Press, 1927–1939

The Dyers sailed to London, although they remained there for only a short time. Melba in 1925 wrote of English conservatism and distrust of experimentation, where audiences asked 'for exactly the same things in music as they demanded forty years ago'.[51] This was what they had fled by leaving Australia. Paris was the place to be for 'the new', with Louise observing 'music in France is a living thing. Paris is the Mecca of musicians. You cannot live there without feeling the vitality which is everywhere striving for expression around you'.[52] Their new apartment was symbolic of their changed life. Their Melbourne home had been an elegant Edwardian mansion, filled with artworks by Australian Impressionists and *fin de siècle* painters. Their Paris apartment, which opened onto a picture view of the Eiffel Tower, was all metal and glass, with the clean lines of contemporary deco style. In her Trocadero apartment she established an informal salon, attracting singers like John Brownlee and Marjorie Lawrence, writers Paul Valéry and James Joyce, artist Max Ernst and musicologists and composers. As a guest inscribed in her visitor's book, Louise the *salonnière* was now in command of dreams.[53] For her housewarming she brought the Holsts to Paris and arranged the premiere of Holst's *Dream City*, the first of twelve Humbert Wolfe songs. Imogen Holst, the composer's daughter, described how Holst was ill at ease when he found himself in the midst of the distinguished gathering Louise had assembled, 'but he forgot his unsuccessful efforts to speak French as soon as Dorothy Silk began singing the songs'.[54] A few weeks later, Silk sang the songs at their first public performance in London's Wigmore Hall.

In these early days in France Louise became interested in the work that Henry Prunières was doing as editor of the journal *La Revue Musicale*. From its first issue in November 1920, this was the most lively music journal of the day and enjoyed the largest circulation of any magazine of its kind. A forum for contemporary music, it featured articles by composers like Bartók and Kodály. In its issues for 1921–22 Nadia Boulanger wrote on Fauré's religious music, Egon Wellesz on Bartók's theatrical work and Calvocoressi on Grove's *Dictionary of Music and Musicians*.[55] The journal particularly reflected

Prunières's own musicological area of expertise: seventeenth-century music, especially French and Italian opera. The first issue featured an article on Louis Couperin by musicologist and organist André Pirro, with a musical supplement of five unedited keyboard pieces.

This interest in early French music was part of a broader movement, which cut across music, the visual arts, historical studies and even theology. A movement inspired by a return *ad fontes*, it argued for a return to sources, and France was at the forefront. In the nineteenth century, the French Benedictine abbey of Solesmes sought to revive the aural landscape of medieval Europe through its promotion of Gregorian chant. Although this tapped into a nineteenth-century fascination with medievalism, Solesmes went beyond mere nostalgia and collected manuscripts for its 'scientific laboratory'. These were transcribed and edited as the basis for determining an authentic performance of chant, freed from the debased traditions of the immediate past. As French monks researched chant, French theologians went back beyond the Middle Ages to analyse and publish the earliest Christian texts. Interest in the past had a contemporary and modernising purpose. The Dominican friars who led the return to sources were not fusty antiquarians, their interest being the contemporary world and its culture. As they brought to light patristic texts they were commissioning artworks from modern artists like Georges Rouault, Fernand Léger, Henri Matisse, Pierre Bonnard and Jean Lurçat and buildings from architects like Le Corbusier.

In music a return to the past was seen as the key to unlocking a new and experimental future. Some musicians had done this, such as Mendelssohn, who revived the work of J.S. Bach. What changed in the early twentieth century was the systematic and scientific way that this was approached, and from that time musicology developed as a distinct discipline. Taking the lead in musicological research was André Pirro at the Sorbonne. His discovery of thirteenth-century manuscripts, unknown fifteenth-century polyphonic works and pieces for organ by the Danish master Buxtehude encouraged others. Libraries in France held a wealth of musical history.

Paris at this time was a mecca not only for classical musicians but also for black singers and performers. The popularity of 'le jazz hot' dovetailed neatly

Louise Dyer's apartment building on the Rue Schaeffer. *Photographed in 2010 by Eileen Chanin.*

with the early music revival. Virtuosity in jazz improvisation encouraged interest in the habits of the players in Lully's time, when musicians improvised while playing, and variations, cadenzas and embroideries were the norm. Baroque composer–performers like Frescobaldi were compared with modern jazz masters. The strong formal qualities of early music were said to provide the bedrock for the filigree of improvisation. This was welcomed after lush, layered romanticism, which appeared rambling by contrast and indifferent to structure. Composers aiming for authenticity in music sought this by carving from the musical bedrock of the past, just as sculptors looked for vitality in direct carving.

The Dyers regularly attended musicological congresses, where Louise made many friends and useful connections. Interest in contemporary music took her to the annual festivals of the International Society for Contemporary Music (SIMC), a significant forum, at which leading contemporary composers met and presented performances of recently composed works.[56] When the SIMC met in Frankfurt-am-Main in June 1927, the gathering included Bela Bartók, Raymond Petit, Aaron Copland, Mario Castelnuovo-Tedesco and Alban Berg.

Two things were quickly becoming clear to Louise as essential to the work of unearthing and promoting early music. The first was scholarly research and access to archives, the importance of which was confirmed when she was invited to the library of the music-collector Paul Hirsch, whose collection of over 20,000 first editions, manuscripts and theoretical writings deeply impressed her.[57] She began hunting for material herself. Over two years, from May 1929, she sourced, with help from Prunières and the Basle merchant Henning Opperman, over two hundred printed works, theoretical writings, libretti and manuscripts.[58] Her collection reflected her principal interest in English and French music, particularly by Purcell, Couperin and Lully. These enabled her to study source material in detail.

The second issue that caught her attention was in the way music was presented. By the nineteenth century, with the advances realised through the Industrial Revolution, music could be reproduced widely and cheaply, but these ugly editions lay browning and crumbling in libraries all over the world. In 1934 Julien Cain, Director-General of the National Library of France, devoted an exhibition of music up to the period of the end of the eighteenth century. The rich store of manuscripts from the Middle Ages dazzled all who visited the show. On display was a manuscript of a *Recueil des Motets* from the library of the Medicine faculty at Montpellier. For Louise this was a manuscript of remarkable interest and beauty: 'I was seized by desire to disinter, not only the manuscript itself, with its delight for the eye, but the music it contained with its charm for the ear'.[59]

Thus began her involvement with the world of publishing, although her first foray into this arena was not entirely happy. She allocated funds to Prunières to publish the complete works of Lully, under the imprint of the *Revue Musicale*. Lully had been a long-term interest of hers and she had featured him in a programme of French music staged in Melbourne in July 1922, when the Alliance Française celebrated the Tercentenary of Molière's birth. Prunières dedicated the first volume of the *Œuvres complètes* to Louise. He then pressed for ongoing funding, which she advanced, but the subsequent volumes were not forthcoming. Louise had originally contracted him to produce the complete works of Lully in thirty-six volumes, to be published in an edition of three hundred. As a major publishing project, this was planned over a twelve-year period, with international distribution by London music publishers Stainer & Bell. When the project stalled and it appeared that no further volumes would appear, she took legal action. The collected edition of Lully's music never eventuated and Louise's case against Prunières dragged on in a protracted affair before the Paris courts.

Her experience using European libraries and in collecting manuscripts prompted her to consider the situation in Australia, which lacked such easy access to resources. She also maintained a strong link with Melbourne through the regular 'Impressions of France' columns she wrote for the Melbourne *Herald*. In September 1930 she offered a collection of music to the Melbourne Public Library. She intended to place there a comprehensive collection of English music, beginning with a complete set of Holst's published scores up to March 1931. Yet, negotiations for her gift dragged on over the duty payable on music imported into Australia. To remedy the impasse, she enlisted help from her friend the Victorian newspaper owner R.D. Elliott, who was a trustee of the Library and Art Gallery. A self-made man, the son of a Northumberland grocer, quick-tempered, with a restless energy, he campaigned for Empire Free Trade. Despite even his support, the duty was never waived. Her catalogue of Holst's complete music was eventually published bearing the name of the Melbourne Public Library, with the credit line 'compiled by Louise B.M. Dyer for the musicians of Australia'. It was the first of an intended series on music by British composers, with a second planned for Elgar.

In 1932 Louise embarked upon the project for which she was to become celebrated worldwide. She launched her own musical press, the Lyrebird Press or Editions l'Oiseau Lyre. Like Melba, Louise never forgot that Australia's sounds, scents, and sights were 'the first bars' written in the impromptu of her life.[60] The emblem of her press combined the lyre, an instrument from antiquity as old as the harp and associated with Apollo as a symbol of art and beauty, with Australia's lyrebird, famed for its showy display and mimicry of calls.[61] She was being provocative, because unlike the lyrebird her endeavour was not concerned with imitation. Lyrebird Press was established to reproduce unpublished or unknown work in modern scholarly editions, thus making early music available. A further aim was to support contemporary composers by commissioning and publishing new works. Announcing the press, she wrote: 'I hope that the Lyrebird will be able to extend his wings without any hindrance, and fly through time and space, and that propitious winds will allow him to alight wherever he recognises his native habitat: the land of music'.[62]

Her first edition was devoted to François Couperin (1668–1733). Interest in his keyboard music had been growing for some time, with the two-hundredth anniversary of his death approaching in 1933. Yet little was known of his other compositions, including his chamber music and two Masses for organ. She decided to publish Couperin's complete works in twelve volumes, reproduced in full for the first time and issued in an edition of 325 copies. Like the complete works of Lully, which she had planned with Prunières, this was an ambitious venture. The first volumes would appear in June 1932 and the last would coincide with the second centenary of his death in the following year. Louise drew on a team of musicologists to prepare the edition from manuscripts and printed sources, engaging the best Parisian designers and craftsmen to produce it. She wanted this to be as perfectly done 'as is humanly possible'. For her, 'Couperin's music is one of the glories of France . . . full of wit, effortless elegance and charm'.[63]

The *Œuvres Complètes de François Couperin* created a sensation. Couperin was resurrected from 250 years of oblivion – and in spectacular fashion. The edition was both sumptuous and scholarly. The twelve volumes, published under the direction of Maurice Cauchie, established a new standard in music publishing. The set was bound in jade green and cream leather, with the feathers of the lyrebird forming a graceful design on the flyleaf and a picture of a lyre on the back cover. The binding was done by Rose Adler, who had been the star designer at the International Book Exhibit at the Petit Palais in 1931 (plate 30). As the London *Sunday Times* noted: 'the volumes are beautifully engraved, on superb paper that will last forever and are exquisitely bound. Mrs Dyer's theory has been that beautiful and precious things, in music no less than in literature, are worthy of the most beautiful presentation possible, their binding, paper and typography'.[64] For Louise, it was no less than the respect owed to music. Couperin was a careful editor of his own work, and Louise's edition reproduced Couperin's original pagination and annotations, thereby enabling the modern student to study Couperin firsthand. The long-term impact of her edition led to an entire reappraisal of Couperin as a composer.[65]

This was a remarkable achievement, at a time of extreme socioeconomic unrest and political uncertainty in France. Rising unemployment fuelled distrust of foreigners and prompted increasingly xenophobic restrictions. Women were particularly vulnerable, unable to have personal bank accounts and without electoral representation. Not even the left-wing Popular Front supported women's right to vote at this time. In the face of these obstacles Louise pressed on regardless, with her aim fixed on historical continuity.

Louise's editions were never intended for trade on the book market. She wanted them placed in the libraries of universities and conservatoriums as a reference for musicians and scholars. To prevent their being traded speculatively, she would not allow them to be sold commercially through the ordinary channels; they were sold by subscription. To acquire them required an application to her press, which would then be assessed. The twelve-volume set of the Couperin was priced at £30.[66] She inscribed a presentation copy to the Melbourne Public Library: 'Number One went to the President of the French Republic. Number Two goes to my own homeland library'. Any profits were devoted to further publications.

To celebrate the launch of the edition she held a dinner at the Cercle Interallié, a recently established hub for officers and diplomats of the Allied nations, of which Jimmy was an active member. Early music luminaries, along with Parisian dignitaries, were present. A Greek dancer performed to music of Couperin played on the clavecin.

The Couperin edition set the tone for the Lyrebird Press, which became synonymous with modern scholarship for its rediscovery of the past and the production methods used in its representation. The Couperin was followed almost annually by other editions, equally impressive in the depth of research required to prepare them and in their production values. In 1934 Egon Wellesz, the Austrian-born British composer and musicologist who had been studying Byzantine music for over twenty years, edited the *Trésor de Musique Byzantine*. Wellesz had been one of the first pupils of Arnold Schoenberg and in 1934 was a professor at the University of Vienna, where he founded the Institute of Byzantine Music. His edition for Lyrebird Press was made using his own modern notation of Byzantine music.

In the same year Louise released the first of Pierre Attaingnant's thirteen books of motets. Louise found special pleasure in reviving editions that Attaingnant, a publisher of music active in Paris during the sixteenth century, had brought out four hundred years earlier. Using single-impression movable type for music printing, Attaingnant was the first publisher to distribute music on a European scale. His innovations halved the time required to set and print music and so paved the way for modern printed music. Albert Smijers, Professor of Musicology at the University of Utrecht, prepared the Attaingnant edition for Louise.

Her most spectacular publication, however, was the Montpellier Codex, which had so inspired her when she first saw it on display at the National Library of France. Compiled around 1300, the codex included over three hundred polyphonic works, most of which had been composed fifty years earlier. Louise published the codex in four volumes over 1935–39, the editor being Yvonne Rokseth, a brilliant pupil of André Pirro at the Sorbonne. While preparing the codex for publication, Rokseth was appointed to the University of Strasbourg, the first woman to teach musicology at a university.

Lyrebird Press first of all published a facsimile of the manuscript, which in the next two volumes was transcribed into modern notation, with critical notes and commentary making up the last. The edition was enclosed in panels of Australian Blackwood. 'Mrs Dyer is always original', the London *Times* reported:

> the scholar, perhaps, would prefer to have his treasures in some solid and unobtrusive binding, but she has wished not only to enrich his scholarship, but also to satisfy her own passion for beautiful books and to express it with some touch of her own patriotism. Let Europe produce its heritage of art to be clothed in the rare products of the antipodes![67]

From the outset, hers was an international press, publishing music ranging from the thirteenth to the twentieth centuries and with subscribers worldwide. Despite Louise having extended the frontiers of music, institutional support in Australia for her editions was limited.[68]

These editions, along with music from the fifteenth-century Burgundian Court (1937), Couperin's harpsichord works (1936) and music by Marchand and Dieupart, were continental in their focus. Yet Louise did not overlook English repertoire. She published sonatas by John Blow (1934), hitherto unknown, and Henry Purcell (1936) and in 1939 engaged the artist Marie Laurencin to design an edition of Blow's *Venus and Adonis*, edited by Sir Anthony Lewis, the English composer, editor and music educator. Nor did she neglect contemporary composers. Young composers published by her included Guillaume Landré (1934, 1936), the Bulgarian Boyan Ikonomov (1937), Henry Barraud (1938), Darius Milhaud (1934, 1938) and Fernand Oubradous (1938). Australian composers Peggy Glanville-Hicks and Margaret Sutherland saw their work issued for the first time through Louise's support. An edition of music for wind instruments, published in 1934, brought together the Australians Arthur Benjamin, Esther Rofe, Peggy Glanville-Hicks and John Tallis.

Anthony Lewis's description of one of his first meetings with Louise provides an insight into her character. She attended a lecture he gave:

At the end of the lecture she asked a very shrewd question which more or less torpedoed what I had been talking about . . . But from then on, we became firm friends, as the years passed, I found myself working for her in various capacities, as music-editor, adviser, sleeve note-writer and the like.

In common with all those who worked for Louise, he soon found that it was almost impossible to say no to her: 'however reluctant or unwilling to become involved one might be, you eventually found yourself doing whatever it was she wanted you to do, and doing it to the best of your capacity, too. She was like that'. Although she was known for being generous and warm-hearted, Lewis recalled that she 'had no use for pretentiousness and incompetence, and would say so with devastating frankness, to the discomfiture of those few who foolishly sought to presume on her.[69]

Amidst this flurry of publication activity she was called back to Australia. Her brother Harold Gengoult Smith had become Mayor of Melbourne in 1931. The press made much of his bachelorhood, despite reports circulating that the other bachelor mayor, Jimmy Walker in New York, was carrying out his duties without the assistance of a Lady Mayoress. The 1934 celebrations marking the centenary of European settlement in Victoria were approaching and Harold asked Louise to assist him in this event. As Lord Mayor during the Victorian Centenary preparations, Harold also became chairman of the centenary committee, following his father fifty-eight years earlier, who had chaired Melbourne's preparations for the 1888 centenary exhibition. Getting wind that Louise might be Lady Mayoress, Keith Murdoch wrote to her from Melbourne 'we want some good people to take the lead in restoring spirits out here'.[70]

The Dyers sailed back to Melbourne in early 1932, after five years away. When the *Oronsay* berthed at Melbourne, the Royal Victorian Liedertafel welcomed them with song. Louise arrived, equipped with recorded lectures by musicians Albert Roussel and Arthur Honneger and by the writers André Maurois and Jean Giradou. She announced these gramophone recordings were intended for use in Australian schools to redress the fact that 'France and Australia are mutually out of touch'. They came with bilingual text in a 'scheme of education whereby the various countries may become more conversant with each other's development'.[71] Harold envisaged more than stereotypical processions and floral pageants for Victoria's Centenary celebrations: he anticipated cosmopolitan events, on a scale which did justice to the occasion, such as the Centenary Air Race of 1934.[72] Yet, unlike the celebrations of 1901, when federalist pride generated an outlook seeking world connections, the 1934 centenary generally fixed on the local. Images of pioneers were widely distributed, and the rhetoric of the celebrations focused on Victorians as the beneficiaries of the past. Developments abroad were met with scepticism. The celebrations seemed decidedly insular compared with those Louise's father had helped to organise in 1901. The principal ceremony was held on 12 November, when the National Shrine of Remembrance was opened. A crowd of 300,000 attended the dedication. Victorians congratulated themselves:

> Melbourne carries her 100 years well. She is a dignified old lady. Her brow is calm and her face is bright. Her figure is good, and her health very sound. Her morals are almost irreproachable, yet, on the whole – in spite of jeers from impolite sister cities – she can claim to have a sense of humour. Her financial position is strong, but her nature is generous. And she is a good Mama to her children.[73]

Harold had hoped that the celebrations would draw worldwide attention to Melbourne, promoting tourism and long-term investment, particularly given the impact of the Great Depression. However, the vision behind the celebrations was local, not cosmopolitan. Louise had made the lyrebird a symbol of what Australians could achieve internationally – in marked contrast to the way the lyrebird was used during the celebrations, where a stuffed specimen was installed on a mound of sand in Melbourne's Town Hall, in a recreated bush environment.[74] Yet younger artists were aware of Louise's worldwide reputation. As a tribute to her one danced as a lyrebird at the Victorian Artists Ball, held for the centenary and organised by Louise's old friend, the painter Louis McCubbin, and young artists Sam Atyeo and Moya Dyring. Atyeo was the artist whom Louise had earlier employed to design the logo for her press (plate 32).

Let's Talk of

Interesting
P·E·O·P·L·E

—Broothort.

WON MANY HONORS.

MRS. JAMES DYER, who is the sister of Melbourne's Lord Mayor, Sir Harold Gengoult Smith, will reach Melbourne on August 27, and remain there till early in 1935.

Mrs. Dyer, who founded the British Music Society of Victoria, and is President of Honor of our Alliance Française, has made her home in Paris for the past few years. She is privileged to write L.A.B. after her name, and is a Gold Medallist of the Royal Academy of Music.

Recently she received the Legion d'Honneur, and she is also an Officer d'Academie avec Palmes.

Mrs. Dyer has published the works of Couperin and other old French and British composers in her own Lyre Bird Press in Paris, and she is the Australian member of the Inter Alia Club of Paris. This is a great honor, as each country is represented by only one member.

Notice of Louise Dyer's return to Australia
(*The Australian Women's Weekly, August 18, 1934*)

No mention was made of the arts and music beyond cinema and radio in the *Age Centenary Supplement*.[75] The *Argus* expressed dismay at what was described as 'divided streams of art'. 'It is perhaps a pity that more of the present-day Australian artists have not devoted themselves to extending its boundaries'. The paper considered that many younger artists in Melbourne were being led astray by sterile artistic speculations, 'and to have been caught up in the backwash of successive European movements, which can have only slight artistic validity in a country which in tradition, experience and complexity has nothing in common with Paris or Berlin'.[76]

Louise braved the celebrations and graced mayoral reception lines, notwithstanding that the press frequently cited her as her brother's wife. On her own initiative she marked the centenary by publishing a book of pipe music written for children by Australian composers (plate 31). 'There is a great need', she said, 'in our own day for people to make music themselves. This is where the musical pipes come in'.[77] Her father had been the first to edit and publish a medical journal in Victoria, and as a partner in several newspapers advocating liberal principles he knew that education was vital to promoting change.[78] Louise's work always had a strong educative purpose to it, and increasingly she recognised that modern gramophone recordings could bring the concert hall into the home and reshape engagement with music. It was a natural step for her to expand her publishing efforts to include recordings; in doing this she was to reach an audience much greater than she first imagined.

At the time Louise founded her press, Emile Berliner's forty-year-old recording system, whereby a stylus etched out recorded wave forms on wax discs, was being converted (in around 1925) to electrical recording. Microphones and triode valve amplifiers introduced for radio broadcasting made recording less cumbersome, while the quality was also vastly improved. The new recording methods, though initially poorer in sound than the old cylinder phonographs, were acoustic and at least gave the suggestion of passionate, human music-making.

As far back as 1902–04, gramophone recordings of the Czech pianist Edward Goll, whom Louise knew in Melbourne, had been made by the Phonotikia Italiana and later in Paris and America by Brunswick. Melbourne critic Thorold Waters advocated the value of the phono as a teaching aid to both singers and instrumentalists. Aware that music on the printed page was only a symbol of the actual music itself, Louise wanted to bring it to life, performed by the finest artists. While her printed editions ensured a permanent record, she saw that she could extend musical knowledge in audiences by authoritative recordings, which would enable people to hear the unfamiliar early music she was reviving. She recognised also that in actual performance the music she had recovered went beyond historical interest and had life as viable as the most recent contemporary work. A new dynamic of space and time was created, for as Harold Arnold, a physicist who had improved the sound quality of gramophones, remarked 'now with one broad sweep the barriers of time and space are gone'.[79] Citing Vaughan Williams's judgement that music does not exist until actual sound is produced, Louise decided that gramophone records would illustrate the Lyrebird publications: she became the first publisher to simultaneously issue printed music and recordings.

Her first recordings were of Noël Gallon's *Récit et Allegro* for bassoon and piano, Vincent d'Indy's *Quintette* (1924) and of Joseph Canteloube, who made his only appearance on record for Lyrebird as the accompanist for a group performing his own folk-song arrangements. The 78" discs, bearing the Lyrebird symbol, presented music by Couperin, Rameau, Lalande and Campra, music that was not represented in the English recording catalogues. When launching the first volumes of the Couperin Edition, she had assisted Henri Sauguet in the preparation of a brief cantata and this was to be his first work to appear on record. *La Voyante* (1932) is a miniature cantata for solo female voice and a small group of ten instruments. Sung by mezzo-soprano Germaine Cernay, with a chamber orchestra conducted by Roger Desormière, this recording quickly became a collector's piece.

Louise went to a great deal of trouble when choosing artists for recordings, using the best instrumentalists, like harpsichordists Ruggiero Gerlin and Isabelle Nef and flautist Marcel Moyse, and they usually played from her latest critical edition of the music. In 1938 she sent Percy Grainger a list of her gramophone records, noting that she was 'illustrating many things that I published by this means. Only experts are used and people steeped in the musical tradition of that time which, as you know, is rare to find'.[80] She asked him to help make them better known, as 'no one more than you can realise the stupendous difficulties of carrying on such an enterprise entirely alone'. Australian duty on foreign gramophone records made almost prohibitive the importation of her recordings into Australia.[81] Louise's self-directed enterprise saw her working as music editor, adviser, sleeve-note writer and publicist. 'I am so particular in watching everything', she confided to music critic Harry Colless.[82] She had one young assistant, Sylvie Belin, whom she trained to be equally conscientious (plate 27). Those working in the industry observed her building up:

> a record catalogue that became the envy of the commercial moguls
> of the gramophone world, whose initial scorn turned into grudging
> admiration and then furtive and finally open imitation. They learnt
> that there was one thing you could not do to Louise Dyer, and that was
> to ignore her'.[83]

Today her recordings are a rich resource for musicologists and musicians.

At this time Jimmy was pursuing the £10,000 he had made available in 1927 to assist in the establishment of a permanent professional symphony orchestra in Melbourne. The fund had increased to £15,000 over seven years, but as nothing had been done to add to the principal, Jimmy approached the Victorian Supreme Court for a variation of the trust. He appealed twice to make the trust over to the British Music Society. This was achieved in 1936: Jimmy gave £10,000 to the BMS, £400 to the Liedertafel and £400 to the Music Teachers Association of Victoria. The remainder of the interest went toward Lyrebird Press publications of neglected masterpieces.

When Max Ernst painted Louise's portrait in Paris in 1933 he emphasised her direct gaze. Ernst saw her as the visionary she was, ahead of her times. While her fellow Victorians fixed on the past, Louise worked to the future. Her achievements were honoured by the French Government when she was awarded the Légion d'honneur by the President of the Republic, Albert Lebrun, in 1935. Saluted as the 'French Lyrebird', she was singled out for the new life she had infused into the rich, but forgotten, repertoire of past centuries.

From the mid-1930s her activities were followed closely across the Atlantic. John Haughton, writing for *Musical America*, America's oldest magazine on classical music, praised her philanthropy and foresight.[84] A letter written to her noted that her work would 'have a deep influence not only on the Australian people but on the world generally'.[85] Her editions were exhibited at the Library of Congress, the Boston Library and at Harvard. When Louise visited America in 1938 on a promotional and lecture tour, Americans noted that she did not accept lecture fees: 'In this profit-seeking era, that seems almost incredible, but it ceases to be when one meets Mrs Dyer and hears the story of her career'.[86] Interviewed in New York, she described her publishing and recording activities as the justification for her existence:

> I do want people to know that I'm not just a rich woman who gives money to a cause. I work at this eighteen hours a day. The Lyre Bird Press is me and one secretary. We have the greatest musicologists in the world prepare our manuscripts, but I've always said I'd never publish a book I did not know and understand thoroughly myself. [87]

In France she received exceptional recognition at the 1937 Paris International Exposition, an exposition presenting visions of the future of modern life and celebrating creativity across nations (plate 33). The Grand Prix for music was awarded to her in the Beaux-Arts section of the exhibition. For a music publisher exhibiting for the first time this was a notable achievement: Louise won the prize in the face of competition from larger music publishing firms, some of which had been in the business for two hundred years or more.

Louise Dyer with niece Marion in Melbourne c. 1937. *Photograph courtesy of Mr & Mrs N Gengoult Smith*

Louise also served, as the only British member, on the committee of patrons of the Versailles Music Festival, which included President Lebrun, the polymath Paul Valéry and the author André Maurois, who were trying to establish a music festival at Versailles.

Concerts from her editions were played in Paris at the Salle Gaveau, a favoured auditorium for chamber music. Attended by the wife of the French President, these were broadcast to Australia. In Melbourne, her old school, PLC, was relocating to new premises and she offered to kick-start a music library by sending it her publications of the last eight years. She considered this would help 'all students of music for the sources they will have access to are important and great research work will be at their disposition'.[88]

Each year Louise penned Christmas greetings from herself and Jimmy to friends and family, written in her firm hand with large upright lettering. Their Christmas card of 1937 featured an excerpt from Handel's *Messiah*: 'For behold darkness shall cover the face of the earth'. She noted that the aria was scored for an alto voice, as sung at the first performance of *Messiah* in Dublin in 1742, and came from the music manuscript in St Michael's College, Tenbury, on which she had begun work. Shortly after, in January 1938, just following their twenty-sixth wedding anniversary, Jimmy died, aged seventy-seven. He had assisted Louise with the press and worked with the Scottish community in Paris. He had followed the dictum of fellow Scot philanthropist Andrew Carnegie, who said that the man who died rich, died disgraced. With Jimmy, Louise had enjoyed companionship and love. He gave her indomitable spirit free rein, ungrudgingly. Together they had been deeply and passionately serious about the art of music, in the service of which they directed their talents and personal wealth. Louise took his ashes back to Melbourne.

Dora Ohlfsen

1. Photograph of herself which Dora Ohlfsen sent from Rome, 22 November 1908.
National Art Archive, Art Gallery of New South Wales, Sydney.

2. Nicholas Chevalier, *Portrait of Christian Ohlfsen-Bagge* 1855. *Image courtesy of the artist's family.*

3. Photograph of herself which Dora sent from St Petersburg, 11 February 1896. *National Art Archive, Art Gallery of New South Wales, Sydney.*

4. Dora Ohlfsen, *The Awakening of Australian Art* 1907. Photograph of Dora's plaster cast for this medal on display at the National Art Gallery of New South Wales, with one of the medals struck from the cast in between the two sides of the plaster medallion. *National Art Archive, Art Gallery of New South Wales, Sydney.*

5. Dora Ohlfsen, *Mother and Child* 1906,
bronze medallion, 9.2 cm (diam). *Collection of the
Art Gallery of New South Wales, Sydney 1210.*

6. Dora Ohlfsen, *Gabriele D'Annunzio* 1909,
bronze medallion, 12.0 cm (diam). *Collection of the
Art Gallery of New South Wales, Sydney 1209.*

7. Dora Ohlfsen, *Ceres* 1910, bronze relief, 9.2.0 x 14.0 cm.
Collection of the Art Gallery of New South Wales, Sydney 1207.

8. Dora Ohlfsen, *Premier Holman* 1913,
bronze medallion, 28.0 cm (diam). *Collection of the
Powerhouse Museum, Sydney 89/328.*

9. Dora Ohlfsen, *Anzac Medal* 1916,
plaster cast of the front of the medal. *National Art
Archive, Art Gallery of New South Wales, Sydney.*

10. Dora Ohlfsen, *Anzac Medal* 1916,
plaster cast of the reverse of the medal. *National Art
Archive, Art Gallery of New South Wales, Sydney.*

11. Composite images showing how Dora Ohlfsen's bronze relief of a chariot race (1915) would have looked over the entrance door to the National Art Gallery of New South Wales. *Images created by Matt Nix.*

12. Dora Ohlfsen, *The Good Shepherd* c. 1920,
bronze sculpture, present whereabouts unknown.
National Art Archive, Art Gallery of New South Wales, Sydney.

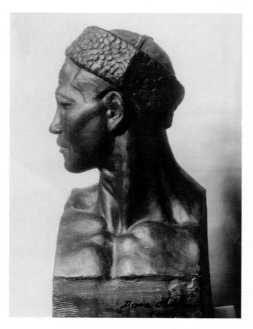

13. Dora Ohlfsen, *Cosacco del Kuban* 1929,
waxed gesso, present whereabouts unknown.
National Art Archive, Art Gallery of New South Wales, Sydney.

14. Dora Ohlfsen, *Dionysius* c. 1931,
plaster, Non-Catholic cemetery, Rome. *National Art
Archive, Art Gallery of New South Wales, Sydney.*

15. Dora Olfsen's war memorial at Formia, Italy, 2008.
16. INSET: Dora Ohlfsen in her studio with the model of her statue *Sacrifice*, 1924.
National Art Archive, Art Gallery of New South Wales, Sydney.

17. The Dedication of Dora Ohlfsen's war memorial at Formia, 18 July 1926, showing Dora Ohlfsen standing next to Tosti di Valminuta in his naval uniform, with the Archbishop of Gaeta.
National Art Archive, Art Gallery of New South Wales Sydney.

18. Dora Ohlfsen with the plaster cast of her commissioned medallion of Mussolini, 1923.
National Art Archive, Art Gallery of New South Wales, Sydney.

Louise Dyer

19. Louise Dyer, c. 1914.
L'Oiseau-Lyre Archive, Louise Hanson-Dyer Music Library, University of Melbourne.

20. Tom Roberts, *Louise, daughter of the Hon. L. L. Smith* 1888, oil on canvas, 102.0 x 77.7 cm.
National Gallery of Victoria, Melbourne. Gift of Mrs James Dyer, 1932.

21. James and Louise Dyer on their honeymoon, 1912.
*L'Oiseau-Lyre Archive, Louise Hanson-Dyer Music Library,
University of Melbourne.*

22. Photograph of Louise Dyer, c. 1914.
Image courtesy of Mr & Mrs N Gengoult Smith.

23. Louise Dyer with sculpture, c. 1920. *Image courtesy of the Bibliothèque National de Paris.*

24. Photograph of Alberto Zelman, c. 1923.
L'Oiseau-Lyre Archive, Louise Hanson-Dyer Music Library, University of Melbourne.

25. Inscribed photograph sent by the composer Albert Roussel to Louise Dyer. *L'Oiseau-Lyre Archive, Louise Hanson-Dyer Music Library, University of Melbourne.*

26. Photograph of the composer Gustav Holst.
L'Oiseau-Lyre Archive, Louise Hanson-Dyer Music Library, University of Melbourne.

27. Louise Dyer with Mlle Belin, Paris, 1930.
L'Oiseau-Lyre Archive, Louise Hanson-Dyer Music Library, University of Melbourne.

28. Louise Dyer in her Paris Apartment, 1929. On the wall can be seen the W.B. McInnes' 1927 portrait of her.

29. Programme designed by Blamire Young for the concert of the BMS on 19 July 1927.
Blamire Young AAA folder, State Library of Victoria, Melbourne.

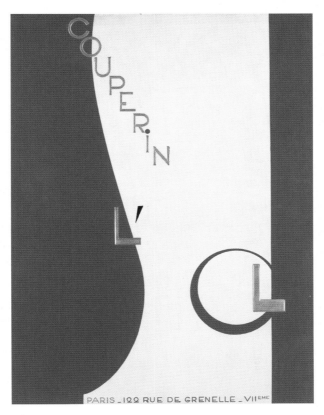

30. Cover designed by Rose Adler for the *Œuvres Complètes de François Couperin* 1932. *Collection of the State Library of Victoria, Melbourne.*

31. The cover to *The Piper's Music Book*
(The Melbourne Centenary Music Book) 1934.
Collection of the State Library of Victoria, Melbourne.

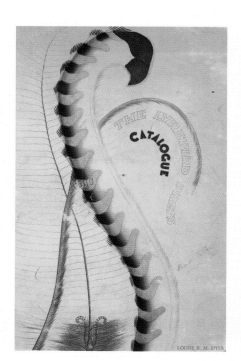

32. Cover designed by Sam Atyeo for the
catalogue of The Lyrebird Press, Paris, 1936.
*Éditions de L'Oiseau-Lyre Archive. Collection
of the State Library of Victoria, Melbourne.*

33. Cover for the 1937 Paris Exposition catalogue.
*L'Oiseau-Lyre Archive, Louise Hanson-Dyer Music Library,
University of Melbourne.*

Clarice Zander

34. Clarice Zander around the time Charles Zander left Australia with the AIF, c. 1915.
National Art Archive, Art Gallery of New South Wales, Sydney.

35. Clarice Zander, c. 1912.
*National Art Archive, Art Gallery
of New South Wales, Sydney.*

36. Charles Zander, c. 1913.
*National Art Archive, Art Gallery
of New South Wales, Sydney.*

37. Clarice Zander (centre) on the beach at St Kilda, Melbourne, c. 1914.
National Art Archive, Art Gallery of New South Wales, Sydney.

38. Clarice and Charles Zander shortly after their marriage, 1915.
National Art Archive, Art Gallery of New South Wales, Sydney.

39. Charles Zander recuperating from
his wounds at Cordes Hall with
Clarice Zander sitting beside him,
1918. *National Art Archive, Art Gallery
of New South Wales, Sydney.*

40. J. S. MacDonald, *Portrait of Clarice
Zander* 1919, pencil on paper.
Collection of Jocelyn Plate, Sydney.

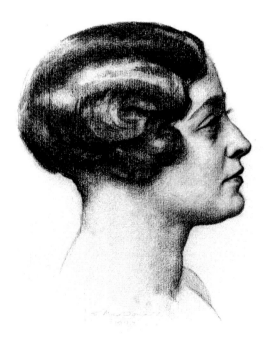

41. Clarice Zander holding Jocelyn
Zander at Red Cliffs, 1922.
National Art Archive, Art Gallery of
New South Wales, Sydney.

42. Clarice and Jocelyn Zander
returning to Australia in 1933.
National Art Archive, Art Gallery of
New South Wales, Sydney.

43. Clarice Zander with Jacob Epstein, 1932.
National Art Archive, Art Gallery of New South Wales, Sydney.

44. Clarice Zander in attendance at the exhibition of British Contemporary Art, Sydney, 1933.
National Art Archive, Art Gallery of New South Wales, Sydney.

45. Clarice Zander during the unpacking of the Chinese exhibition at the Royal Academy, 1935.
National Art Archive, Art Gallery of New South Wales, Sydney.

46. Amy Browning, *Clarice Zander sick in bed* 1938, oil on canvas. *Collection of Jocelyn Plate, Sydney.*

47. Clarice and Jocelyn Zander at Brook Cottage, 1940.
National Art Archive, Art Gallery of New South Wales, Sydney.

Mary Cecil Allen

48. Mary Cecil Allen, Melbourne, c. 1926, *Allen Papers, State Library of Victoria, Melbourne.*

49. Mary Cecil Allen, *Portrait study* c. 1920, oil on canvas, 76.5 x 64.0 cm. *Castlemaine Art Gallery.*

50. Mary Cecil Allen, *Hilda Elliott with black shawl* 1926, oil on canvas, 152.5 x 122.0 cm.
Collection of the Mildura Art Centre, Hilda Elliott Bequest 1970. Photographer Krystal Seigerman.

51. Mary Cecil Allen, *The Lake, Melbourne University* c. 1921, oil on canvas, present whereabouts unknown.
From slide in the Frances Derham Papers, University of Melbourne Archive.

52. Mary Cecil Allen, *Sketch of Miss Audrey Stevenson as Circe* 1930, oil on canvas, 41.0 x 36.0 cm.
Collection of the National Gallery of Victoria, Melbourne, gift of Miss Beatrice Allen in 1972.

53. Mary Cecil Allen, *Portrait of Jessie Brookes* 1928–9, oil on canvas 62.0 x 42.0 cm.
Private collection, Melbourne.

54. Mary Cecil Allen, *Reclining Blue Figure* c. 1930, watercolour over pencil, 60.2 x 57.6 cm.
Collection of the National Gallery of Victoria, Melbourne, purchased 1972.

55. Mary Cecil Allen, *New York* c. 1933, oil on canvas, present whereabouts unknown.
From slide in the Frances Derham Papers, University of Melbourne Archive.

56. Mary Cecil Allen, *The crazy stairs I see from my studio* 1933, oil on canvas, present whereabouts unknown.
From slide in the Frances Derham Papers, University of Melbourne Archive.

57. Mary Cecil Allen, *Folly Cove* 1935, thinned oil on paper, 38.0 x 51.0 cm.
Cruthers Collection of Women's Art, Perth.

58. Mary Cecil Allen, *Screen; five panels, a design of seven kangaroos* c. 1941,
oil on cardboard mounted on a wooden frame, 183.0 x 60.0 x 2.5 cm (each).
Collection of the National Gallery of Australia, Canberra, gift of Lady Casey 1979.

Part 3

THE PUBLICIST
CLARICE ZANDER (1893–1958)

Courage a grace, 1893–1932

If there is truth in the psychology of names, those given to Alleyne Clarice Zander were particularly appropriate. Friends knew her by her second name Clarice, derived from the Latin for 'bright' or 'clear'. Her Celtic first name embodies notions of concord and harmony. A handsome and gregarious woman, with a warm-hearted disposition, she disliked discord, preferring harmonious relations based on clear communication. Her surname, from the Greek, is a variation of Alexander, the protector and helper. She became an ambassador for Australian art in the first half of the twentieth century and a mentor to countless young Australians arriving in London with little other than their artistic talent, which she ensured was nurtured.

She was born at Coleraine, in the picturesque Wannon River valley of southwest Victoria, where the wild sandstone formations of the Grampian Mountains mark the western extremity of the Great Dividing Range. Her parents had moved there shortly after their marriage in 1892, seeking clean air for her father's tuberculosis. Catherine Louise Campbell was aged twenty-five when she married Benjamin Thomas Peel, an Englishman from Manchester, eleven years older and distantly related to the past British Prime Minister Sir Robert Peel. He was working in Australia as an agent for brass manufacturers. Their wedding photograph shows Catherine Louise, slender, doe-eyed, stylishly groomed. He is shorter, of stocky build and dark complexion. On 9 February 1893, their only child, Alleyne Clarice Peel, was born. Clarice, as she preferred to be called, spent the first thirteen years of her life in Coleraine.

Clarice Zander at St Kilda, 1915. *National Art Archive, Art Gallery of New South Wales, Sydney.*

The small town, memorialised in paint by Louis Buvelot and in verse by Adam Lindsay Gordon, was home to a number of memorable women.[1] The popular novelist, English-born Ada Cambridge Cross, was the wife of the Anglican vicar. Her first novel *Up the Murray* was published shortly after she arrived in Australia in 1870 and serialised in the *Melbourne Weekly*. Numerous novels, short stories, essays and poetry followed. She was a strong-minded woman, like many of her heroines, championing women's suffrage and emancipation. Two years after Clarice's birth, the Polish-born Helena Rubinstein arrived, escaping an arranged marriage. Rubinstein lived with her uncle, who was a storekeeper and part-time oculist in Coleraine. He was known to the Peels, who also kept a store in the town. The exotic Rubinstein created a stir with her fashionable foreign clothes and forthright opinions. She went on to found a global cosmetics company.

Whether or not the achievements of these Coleraine women provided Clarice with models of enterprise, the women in her immediate family certainly did. From birth, a pattern of single-minded endeavour was set for her life, modelled upon the women on her maternal side. Her great-grandmother, Catherine Bloomfield, came to Australia at the time of the potato famine in Northern Ireland. Quick to improve her position, she landed in Australia, married to the captain of the ship transporting her. Her daughter, Catherine Davies Campbell – Clarice's grandmother – married, but was abandoned by her husband at the time of the Victorian gold rush. Left with a daughter – Louise, Clarice's mother – she returned to her mother, who by now lived in some comfort. Catherine Campbell quickly remade an independent life for herself and for her daughter. Clarice was destined to resemble these capable, spirited and resourceful women.

Clarice was twelve years old when her father died, in 1905, aged only forty-six. Her mother moved to Melbourne. An estate valued at nearly £2000 left them with some security, which Clarice's mother consolidated by opening a shop. The business was successful, enabling the purchase of the elegant house, Nigretta, on Burke Road, East Malvern, and Clarice's schooling at the prestigious Oberwyl Ladies College in St Kilda. This school, established in 1867 by the Swiss art patron Madame Elise Pfund, had been acquired in 1885 by Berthe Mouchette and her sister Marie Lion. Madame Mouchette was an artist who had exhibited at the Paris Salon (1878–81). The sisters enjoyed the patronage of the wife of the Victorian Governor and were founders of the Alliance Française in Melbourne. By the time Clarice arrived they had sold the school to new owners, Misses Garton and Henderson, who built upon its traditional strengths, promoting the study of languages, literature, music and art.

Photographed in 1907, aged fourteen, Clarice is a picture of Edwardian elegance. Her chic clothes suggest that she was indulged by a mother determined that her daughter should have the best start to life, although

Alice Mills [Melbourne] photograph of Clarice Zander in June 1907.
National Art Archive, Art Gallery of New South Wales, Sydney

Louise's intentions for her daughter went beyond superficial styling. Oberwyl was a school 'for daughters of the foremost Victorian families', and its insistence on cultivating social graces equipped Clarice for life.[2] She also made lifelong friends at the school, among them Dorothy Blanchard (later Mrs Oscar Hammerstein).[3] School reports note that Clarice was 'always well prepared – an excellent student', distinguishing herself in English, literature and scriptural studies.[4] Oberwyl girls had a keen sense of the world beyond Victoria, a world Clarice was restless to discover and made more real in 1908 when the American fleet of sixteen vessels cruised into the waters of Port Phillip Bay, engaged on a world tour to 'show the flag'. Clarice watched the torchlight procession through the streets of Melbourne, when the largest crowd Melbourne had ever seen – about 600,000 – welcomed the troops.

In the following year her mother remarried. Alfred Cope, widowed the year before, was seventy, nearly thirty years her senior. Although her mother found companionship and security in the marriage, Clarice felt constrained at home, with shelves now full of patented medicine for the hypochondriachal Mr Cope. His three children had long since left home and he was not enthusiastic about acquiring a young and opinionated step-daughter.

Art studies at the new Eastern Suburbs Technical College and Art School provided an escape from home. This school, boasting instruction in drawing, painting, designing, modelling and craftwork to artists and artisans, was in nearby Hawthorn. Clarice achieved considerable success as a freelance illustrator and commercial artist, creating fashion drawings for the Melbourne department store of Buckley & Nunn. She earned £10 a week, a substantial sum for a woman when the Commonwealth basic wage was eight shillings a day.[5]

It was around this time that she met Charles Noble Leonard Zander (plate 36). He was two years older than Clarice, born in 1890. The maternal side of his family traced its roots back to the early settlers in Australia. His mother, Rebecca Francis Britten Beasley, had married John Bernard Zander in 1885. They moved into the neoclassical house, Virginia, in Queens Road, St Kilda, where they reared four children, Charles being the youngest.

The Zanders, Charles's paternal family, came originally from Schleswig-Holstein, then part of Denmark. Charles's father, John Zander, was a wool broker, operating a successful business from Zander's Bond Store in Melbourne. His real passion, however, was racing. He owned a trotting stud at Bundoora, thirteen miles north of Melbourne, and was President of the Victorian Trotting Horse Association. From 1908 until 1918, Zander and his stud were major forces in Melbourne racing, importing prize stallions. Contemporary sources paint a portrait of a flamboyant Zander: when times were good, he spent up big and was showy with his money. He was also generous. When Charles enlisted in the Australian Imperial Force (AIF) he donated the valuable trotting stallion Prince Maurice to a fund for sick and wounded soldiers.

Charles did not share his father's passion for racing or his willingness to be in the public eye. From an early age he cultivated an independence from his family. Being born on St Patrick's Day, he was known in the family as 'Mickey', a reminder of the sectarian divisions which defined Melbourne society at the time. The Zanders, nominally Presbyterian, were part of the city's affluent and enterprising business class, distinct from the establishment Anglicans and the working-class 'Mick' Irish Catholics. After working briefly as an itinerant labourer on the railways, Charles trained in the wool trade as a classer and buyer. He was employed for a time in Northern France with the French textile firm the House of Rodier, which was then developing experimental textiles.

He returned to Melbourne well travelled, speaking fluent French, quick in his uptake of modernity. Family photographs capture a dapper young man, smoking a pipe, leaning against the latest model Norton motorbike. His urbanity and world experience appealed to Clarice. They were a handsome couple: she 5 feet 5 inches, a grey-eyed brunette, stylish and confident; he 5 feet 9 inches, fair, green-eyed, strikingly handsome. They were married on 9 October 1915 at Clarice's home and moved into rented rooms in a grand bluestone house not far from Charles's family, on the east side of St Kilda Road.

Charles had enlisted in the Australian Imperial Force before his marriage, which meant that he and Clarice only had four months of married life before he departed for Europe (plate 38). Photographs taken of him in uniform show his face with the unblemished skin of youth, but sporting a pencil moustache, perhaps to appear older than his twenty-five years. Other photographs, taken on departure day, speak eloquently of the loss that was to befall their generation. Charles Zander's photographs show crowds of volunteers aboard ship.[6] Colonial boys, still largely unaccustomed to uniform, swarm on the wharves and cram into lifeboats with youthful enthusiasm. His ship left Melbourne on 10 March 1916. It sailed for Egypt where, as part of an AIF restructure, Charles was incorporated into the newly formed 55th Battalion. This battalion was made up of Gallipoli veterans and the newly arrived recruits and destined for despatch to Flanders Fields.

Arriving at Marseilles on 29 June 1916, Charles entered the frontline trenches on 12 July. A week later his battalion fought its first battle at Fromelles, where over five-and-a-half thousand Australian soldiers were killed, with another four hundred taken prisoner. It was the bloodiest twenty-four hours in the history of the Australian Army. Charles was lucky to survive, suffering serious wounds to the right shoulder and to the head, causing the loss of his right eye. He was transported to England on 22 July and admitted to the Third London General Hospital at Wandsworth. Clarice, who was informed by telegram of his injury on 1 August, was sailing to join him within a week. It was a testimony to her powers of persuasion that she so quickly negotiated passage at a time when shipping was necessarily restricted.

In October they were reunited in Sunninghill just outside Ascot, Berkshire, where Charles was convalescing (plate 39). The grand house just beyond the village, Silwood Park, where Prince Edward and Princess Alexandra stayed during the racing season, had been turned into a nursing home for colonial officers. Photographs show Charles and his wounded compatriots, bandaged and with limbs in slings, attempting to return to normal civilian life with sedate park strolls and picnics. Yet the strain upon Charles is evident. Years later Clarice wrote a number of short stories in London under the pseudonym of Dennis Aiken. In one of these – the autobiographical 'Ever After?' – she described her husband: 'Very thin, his face in spite of its bronze was haggard. A different man from the day, not quite two years ago, when she had first met him . . . even his indomitable spirits seemed to flag'.[7]

Clarice found friendship in the company of Dorothy Cordes, whose mother owned the estate. The grand-daughter of Sir Alexander Milne, GCB, Admiral of the Fleet, and daughter of a prosperous Monmouth nail maker, Dorothy had a broad range of friends among the aristocracy and fashionable set. In 1925 Dorothy married Bertram Freeman-Mitford, who later became the 3rd Baron Redesdale. A lifelong friend, she provided Clarice with invaluable connections. Charles was granted convalescent leave in April and May of 1917, and the couple travelled to London to enjoy the wide range of entertainments the capital still offered. Charles was declared fit for home service only; after London he was sent to the AIF training headquarters in Codford. By early 1919 they were on their way back to Melbourne, where Charles was discharged on 27 October.

Charles was expected to return to civilian life and pick up where he had left off in 1915. But he was a changed man. He joined seven hundred other diggers who decided to begin anew on the land, applying for a soldier settlement block 544 km northwest of Melbourne, at Red Cliffs, near Mildura. This was a plan to convert bushland into a thriving irrigation settlement; some veterans of Gallipoli had already been established on properties in the Mildura district, growing citrus fruits and grapes for the dried fruit industry. In 1919 the government decided to extend the project to what was judged superior land at Red Cliffs. It purchased 33,000 acres and made available over half of this for the scheme, in blocks averaging sixteen acres. The area was surveyed and a township laid out using the labour of over a thousand men, mostly returned soldiers. The first allocation of lots was made in December of 1920.

Charles may have been influenced in his decision to move to Red Cliffs by other members of his battalion. Two had been block labourers at Mildura before the war. They knew the area well and the type of work that would be involved, as well as the expected benefits. Charles secured a standard-size block opposite the railway crossing at Sunnycliffs.[8] Land was allocated under the *Discharged Soldier's Settlement Act 1917*, which required each applicant to hold a qualification certificate, with government, professional and character references. George Picton of the Repatriation Commission wrote that he had known Charles 'long before Red Cliffs' and that he was 'very intelligent'.[9] His application declared assets of £1300 and a total pension of £3 a week, placing him among the most affluent of the settlers.

Propaganda for the settlement pictured it in heroic terms. A correspondent in the *Age* expressed the general optimism: 'As far as the eye can travel . . . are the sweeps of ploughed land . . . it is here the digger begins life all over again, dreaming of progress where there are no restraining nightmares'.[10] Artist Jessie Traill recorded the construction that was taking place. In etchings such as *Testing the new turbine, Red Cliffs Pumps* (1922) she depicted the workmen as patriotic heroes. Many of the men had demonstrated leadership during the war, with many decorated for bravery and a large number badly wounded like Charles. Jessie Traill recorded her impressions of Red Cliffs in 1922: 'Youth, Activity, Haste – should be written after Red Cliffs'.[11] Yet conditions on the Mallee, with the wounds of war still fresh, made life very raw.

Charles and Clarice built a house of three rooms with a front veranda constructed initially of saplings and with walls of hessian. In order to plant grapevines they had to dig out the tenacious mallee roots. This task – nicknamed 'emu bobbing' – usually fell to the women. Clarice wrote:

> While their husbands staggered after the plough that leapt and bumped over the huge roots . . . the women patiently gathered up what they were able of the roots flung about like tremendous tentacles . . . When these heaps had been burnt off, the ground was ploughed again. This time the pieces of root were not so long and the women patiently stooped, or followed the furrows on their knees, gathering the pieces. A back breaking effort.[12]

Clarice would then rake up the roots and burn them, taking great care that 'the fires did not spread . . . Sometimes a standing tree would catch fire, and blaze like a Christmas tree. All the trees were full of oil and easily inflammable'. The house of their neighbour Jim Doyle was completely destroyed by fire. Beyond accidental fires, more suspicious fires were common, when insurance money gave some settlers just enough to release them from an untenable commitment.

The blocks were too small to be immediately profitable. Most of the 1921 plantings were lost and it was not until 1924 that the first consignment of sultanas was sent overseas, although by this time prices for dried fruit had plummeted. The government administrators of the scheme were unsympathetic to the settler, who was barely subsisting on the land. Suicides resulted. A Royal Commission in 1925 found that many men were physically and mentally unfit for the strenuous conditions, which was certainly true of Charles. Sly grog was widely available and, like others, Charles took to heavy drinking. It was a way of anaesthetising the pain that Charles, and many like him, carried from the war, but which – as Mary Gilmore noted – they were expected to bury.

> Never admit the pain,
> Bury it deep,
> Only the weak complain.
> Complaint is cheap.
>
> Cover thy wound, fold down
> Its curtained place;
> Silence is still a crown
> Courage a grace.[13]

Charles's drinking saw him involved in incidents of increasing seriousness and on several occasions he was hospitalised. Emu-bobbing and living between white-washed sacking was not Clarice's idea of life. Having endured two winters and one summer, she baulked at the thought of a second summer, particularly with their first child on the way. She returned to Melbourne (plate 41). Charles soon followed, leaving their block in the care of neighbours. On 29 November 1921 their daughter, Jocelyn Britten Zander, was born. The birth of a daughter and the move to Melbourne did not resolve Charles's problems and a neurologist at the Repatriation Department recommended a complete break. 'Zander is suffering from chronic nervous instability, and is liable to recurrent attacks of mental depression', he reported. 'I have advised him to take a long trip and complete change of environment for a prolonged period.'[14]

In 1925 Charles left for Europe, after which he travelled to Canada. In 1926 Clarice was given power of attorney and in 1928 she sold the block. By then she had returned to her family, living at a house in South Yarra. She became the family provider, responsible for her daughter Jocelyn as well as for her mother and grandmother. Her mother Louise Cope had developed Parkinson's Disease and was increasingly infirm. Clarice's grandmother Catherine Bloomfield, stone deaf since the age of twenty-six from rheumatic fever, helped to nurse her invalid daughter and to mind her great grand-daughter, assisted by some paid help.

As the household's sole breadwinner, Clarice held several jobs at once. She returned to fashion drawing and for a time ran a beauty parlour. She also managed the lending library of the Leviathan bookshop in Bourke Street, a useful place for meeting key figures from law and politics. Her most important job, however, was as manager for five years of the New Gallery, a venture established by Melbourne-born artist and critic James Stuart MacDonald and his American-born wife Maud. Jimmy MacDonald was a respected authority on art and a promoter of Australian artists. He had studied in Paris where he met his wife and had taught art in New York.

The gallery, of which most of the leading artists of Melbourne were shareholders, opened on 56–62 Elizabeth Street in mid-November 1923 with a group exhibition, followed by a posthumous exhibition of work by Frederick McCubbin. In January 1924 it relocated to the Robertson and Mullens Building at 107 Elizabeth Street, opening there with an exhibition by the Sydney modernist Gladys Owen. Ten exhibitions were staged during 1925, nearly all of them solo exhibitions, including shows by Dora Wilson, Ethel Carrick, Phil May, Ethel Spowers, Blamire Young and Lionel Lindsay. The gallery was a lively centre of new work. It capitalised on a growing public interest in art, only closing at the end of 1928 when MacDonald was appointed to the position of Director and Secretary of the National Art Gallery of New South Wales in Sydney.

Change was in the air, with the city, fashion, the arts and social behaviour undergoing significant transformation. As post-war Australia set about reconstruction, Clarice sought to build a new life for herself and her daughter. While the Jazz Age trumpeted around her at tea dances, dinner dances and supper dances, 'It ain't gonna rain no mo' no mo', it ain't gonna rain no mo', Clarice – always attentive to appearance – cut her long hair into a bob, declaring she was unambiguously modern and emancipated (plate 40).

In 1926, while working at the New Gallery, she met the celebrated artist Will Dyson. McDonald was a good friend of Dyson and had recently written an extended piece on him for *Art in Australia*.[15] Dyson had been brought up in a mining district near Ballarat in Victoria, and was familiar with the difficulties of labouring men and women, becoming a lifelong champion of the underdog. His full genius was expressed in his cartoons, for which he was celebrated as the most trenchant satirist of his day. Melbourne writer Robert Croll described Dyson's work as 'epigrammatic, concise, mordant and often bitter, [which] in subject and in its accompanying text, disclosed a powerful logical mind and a fine gift of expression'.[16] His brother-in-law Lionel Lindsay believed that Dyson's drawings introduced 'a new element of psychological import' to Australian journalism.[17]

Photograph taken of Bill Dyson on 12 April 1935.
National Art Archive, Art Gallery of New South Wales, Sydney.

Clarice and Dyson were both nursing loss when they met. Dyson's much-loved wife Ruby Lindsay had died of the Spanish influenza in early 1919. Left in London with their young daughter Betty and disillusioned by the shift of the labour paper, the *Daily Herald*, towards the Right, he was lured back to Australia to work on the staff of Melbourne's *Herald and Weekly Times* and *Punch*. However, his experience over five years in Australia was not happy. He felt that Keith Murdoch, the Director of the *Herald and Weekly Times*, pressured him to dull his critical edge. Australia too had changed during his fifteen years abroad. He quipped: 'I found the good old honest defamation of one citizen by another was ruled out of the higher walks of journalism with a completeness that made life unbearable for one who had been a defamer all his life and was too old to change'.[18]

Dyson was a natural performer, but an unremitting round of social engagements, along with heavy drinking and smoking, was ruining his health. Clarice took him in hand, caring for him and sheltering him from the pressures of his celebrity status. For Clarice, Dyson brought intellectual interest as well as companionship. They increasingly spent time together, although discretion was all-important. Clarice was still a married woman and Dyson's headstrong fifteen-year-old daughter Betty bitterly resented her.

At the end of 1929 Clarice learned that Charles had died in Canada. He had been killed in a drunken brawl in Montreal. She was aged thirty-seven. A few months earlier her parents-in-law had died, severing ties with the Zander family. She discussed with Dyson the possibility of relocating to England. To do this, she needed to provide for her mother and grandmother. She bought the house, Clifton, in Kooyong Road, Armidale, and set it up as a small nursing home. Tenants lived in the old servants' quarters and in the sleepout at the back. Her mother and grandmother lived in the front of the house with a female lodger, who nursed them in lieu of paying rent. Although she ensured they were comfortable and well looked after, Clarice always carried a sense of guilt for leaving them.[19]

With her eight-year-old daughter, Clarice followed Dyson to England, arriving in March 1930. He had sailed ahead of her. It was not the most opportune time to arrive or the most cheerful. Sergei Diaghilev, the great

Russian impresario whose Ballet Russes had spawned artistic advances and gripped audiences worldwide, had died in August 1929 and D.H. Lawrence, who had championed sexual freedom, in March 1930. Their deaths marked the close of the 'Amoral Decade' or the 'Sweet and Twenties', as the immediate post-war period were called.[20] In early 1930 Britain was in the grip of the Great Depression.

Clarice's anticipated employment in London with a women's magazine never eventuated. To her dismay, the magazine had given the promised position to someone else. To make matters worse, the Australian currency had been devalued dramatically while she was aboard ship and she arrived with much less capital than when she had set out. She had been refused a pension following Charles's death, as he had been buried incorrectly as a single man.[21] She faced an anxious future, with just £200 in savings.

Dyson's extensive connections in London, along with those she had made during 1916–18, proved invaluable. She worked initially as a freelance journalist, yet financial insecurity continually dogged her, a recurrent theme in the short stories she wrote at the time. Her characters are defined by poverty, living in boarding houses, struggling to make ends meet and trying to present themselves more sharply than their impecunious circumstances allowed. A priority was to provide for her daughter Jocelyn. Clarice's views on education were progressive, favouring child-centred education. Prepared to make similar sacrifices to those her own mother had made for her education, Clarice sent Jocelyn to the experimental Farmhouse School, which social reformer Isabel Fry had established at Mayortorne Manor in Buckinghamshire.[22] Later Jocelyn won a scholarship to Bedales, the first coeducational school in England.

While Clarice worked to establish herself in London, Dyson enjoyed a sell-out exhibition of his drypoints at Ferargil Galleries in New York. The *New York Times* compared him with Daumier. He held a similar exhibition in London in November 1930 and further successful shows followed in 1931, in both London and New York. However, the pressure of press deadlines and irregular hours, with alcohol and nicotine, had taken their toll. At the end of 1931 he was admitted to a nursing home. Clarice was kept at a distance and prevented from nursing him by his daughter Betty, who lived with him in

Netherton Grove, Kensington. Playwright and author Eric Ambler thought they were 'more like a couple who had finally decided to get a divorce than a father and daughter'.[23]

By now, Betty was emerging as a notable theatrical designer but she alienated many with her brusque manners and bad temper. Her cousin Philip Lindsay described to his father Norman the hold she had on Bill. He called her a 'bullying bitch . . . she was mad with an unconscious Electra complex and gave poor Bill hell. Whenever I met them he would sit sadly smiling while she acted her chosen part, demanding all attention'.[24] Betty aside, social mores prevented Clarice from living openly with Dyson in London. She could not afford to have her reputation compromised. The successful author H.G. Wells, a friend of Dyson, had been sharply criticised for his portrayal in *Anna Veronica* (1909) of a 'new woman' who lives with an older married man. Clarice purchased a stone and thatched cottage in secluded Empshott Green in Hampshire, where she and Bill could be together. Towards the end of 1930 Clarice became secretary and manager of the Lord Alington Gallery in Bond Street, founded

Brook Cottage c. 1936. *National Art Archive, Art Gallery of New South Wales, Sydney.*

in September 1923 as a small artists' cooperative. The gallery was named after Napier Sturt, the 3rd Baron Alington, a cultivated arts benefactor and friend of the painter Augustus John. By 1931 the New Zealander Rex Nan Kivell was the managing director of the gallery, which was renamed the Redfern Gallery. That September Clarice promoted the Australian artists Derwent Lees and Roland Wakelin in the gallery's Summer Salon Exhibition. And so Clarice began the networking for which she became celebrated, eventually introducing Australians Donald Friend, Sidney Nolan and Loudon Sainthill, amongst others, to the gallery.

Alongside the connections which Clarice began making through the Redfern Gallery, there were Dyson's wide circles of contacts from press and literary circles, as well as from the Chelsea Arts Club, albeit a generally all-male milieu. Dyson moved in the world of London's *Daily Herald* newspaper, which in 1933 was the world's best-selling daily newspaper, and mixed with progressives from A.R. Orage's *New Age* journal (1907–24) and the recent *New English Weekly* (from 1932). This group, which included A.E. Randall, Wyndham Lewis, Ezra Pound, Beatrice Hastings and T.E. Hulme, met every Monday afternoon at a Chancery Lane café to debate politics, arts and society. Clarice and Bill were also regulars at the Café Royal, the Regent Street centre at which London's bohemian writers and artists gathered. More salubrious were the annual soirees to mark the Royal Academy Summer Exhibitions.

Dyson and Clarice enjoyed a particularly close friendship with the notable intellectual Alfred Orage and his American wife Jessie (Richards Dwight). Deep desire for social reform cemented the friendship between Orage and Dyson. Both enthusiastically supported Social Credit, the economic philosophy of British engineer Clifford H. Douglas, which offered an alternative to traditional Left and Right ideas on the management of the economy, wealth, debt and socioeconomic breakdown.[25] T.S. Eliot thought Orage 'the finest critical intelligence of our days' and others said that he was best talker in London since Wilde.[26] Clarice and Dyson holidayed with the Orages, who were also regular weekenders at Clarice's Hampshire retreat. They were often joined there by Hungarian writer Joseph Bard and surrealist painter Eileen Agar, friends of Man Ray and Roland Penrose.

The Zandrian wars, 1932–1933

Not long after arriving in London Clarice received news from Australia that both her mother and grandmother were ailing. She recognised that she had to return to Melbourne but she decided to take advantage of the situation and return with an exhibition of contemporary British art. The connections made through the Redfern Gallery along with her own friendships with leading artists enabled her to assemble an important show in a short time. It would display British artists, many of whom were associated with Roger Fry's Omega Workshops and the later London Group: Mark Gertler, Edward Wadsworth, John and Paul Nash, Christopher Wood, Stanley Spencer; Bloomsbury School members Duncan Grant, Vanessa Bell, and Henry Lamb; the expressionist Matthew Smith and the younger abstract painter, Ben Nicholson.

The star of her venture was Jacob Epstein, who told the London *Evening Standard* that he was contributing three of his works to the exhibition (plate 43).[27] Clarice attributed the genesis of her exhibition to Epstein, since she had originally intended to exhibit only his work.[28] She had come to know him well in 1932 while organising an exhibition of his watercolour illustrations to the Old Testament, the first time he had exhibited anything but sculpture. To associate her travelling exhibition with Epstein was astute, with reports of his bohemian life and the controversies surrounding his sculpture commanding attention worldwide. He was considered to be more reviled than any living artist and it was said that the man 'whose doings have the greatest news value of anyone in England – barring the Prince of Wales – is the sculptor, Epstein'.[29]

It was a difficult time to be promoting art, let alone British art. Australia in the early 1930s was still in the grip of economic depression. Presenting a large-scale exhibition of 184 works was costly and risky. The list of those who gave Clarice work indicates how well established and regarded she had become in London. Lord Alington and Rex Nan Kivell of the Redfern Gallery were key to her endeavour. Help also came from other dealers: Arthur Tooth & Sons, the French Gallery, Reid & Lefevre and Agnew & Sons. James Bolivar Manson, Director of the Tate Gallery from 1930, and his assistant H.S. (Jim) Ede, an enthusiast for modernist art, gave their help. Private collectors who lent works included Edward Marsh, who owned a remarkable collection of contemporary art, and Samuel Courtauld, who endowed the Courtauld Institute of Art, Britain's first specialist centre for the study of the history of art.[30]

Clarice's Australian connections also proved useful. Colin Anderson of the Orient Line backed Clarice's venture by waiving the usual charges for freight.[31] In the 1920s Anderson had joined the family firm that ran passenger ships to Australia. In 1932 he married an Australian and began applying his interest in art to his ships. A committed patron of modern design, he was then engaged in fitting out a new 'floating hotel' – the *Orion* – when Clarice met him. A team of young artists, including Ceri Richards and John Piper, were commissioned to work on the interiors for the new liner.

Before leaving London, a reception was held for her at the Redfern Gallery. Present were the Epsteins, Harrison Owen (who wrote *Dr Pygmalion* for Gladys Cooper and who was married to Dyson's sister Etty), the *Evening Standard* cartoonist David Low, the etcher Muirhead Bone, the artist Christopher Nevinson and his ally, the progressive art critic Paul George Konody, Lord and Lady Edward Gleichen (brother of the noted sculptress), and the husband and wife artists, Thomas Dugdale and Amy K. Browning. Konody had helped Penleigh Boyd assemble 345 works for his exhibition of *European Art for Australia*, which was exhibited in Melbourne and Sydney during 1923. He admired Australia's black and white artists like David Low and Will Dyson.[32] Nevinson and Bone had been exhibited before in Australia, as had Epstein, who with Augustus John took a deeper interest in Australia. 'They are both interested in the primitive aspects of things,' noted Clarice. 'Already they know far more about our aborigines than I do, but I am commanded to take back all the information on them that I can get together.'[33]

The London *Evening Standard* judged 'so far as paintings in oil and water-colours are concerned, it would not be easy . . . to give a fairer impression of contemporary English talent'.[34] The London correspondent for the *Home* called Clarice's selection a 'pictorial modern cocktail which will buck up art lovers'. She was dubbed the 'Moving Picture Queen'.[35] The press in Australia picked up the story during the months of preparation, adding to the anticipation of the show. When Clarice arrived in Sydney, Walter Taylor

The Redfern Gallery, London 1932, with some of the works Clarice Zander
took to Australia for her exhibition of British contemporary art.
National Art Archive, Art Gallery of New South Wales, Sydney.

hosted a welcome for her at his Grosvenor Galleries. She endured, for the sake
of the extended publicity, the trivialising reports of the Australian press, which
routinely reported on the appearance of women over their achievements. The
Bulletin, patronising her as 'a pretty girl whose passage brightened Sydney',
had little to report about her exhibition beyond saying 'She knows more about
Art in London of to-day than probably anybody else in Australia'.[36]

As selected, Clarice's exhibition was far from extreme. English critics like
Clive Bell thought that English art was, after all, little more at this stage than
a footnote to continental artistic advances.[37] However, Clarice was aware of
the disquiet that then existed in Australia over 'modern art'. The editorial for a
1929 issue of *Art in Australia* argued for a more measured approach to modern
art in Australia. 'An unfamiliar turn of style can give rise to vague but sinister
suspicions in this country', wrote Basil Burdett. 'An entirely traditional artist
such as George Lambert is viewed with suspicion and disapproval', Burdett

continued. 'It is interesting to note a certain parallel between the essential phase of Australian art at present and the reaction after French impressionism in Europe.'[38] Fear of the new was difficult to understand, given how quickly Australians adopted the modern in anything but art.

Clarice was in fact presenting two selling exhibitions: one of paintings and another of prints. 'I have been at pains to make both shows fully representative of the work that is being done in Britain', she explained.

> As regards the paintings, they will cover a period of about 40 years. After all, most of the really significant artists of the nineties are still alive. With the help of the Contemporary Society, I have been able to obtain pictures which are really representative of the modern school.[39]

The print exhibition, *Modern Colour Prints and Wood Engravings from the Redfern Gallery*, was first exhibited in Melbourne during December 1932. It was a large show, hung in the two galleries of the Arts and Crafts Society in Collins House and Cynthia Reed's Gallery in Little Collins Street. The catalogue included a foreword by Claude Flight, the inspirational teacher of linocut at London's Grosvenor School of Modern Art.[40] Although numerous shows of British and European prints had been held in Australia prior to Clarice's show, none had been quite as up to date as hers, including as it did all the stars of the Grosvenor School, which had been established in London in 1925. Influential Melbourne teacher and critic George Bell thought works by Grosvenor artists Claude Flight, Cyril Power, Sybil Andrews and Lill Tschudi the exhibition's highlight.[41] Those who, like Bell, admired the firm outlines and bold colours of these prints thought they were 'wonderfully simple and direct in appeal' and represented the best of contemporary art.[42]

Lieutenant-Governor Sir William Irvine opened the exhibition, directing attention to Sybil Andrews's linocut *Steeplechasing* (1930), an impression of which had recently been purchased by London's Victoria and Albert Museum. Irvine thought that the novel production of the work, made from three colour blocks of chinese orange, alizarin purple madder and prussian blue printed on buff paper, would cause argument: 'I have no doubt that the majority of these pictures will be made the subject of keen criticism and debate'.[43] No notice appears to have been taken of the fact that the exhibition was one of several similar exhibitions which the Redfern Gallery had staged separately in many cities worldwide in order to publicise and market the linocut internationally. These exhibitions made extensive tours of British regional centres between 1929 and 1931 and were also held in the United States (1929, 1934), China (1931) and Canada (1935–36) as well as Australia.

The 1920s had seen a renaissance in printmaking and the development of a significant print market. The first exhibition of the Australian Painter-Etchers Society in 1922 yielded £1600 in sales (equivalent today to close to UK£50,000). Clarice had seen these successful sales, including to the Felton Bequest, when at the New Gallery, where the Society of Painter-Etchers exhibited annually.[44] According to Sydney Long, 'the one-man shows of the foremost etchers seldom realised less than five hundred pounds in sales'.[45] Clarice was hoping that the sales of prints might make her exhibition, if not profitable, at least financially viable. She brought to Australia as many impressions of a print edition that each artist would allow, distributing these widely and sending impressions to those who could sell them: to Daphne Mayo in Brisbane, to Margaret Jaye in Sydney and to Henry E. Fuller in Adelaide.[46]

Australia's obsession with market protectionism saw a ten per cent tariff applied to oil paintings and watercolours imported from the United Kingdom. Prints and photographs were taxed at a higher rate – thirty per cent of their determined value. 'People told me I should encounter great difficulty with the Australian Customs Authorities', Clarice said, 'but I have found them most considerate and reasonable. They fully realize the educational value of the exhibition'.[47] She hoped to deflect Customs charges by stressing the educational value of the exhibition, but was unsuccessful, which forced her to resort to a little guile. Determined to conceal from Customs some of the prints she brought with her, she hid them between pages of the *Bulletin* and sent her daughter to post them to Melbourne from their ship in Perth before Customs officers made their inspection. Clarice confided to J.S. MacDonald, now Director of the National Art Gallery of New South Wales, that had she realised how difficult Customs regulations and restrictions would be, she would not have proceeded with her exhibitions.[48] They cost Clarice dearly. She was required to advance a bond of over £2000 (equivalent in 2005 to UK£66,840) on the shows and had to pay someone from the Customs Department to check her accounts, because they would only refund the bond on unsold work. It took her years to overcome the strain the venture put on her finances.

The more prestigious exhibition of paintings and sculpture by more than fifty artists opened in Melbourne on 8 March 1933 at Newspaper House, the *Sun*'s new building on Collins Street. The invitations to the show singled out Augustus John, Jacob Epstein, Richard Sickert, Frank Dobson, Paul and John Nash, Derwent Lees, Lucien Pissarro, Duncan Grant and Eric Gill. In the foreword to the catalogue Clarice noted that the collection 'is a survey of the work of the most significant artists of the last forty years who have refused to continue paraphrasing their art on traditional lines'. The exhibition included an uncatalogued section of textiles, furniture and applied art drawn from Cynthia Reed's gallery, including fabrics by Michael O'Connell and furniture by Fred Ward and Mark Bracegirdle.[49] In bringing art and design together, dissolving the traditional division between fine and applied art, the exhibition became a full celebration of creative modernity.

Installation view of the *Exhibition of British Contemporary Art*, Melbourne, 1933.
National Art Archive, Art Gallery of New South Wales, Sydney.

Over five thousand people visited the show during its three weeks in Melbourne and average daily attendances of five hundred were recorded in Sydney, where the show opened in April 1933 at the Blaxland Galleries in Farmer's Department store (plate 44). Clarice arranged events in the exhibition space, from talks to practical demonstrations of printmaking, encouraging school groups to take advantage of these. Lectures on modern art were given in Melbourne by George Bell, Arnold Shore and Blamire Young and in Sydney by Thea Proctor, Margaret Preston and Gladys Owen.

The exhibition included Australian artists little known in their own country such as Maurice Lambert and Derwent Lees. Lees had studied art in Paris and at the Slade in London, where he became Assistant Drawing Master (1908–15) to Henry Tonks when aged just twenty-three. The Tate and other English galleries held examples of Lees's work. His sister in Australia had not seen her brother since he had departed for studies in England at the age of nineteen. Visiting the exhibition she got her first glimpse of her English sister-in-law Lyndra through Lees's paintings. A letter to the Melbourne *Herald* urged the National Gallery of Victoria to buy Lees's *Lyndra by the Pool*, as a work by an Australian artist little known in his home country but who had achieved success overseas.[50]

Lees's work was returned to England with most of the collection. Just twenty-eight works sold – fifteen per cent of the show – with sales totalling £1082.[51] These sales included five works whose prices had been negotiated downwards: Henry Lamb's *Portrait of Edwin John* (1908) was priced at seventy-five guineas in the catalogue, but was sold to Keith Murdoch for £48. Private collectors were the most adventurous buyers from the show. Two works by the English Cubist William Roberts, a key figure in Wyndham Lewis's vorticist movement, were purchased by Justice Evatt and Professor John Anderson of Sydney University, both known as supporters of experimental art.[52] Ben Nicholson's *Fireworks* (1929), which reportedly left some viewers 'speechless', failed to find a buyer.[53]

The most expensive works in the exhibition were the five oils by Augustus John, followed by the four Epstein and two Frank Dobson bronzes.[54] One of these, Epstein's *The Beautiful Jewess (La Belle Juive)* of 1930, was sold to the National Art

Gallery of South Australia for £210. This was the most important sale from the exhibition, prompting Clarice to declare that 'Adelaide thus lives up to its reputation as the most progressive and enlightened culturally of our States'.[55]

In Melbourne, architect Norman Macgeorge wrote to the *Herald* urging the state gallery to buy Richard Sickert's *Barnet Fair* (1930), which he considered one of Sickert's best works.[56] At the time, the National Gallery of Victoria did not own any work by Sickert, an artist who had inspired and influenced successive generations of British and Australian painters. Although Australia's richest public gallery, it bought only two descriptive etchings from the exhibition.[57]

The trustees of the Queensland National Art Gallery purchased a pencil study by Clara Klinghoffer.[58] Sent to them on approval was Gilbert Spencer's *Terraced Houses Nottingdale* and R.O. Dunlop's *Eileen*. They bought both. The Spencer is a curious choice for Brisbane, being a window view of London terraces in winter. Perhaps it was bought speculatively, due to Spencer being thirteen months younger than his brother Stanley and, as the *Daily Telegraph* noted, was a much-discussed young British artist.[59] Dunlop's portrait of Eileen Hawthorne had more Australian relevance. She was a Melbourne artist's model who had achieved celebrity status in London and was later assisted by Clarice.[60] She had been Augustus John's mistress during the 1920s and was known to the newspapers as the girl of a thousand faces, being able to alter her features from day to day with cosmetics; it was said that she painted herself more fluently than he did.[61]

No purchases were made by the National Art Gallery of New South Wales, and the trustees were criticised for this.[62] Clarice's exhibition became a focal point for the disaffection younger artists had felt for some time about the gallery, prompting a confrontation between the old and the new. John D. Moore wrote to the *Sydney Morning Herald* criticising the Sydney trustees:

> They have failed, as leaders of artistic thought, to help make our art galleries representative of the vital art of our time. Instead, we find in our collections, with a few exceptions, lifeless examples of the work of artists who, though physically alive, are mentally dead.[63]

John Sulman, President of the trustees, countered criticism by highlighting the effect of the Great Depression upon purchasing funds and by arguing that purchases were being made in Europe, where trustees were free to select 'from the whole field of art', adding that such purchases were free from tariffs.[64] The situation with tariffs was complicated. Clarice believed that all purchases by public galleries were free from duty, although this was not entirely the case. In some instances exemptions were granted for educational purposes. Clarice told Sulman that the trustees could signify their real appreciation for her exhibition 'by buying from it for their private collections'.[65]

Looking back on Clarice's exhibition in 1940, the *Sydney Morning Herald* credited it as being 'the first exhibition of modern art seen in this country', ahead of the legendary 1939 Herald Exhibition.[66] In the paper's estimation, Clarice's exhibition was the most important exhibition of contemporary work seen in Australia up to that time and echoed the opinion of journalist Colin Simpson, who in 1933 called it 'the most important art show this city has seen'.[67] A piece written for the *Sydney Morning Herald* at the end of 1933 entitled 'The year's violent art controversies' described 1933 as 'one of extraordinary significance in the development of pictorial art in Sydney'. It described Clarice's show as a 'turning-point', when 'artistic ideas from overseas made a powerful drive against the insularity of the local outlook', leaving every artist 'in a constant state of argument, and in many cases, of unrest'. The year had been, the press quipped, one shaped by the Zandrian wars.[68]

In the Zandrian wars Clarice found herself pitched against her old colleague, Jimmy MacDonald. Both believed that 'art is a delicate and responsive barometer' (as MacDonald put it), but he denounced the 'modernistic school' in painting as 'trash' that was 'being compelled by the present economic depression'.[69] Lecturing in Sydney at the bohemian Pakie's, a meeting place for artists and intellectuals in rooms decorated by Roy de Maistre, MacDonald said that he could not understand how anyone could get inspiration out of modern art since all it represented was an attempt to be exciting. He lamented the recent intrusion of women into art, characterising them as 'very slick as students' and 'grim and determined [in their drive] . . . to secure a place in the painting world'.[70] Here he was making a reference to the predominance of women in the Contemporary Group, which exhibited annually. Most vocal among them were Thea Proctor, Margaret Preston and Gladys Owen, the three women who had lectured at Clarice's exhibition in Sydney.

Clarice replied by addressing the National Council of Women at Melbourne's Lyceum Club. She said that Australia's lack of a long historical perspective led to a lack of appreciation of contemporary achievements in the arts.[71] Contemporary artists were moulded by the work of the past, but not simply that of the immediate past: their inspiration could be Romanesque art or Cycladic Greek sculpture. She argued that because Australia had a short history of making art, technical perfection was valued more highly than 'the spirit force which expresses the individuality of the artist'.[72] She directly countered MacDonald's criticism of modern art by pointing to the number of modern artists who were applying technical ability to expressive ends. 'Painting has shed accuracy, correctness, and conventional laws in an effort to live again after a long period of spiritual deadness.'[73]

Many artists supported Clarice's views. By 1933 they had become convinced that those in charge of national collections were 'not equipped with the necessary artistic knowledge to administer their trust . . . to make our art galleries representative of the vital art of the times'.[74] Inspired by Clarice's exhibition, a letter signed by seventy-three artists and 198 art students was sent to the trustees of the National Art Gallery of New South Wales urging them to obtain a collection of modern art prints and to set aside a section of the gallery where these could be permanently displayed. They argued that such an action would raise Australian standards. Among the signatories were John D. Moore and Gladys Owen, Dattilo-Rubbo, Thea Proctor, Rayner Hoff, Roland Wakelin, Grace Cossington-Smith, Maud Sherwood, and the entire staff of the East Sydney Technical College.[75] The Zandrian wars had brought to the surface the widespread discontent among artists with the values and priorities of the art establishment.

Royal Academy Public Relations Officer, 1933–1939

In mid-1933 Clarice returned to England with Jocelyn. Fellow Australian artist George Duncan travelled with them. En route they met Sidney Michael Cooper in Ceylon, a descendant of Sir Daniel Cooper, one-time Speaker of the New South Wales Legislative Assembly. Cooper had no interest in politics, being an aesthete and a sybarite for whom life was about living stylishly. Cooper moved to Peking, where he assembled a fine collection of Chinese art, most of which would be left to the Art Gallery of New South Wales. Clarice and Cooper became close friends, with Cooper eventually buying Clarice's country cottage, enabling her to afford a home in London.

Clarice disembarked at Toulon to holiday at Cannes with Bill Dyson, his sister Ett and brother-in-law Harrison Owen, leaving Jocelyn to sail with Sydney artist George Duncan to England. Even in the south of France Clarice sensed the growing anxiety over recent events in Europe. In March 1933 the Reichstag passed the Enabling Act, giving Adolf Hitler absolute power. Less than one month later, the recently elected Nazis unleashed a wave of anti-Semitism, which began with a one-day boycott of all Jewish-owned businesses in Germany. Trade unions were banned and the Gestapo was established. Early in May that year the Nazis staged massive public book burnings. As Clarice was sailing to London from Toulon half a million people demonstrated against anti-Semitism in London's Hyde Park.

Her friend the Australian interior decorator Arthur Boys had found a rental flat for Clarice in London at 6 Queensbury Mews West in South Kensington. Entry to it was gained by stairs outside the building; the flat had originally been a storeroom above stables. With a hole in the floor, it was draughty and hard to keep warm, and below could be heard the tinkerings in the garage that now occupied the former stables. Although the flat was tiny, Clarice set about decorating it with relish.

During the years 1933 to 1935 she was a roving correspondent for the *Star*, being the Melbourne paper's representative in London and Paris. She experienced at firsthand the mounting tensions in Europe when she was in France in February 1934 to write a number of feature articles. She was caught up in the riots which erupted over the Stavisky Affair, narrowly escaping being shot when fleeing from gunfire in the Place de la Concorde. A young woman alongside her was killed.[76]

Paris riots, 1934. *Image courtesy of Everett Historical Photographs.*

She also wrote regular features for the Melbourne *Argus*. Clarice's articles, for each of which she normally received a guinea, covered everything from art to society gossip, fashion to education, ballet to mixing modern cocktails. Her writing shows the breadth of her interests and her observations indicate her alert eye and humour. Writing brought her into contact with a wide range of people. 'Beside me sat Serge Lifar, the famous Russian dancer', she wrote. 'Just one away sat Madame Chanel . . . young, dark, and incurably original in her dressing, with a characteristic elfin humour that remains unbroken throughout the gruelling business of "creating" clothes'.[77] All the while Clarice promoted Australian products. She brought to notice Australian timbers in articles on modern furnishings. She chronicled the achievements of Australian artists and promoted Australian talent in general. 'A young man whom Melbourne remembers for his talent as a dancer is now proving his ability', she wrote from London in 1934, 'Bobby Helpmann, the dancer in question, has developed out of all recognition'.[78]

In March 1934 Clarice began working for the Royal Academy of Arts. The Academy had first appointed a press agent to publicise the exhibition *British Art* in 1933, but this arrangement was not continued once that year-long contract expired.[79] Academician Algernon Talmage recommended Clarice as press agent to Sir William Llewellyn, President of the Academy, and its long-serving Secretary, Australian-born Walter Lamb. After an interview with Llewellyn, Lamb and the Academy's treasurer, Clarice was appointed for five months on £150. Her first task was to manage the press for the Academy's annual Summer Exhibition.

Among the original objectives for the Academy's foundation was the presentation of the Summer Exhibitions, and these had continued without a break for two-and-a-half centuries. Around the time of Clarice's appointment over ten thousand works were submitted to the Summer Exhibition every year. Each member of the Academy was allowed to send up to six works, while any other person, without restrictions on age, experience, nationality or domicile, could submit three. A selection committee, composed of Academicians working in rotation, selected around twelve hundred works from the submissions for display. No commission was charged on work sold from these exhibitions.

The Academy, founded in 1768 by George III 'for promoting the Arts of Design', included substantial galleries, a library, meeting rooms and a school of art, the oldest in Britain.[80] It was to British art what Ascot was to horse racing and Lord's to cricket. By the early 1930s, however, the Academy was very much a genial old boys club and was increasingly criticised for its entrenched conservatism. Younger artists derided an institution where top hats and tail coats were the required dress on private view days. 'In our eyes the R.A. was so bad that no self-respecting artist would be seen dead in it', said Augustus John, 'and yet among its more outstanding corpses are to be numbered those of Reynolds, Gainsborough, Hogarth, Lawrence, Turner and Constable'.[81] There was little evidence at the Academy, according to Frank Rutter, critic for the *Sunday Times*, of 'new inventions in paint, in the evolving of new styles, new manners and new theories of art'.[82]

Notwithstanding, as the principal society of artists in Britain, election to membership of the Academy remained prestigious. The New English Art Club had been organised in 1885 as a protest against the narrowness of the Royal Academy, yet by the 1920s works by most New English Art Club exhibitors now hung at the Academy. The challenge the Academy faced was that of updating itself and reaching new audiences, while remaining true to its charter of promoting the best in the fine arts in Britain. As Llewellyn put it: 'The Royal Academy of Arts will continue to exhibit pictures and statues; and some will continue to rail at it as old-fashioned and unintelligent, and others will continue to hold that, once it takes its foot off the brake, it will have betrayed its trust'.[83] He believed that more effective public communication about the Academy and its activities was essential.

Clarice was more than capable of handling this challenge. She had press and gallery experience, was acquainted with Academicians and artists and was well informed about art and literature. She was accustomed to facing difficult circumstances and forceful male characters; she was not easily overawed. She was able to mix easily in different circles and was engaging; modern but not extreme. Her deft touch suited the Academy, which was eager to counter the adverse publicity of recent years, while her colonial status probably also worked in her favour. The attributes of colonial women had been praised by English authors for some time. Trollope considered the 'colonial born' had the edge over English women, thinking 'girls born in the colony have the pre-eminence . . . They are bright and quick'.[84] R.E.N. Twopenny wrote of their 'frankness and good-fellowship', finding them 'rarely affected'.[85] Colonial women were free of the class restraints applying to English women. 'If I had to be in a tight corner with a woman, I would not mind if she were an Australian', wrote the journalist Tom Clarke in 1934. 'They are so independent, so self-reliant, so strong. They can do most things . . . They need no lesson from the much publicized Bright Young Things of London.'[86]

Clarice eventually worked on every Summer and Winter exhibition from mid-1934 until the outbreak of war. She was not a full-time member of staff, but was engaged as a consultant on a contract. Her work differed substantially from public relations as understood today. Today she would be called a gallery educator, coordinating and writing public programs, roles as yet generally not developed by museums in the 1930s. Clarice was required to shape and direct public access to the Academy, write articles for the press, put together educational 'kits' and guide visitors from the press through an exhibition, all of which required expertise in art history and in public relations. 'When I took my first post as Relations Officer to the Royal Academy, it was an almost unknown profession', she said. The tasks called for intellectual as well as interpersonal qualities. 'My work calls for great adaptability and speed', she added, 'working with the press and radio . . . audacity and invention are essential'.[87]

Her work was all-consuming. The Summer show of 1934 opened to the press on the first Wednesday and Friday of May. The annual dinner was held on the Thursday between these days and was attended by the Prince of Wales. The King and Queen, accompanied by other members of the court, attended the exhibition on the Sunday. A soiree was then held for nearly two thousand guests. Clarice was expected to be in attendance, liaise with the press and members of the Royal household, represent the interests of the Academicians to relevant third parties and to prepare and issue material that was comprehensible to the information-hungry public. She became the public face of the Academy. By the close of the show, paid admissions totalled 129,595, an increase of 5236 on 1933.

Her efforts did not go unremarked. In the press the Academy had often been the butt of criticism for failing to foster an interest in art 'beyond the narrow circle which on Private View Day has a free peep at the works which ordinary members of the public must pay to see'.[88] The Academy was characterised as both ossified and elitist. With Clarice there, the press noted that the entrenched order of Burlington House was attempting to recover the institution's steadily declining patronage. It now had 'an admirably conducted campaign, which brought the Academy into touch with an immense newspaper-reading public, without doing anything to impair its somewhat intimidating conception of its own dignity'.[89]

Her success gave her some leverage in negotiating her salary. It was agreed that she would be paid between £100 and £250 on an exhibition-by-exhibition basis. The years from 1934 to 1939 were significant at the Academy, in that

Clarice Zander on holiday in France, c. 1934. *National Art Archive, Art Gallery of New South Wales, Sydney.*

it staged a number of international exhibitions which were unprecedented for their quality and comprehensiveness. 'In addition to their educational value', said Sir William Llewellyn, 'such exhibitions tended to promote a better, happier, and healthier feeling between nations and assisted towards mutual esteem and understanding'.[90] The logistics involved brought Clarice into contact with a wide variety of people. 'Many extraordinary events and people have crowded into my life as a Public Relations Officer', she later wrote, 'there are so many that it has the colour and variety of a kaleidoscope'.[91] Close ties were established with landscape and architectural etcher (later Sir) Henry Rushbury, who occupied a studio in Dyson's Chelsea house. The art critic Alan Clutton Brock, who wrote for the *Times* from 1930, became a good friend. Ernest Wright, Librarian of the Academy from 1905, became infatuated with Clarice. She admired him for his scholarship, old-world manners and tremendous kindness. When he died in 1955, aged seventy-six, he left a third of his estate, a £10,000 windfall, to her daughter Jocelyn.[92]

At the end of 1932 the Royal Academy Council considered a proposal from Sir Percival David and the collector Sir George Eumorfopoulos for a comprehensive international exhibition of Chinese art, to be held as the Winter show from November 1935 to March 1936. The exhibition would centre on the Eumorfopoulos collection, the foremost collection of Chinese art of the time. The acquisition of a portion of this collection for the nation in 1934 was considered as significant as the British Museum's acquisition of the collection of Sir Hans Sloane. Preparations for the exhibition overlapped with the 1935 Winter Exhibition, *British Art in Industry*. Jointly arranged by the Academy and the Royal Society of Arts, *British Art in Industry* illustrated recent collaborations between British manufacturers and artists, demonstrating to the public the importance of good design. Both exhibitions were vast in scale, requiring skilled management and organisation. Clarice provided information about both shows and organised lecture programmes and the associated ancillary events.

In the midst of all this activity, Clarice and Dyson were shocked to lose their close friend Alfred Orage. He died in his sleep on 6 November at the age of sixty-one. Only a few hours earlier, he had given a broadcast, 'Poverty in plenty'. Dyson arranged the funeral, with the literary world paying Orage a spectacular tribute in the next issue of the *New English Weekly*: forty-nine tributes appeared including from Bernard Shaw, G.K. Chesterton, T.S. Eliot, H.G. Wells, Llewellyn Powys, Augustus John and Ezra Pound.

Throughout 1935 the *Times* wrote about the mounting excitement over the coming Winter Exhibition at the Academy: 'never before have so many and such valuable objects representative of the art and culture of China been assembled together in one place'.[93] About a third of the exhibits had been lent by the Chinese Government. Others came from the royal residences in England and private and public collections in Europe, the United States, India,

Japan and the Near East, including from the exceptional collection of George Eumorfopoulos. A much-discussed exhibit was the colossal marble statue of Buddha from the late sixth century, which stood 19 feet high in the central hall. It was the first work seen on entering the exhibition. Weighing over 36,000 kilograms, it required the floor to be strengthened by massive girders installed in the basement.[94]

The exhibition was a spectacular success, attracting over 422,000 visitors. The organisers had not envisaged such public enthusiasm for oriental art. The Academy praised Clarice's contribution to raising this interest:

> she was indefatigable in interpreting for the ordinary observer the beauties of a display which might otherwise have attracted, not so much the general public, but artists, Orientalists, archaeologists and scholars. The contacts she established enabled her to realize what a wide interest there was in Chinese art, particularly in its earlier forms.[95]

Clarice was aware of the hunger that the general public had, 'who want badly to understand a great variety of things particularly on subjects of art and archaeology'.[96] Over 50,000 inches of editorial space had been devoted to the exhibition in British papers alone, with almost as much again in foreign newspapers. Although 'worn to a shadow', as she wrote to Basil Burdett, Clarice rightly prided herself on her part in this achievement.[97] The Academy awarded her a bonus honorarium of £150 for her exceptional work on the show, supporting the press's judgement that 'much of the praise for the success of the show goes to Mrs Zander, propaganda and publicity chief at Burlington House . . . she does not believe in half measures' (plate 45).[98]

Following the exhibition, Clarice considered taking a curated selection of Chinese art to Australia during 1937. This never occurred. The difficulties of transportation and display – including, again, customs – made it impractical. The first comprehensive exhibition of Chinese art in Australia did not take place until the 1970s.[99] She did manage, however, to include Chinese artworks (many of which were borrowed from Sydney Cooper) in an exhibition organised by her for the David Jones Gallery in Sydney: *An Englishman's Home from 1700 to 1941.*

Work on the Academy's Chinese exhibition confirmed her ideas about the cultural context in which art was made and judged. She became a persuasive advocate for the study of non-Western art forms for their intrinsic worth. She considered that such study was particularly important for Australia, writing: 'Thrust into the life of the world we must learn more of the thoughts and ways of life of our Pacific neighbours by studying their arts'. Back in Australia, a number of artists were already doing this, studying Australia's Indigenous art in particular. This interest eventually led to the 1941 landmark *Exhibition of Australian Aboriginal art and its application* at the David Jones Auditorium in Sydney. This exhibition problematically appropriated Aboriginal images, which Australian artists imitated. Clarice was wary of such appropriation. She wrote, 'we should guard against adaptations and distortions'.[100]

Clarice sensed that the holiday escapes that she enjoyed on the continent with Dyson and Jocelyn were nearing an end. Fascism was on the offensive everywhere. In the Spring of 1936 Ethiopia fell to the Italians and Hitler marched into the Rhineland. British Tories stood nervously by with little protest and the Prime Minister Stanley Baldwin became known as 'Old Sealed Lips'.[101] Dyson railed against the cowardice of the 'Yellow Press'. Seventeen years earlier he had predicted the failure of the Treaty of Versailles. In 1919, Dyson drew Europe as a weeping child: the League of Nations was being established simultaneously with the rise of Hitler's National Socialist Workers Party and Mussolini's Fasci di Combattimento. He anticipated then that peace in post-war Europe would be short-lived.

As the 1930s drew to a close, war seemed inevitable. There was a sense of disillusionment that all efforts for peace and international cooperation had proved futile. Londoners were shocked on the 30 November 1936 when the Crystal Palace, designed by Joseph Paxton to house the Great Exhibition of 1851, burned down. The structure epitomised the country's past sense of optimism and achievement, and rumours circulated that the building had been deliberately lit because it was a landmark for German bombers in the event of war. Just ten days later Edward VIII abdicated, announcing that he was renouncing the throne to marry an American divorcee.

Instability in Europe prompted the Academy to mount exhibitions

PEACE AND FUTURE CANNON FODDER

The Tiger: "*Curious! I seem to hear a child weeping!*"

Will Dyson, *Peace and future cannon fodder*, 17 May 1919. *State Library of Victoria, Melbourne.*

which could be easily assembled in Britain, such as shows of modern British architecture and of seventeenth-century art.[102] While working on these, Clarice travelled to Munich with her Melbourne friend the pianist Mancel Ellery, whose mission there was to collect a new clavichord. Clarice was curious to put into context the vexing question of art in Germany, as she was organising publicity for an exhibition of 'degenerate' German paintings, condemned by Hitler and scheduled for London in 1938. In connection with this project she met Gauleiter Wagner, the Bavarian Minister for Culture. He had been one of the organisers of the notorious 1937 Exhibition of Degenerate Art in Munich.

Thomas Dugdale, [*Will Dyson after death*], pencil on paper, 1938.
Collection of the State Library of Victoria, Melbourne.

On 21 January 1938 Dyson collapsed in his studio from heart failure and died. He was only fifty-seven years old. Clarice was devastated. 'As you may have seen in the papers, Bill has died', she wrote home to Australia. 'For me the end of everything.'[103] He had hidden the seriousness of his failing health from everyone, including Clarice. He was buried at Hendon Park Cemetery. Five days later Clarice was admitted to hospital for a previously scheduled hysterectomy. She was concerned about Jocelyn and ensured that her affairs were in order, organising for close friends Eileen and Laurence Heyworth to take care of Jocelyn, should anything befall her. She was overwhelmed with grief and a sense of purposelessness for, as she told the Heyworths, 'Bill had been the "aim and object" for so long, twelve years to be precise' (plate 46).[104]

Dyson died leaving an unsigned new will: a careless lawyer had left it unattended for two months. Although he had bequeathed a portion of his estate to Clarice, Betty laid claim to the entire estate. Clarice was in no condition to argue about finances and simply accepted the situation. Tom

Dugdale gave her a sketch of Bill made after his death, a memento she always treasured.[105] She also felt close to Bill at the Hampshire cottage, which she kept, as they had decorated it together, its interior walls washed in pink, green and primrose and its window frames painted a bright apple green.

Friends nursed her through this time of grief and, as is often the case, she turned to work for distraction. The Royal Academy had appointed her to its full-time staff just before Dyson's death and she was now employed for five years on a salary of £200 per annum with separate contracts to be negotiated for her work on significant loan exhibitions. An indication of how the Academy appreciated Clarice was revealed in a letter to her from Llewellyn. He was pleased she was back at work and wrote to 'express the hope that you will now enjoy good health and be free from worries of any kind'.[106] Included in his letter was a comment that her discretion about sensitive issues was welcomed, the sensitive issues being the debate aroused in April when the Academy jury rejected Wyndham Lewis's portrait of T.S. Eliot (1938). It had been submitted for the Summer Exhibition, after Lewis had published his book *Hitler*, in which he praised the German leader. Augustus John resigned from the Academy in protest.[107] Those who sided with John held the view that art should be above politics, but to no avail.

Clarice continued her work as a freelance publicist on the *Exhibition of Twentieth Century German Art*, which opened in July at the New Burlington Galleries.[108] The exhibition had been organised by a committee chaired by Herbert Read, an early critic of Nazism. Under discussion for between ten and fifteen years, the exhibition had been conceived historically, to represent German art from impressionism to surrealism. It was a sensitive time to be staging the show and the catalogue specified that 'no artist still living in Germany has been asked to participate in the exhibition'. The exhibition included important works by Max Beckmann, Otto Dix, Lyonel Feininger, George Grosz, Wassili Kandinsky, Kathe Kollwitz, Hans Liebermann, Emile Nolde and many others.

At the beginning of 1939 Basil Burdett arrived in England to organise his exhibition of European art for Australia, with the financial backing of Keith Murdoch. He was among the many Australians whom Clarice assisted on their visits to London. Burdett wished to learn from the experience she had gained from her exhibition in Australia six years earlier. By this time Clarice was living in a tiny, dilapidated house, with no power and no bathroom, which she had bought in Bloomfield Terrace, off Pimlico Road in Chelsea. 'One of four little houses in a row', Clarice wrote, 'three floors with two rooms on each give a very narrow front, set over a basement'.[109] She took lodgers on the top floor to cover costs. She thought it a good omen that it adjoined a house where Mozart had once lived and that her new street bore the same name as that of her Irish great grandmother, Catherine Bloomfield.

That April she initiated the first televised programme from the Royal Academy. The world's first regular television service had begun in 1936 with BBC1 broadcasting from Alexandra Palace. Outside broadcasts had become common by 1939 and television became another medium, apart from the press and radio, to which Clarice regularly provided publicity. She convinced the Royal Academy to allow the televising of a non-members 'Varnishing Day'. The half-hour programme showed some exhibitors putting final touches to their pictures and included interviews with artists, Eric Gill among them.

Her contact with notable artists brought her a steady flow of freelance work. Dame Laura Knight, the first woman to become a full member of the Royal Academy (1936), was one of her clients, as was the landscape painter and printmaker Sydney Lee. He thanked Clarice for her promotion of his 1937 exhibition at the prestigious New Bond Street art dealership of Colnaghi's. 'But for your efforts and my own I feel Colnaghi would not have got it well started at all', he wrote, 'they don't seem to understand this part of the business'.[110] She arranged the publicity for Epstein's solo exhibition at the Leicester Galleries and agreed to handle the promotion of the one-year-old musical festival at Lucerne. She convinced the organisers of the 1939 festival to have the programme, with performances by Toscanini and Bruno Walter, broadcast worldwide by seventy-two radio stations. This was a significant political statement, because Toscanini, widely considered the world's foremost conductor, represented opposition to Nazi Germany and Fascist Italy. He refused to conduct at the Salzburg Festival after the Anschluss and at his own expense led a new orchestra (later the Israel Philharmonic), mainly composed of Jewish refugees.[111] Clarice had had personal contact with the maestro in the past, working as publicist for an exhibition of works by his son-in-law at the Leicester Galleries.

On the nights of 10 and 30 September and again on 15 November the Academy schools and galleries were damaged by bombs exploding in Burlington Arcade. At the time Clarice was helping to arrange an Academy benefit show for the British Red Cross. Suggestions that Clarice return to Australia weighed on her. Jocelyn, now nineteen, barely knew Australia and so in June 1940 Clarice took leave from the Royal Academy and sailed to Sydney. As had happened in the First World War, this was to draw a sharp line across the story of her days.

The Royal Academy bombed. *Photograph courtesy of the Imperial War Museum, London.*

Part 4

THE EDUCATOR
MARY CECIL ALLEN (1893–1962)

The golden light of Truth, 1893–1916

'The number of "Shows" held in Melbourne, which in earlier years was confined to two or three displays yearly, with a sprinkling of auction sales, has now greatly increased', Melbourne critic Alexander Colquhoun wrote in 1923, 'and purchase records have run to figures which would have been deemed fabulous twenty years ago'.[1] Mary Cecil Allen began her working life in this boom atmosphere, where art was being made in a climate polarised by competing views. Opinion was divided over the nature of art and the purpose it should serve, and this clouded art appreciation. It was here that Mary Cecil Allen's artistic talent, expertise and eloquence were realised. She led many to an enhanced understanding of art, both in the experience of making art and in its appreciation.

Mary's family background prepared her for her later role in educating art audiences. Mary's mother was governess to the children of the Countess of Jersey and came to Australia with the family when Lord Jersey was appointed Governor of New South Wales in 1891. Paris-educated, twenty-nine-year-old Ada Mason was a sensible woman of firm character – as required to satisfy Lady Jersey's robust expectations. On board the ship to Australia Ada 'collected an admirer, a professor, whom she married' on 11 November 1891 at the governor's summer residence.[2] Harry Brookes Allen, Mary's father, was eight years older than his bride and well established in Melbourne. His father, however, had been in trade as a shoemaker. He believed that education would give his two boys the opportunities he had not received, and the sacrifices made

Mary Cecil Allen at the National Gallery of Victoria School, c. 1916. *State Library of Victoria, Melbourne.*

by him to this end were rewarded. Harry was at the top of his class in medicine each year and graduated in 1876 with first class honours. His brother George became the first secretary of the Commonwealth Treasury and was key in establishing the tax office, pensions, public service conditions and a system of federal financial auditing.

After graduating, Harry began to play a leading role in the medical affairs of Victoria. At twenty-eight he became Professor of the recently established Department of Descriptive and Surgical Anatomy and Pathology at Melbourne University. He edited the monthly *Australian Medical Journal* and was a pathologist at Melbourne Hospital. Gifted as a teacher and organiser, he took a leading role in medical education and the raising of medical standards in Victoria. He was on the state's Central Board of Health and presided over a Royal Commission into Melbourne's Sanitation (1888–89), as well as being General Secretary of the Second Inter-Colonial Medical Congress of 1889.

The Allens set up house in the grounds of Melbourne University, in the last of the semi-circle of professors' residences near the university's city boundary known as 'Tin Alley'.[3] Mary Cecille, the second of their three children, was born there on 2 September 1893. She had an older sister, Edith Margaret, who was born on 4 June 1892, and a younger, Beatrice Bicknell, who was born on 7 November 1897.

During 1897, Allen journeyed to England for a second time. This was an important trip, as his objective was to secure full recognition for the medical and surgical degrees awarded by Melbourne University. He was the only local graduate to hold a chair at the university and his success in having Australian degrees recognised as equal to their British counterparts reflected his world outlook and his persuasive skills, as did the professional regard with which he was held worldwide.[4]

Ada Allen, like her husband, possessed a high sense of public duty and applied her organisational ability to the life of the community in Melbourne, gathering its leading women around her to benefit community causes. She was a foundation member of the Victoria League in Victoria, a long-serving president of the Mothers Union, a prominent worker for hospitals and the Red Cross, a council member of the Diocesan Board of Education and a foundation

Lady Allen and her daughters, c. 1907. *State Library of Victoria, Melbourne.*

member of the University of Melbourne's Women's College.[5] Women's clubs were important at the time as a place where women could socialise and through which they could organise charitable and educational events, both for themselves and for others. The Austral Salon was founded in 1890 for women writers and those interested in the arts. The Women Writers Club followed, with Ada Cambridge the first president. This became the Lyceum Club, requiring distinction in the professions, law, the arts or public service for membership.

The three Allen girls were privately educated in the university environment. Though privileged in many ways, a professor's salary made sure they were not spoilt. Years later, watching a bevy of young girls in their gaily printed cotton frocks, Mary remembered she and her sisters 'had only two cotton frocks each summer – in plain colours'.[6] The values that were promoted in the family home were piety, wide and interesting cultural pursuits and creativity. Sir Roy Cameron, an Australian pathologist who went on to a distinguished career in England, said that until he met the Allens he did not know 'what true culture, wit and charity could be'.[7] The Allens gave their daughters a childhood rich in imaginative play, intellectual stimulus and social engagement. Family papers suggest that their childhood was idyllic. Photographs picture them at dress-up parties in the gardens of the university, while musical scores illustrate the compositions for small orchestras by which they entertained themselves and the many guests hosted by the Allens. Harry shared poems he wrote, based on his love of nature and the bush, and Ada's scrapbooks show their pride in their gifted daughters.[8]

All three achieved distinction in their chosen fields. As a specialist in the domestic arts, Edith took to journalism, first with the *Australasian*, and later writing as a housecraft and social reporter for the *Argus* for seventeen years under the name of 'Vesta'.[9] She was also the cookery expert for the Melbourne *Herald* for twenty-four years, writing as 'Sarah Dunne'.[10] Beatrice, who was known as Biddy, was a pianist and music critic, giving recitals from the early 1920s, including for the British Music Society. She also led Melbourne's Roussel Trio, which enthralled audiences with their performances of Couperin, Ravel and Debussy.[11] She published with the *Argus* and the *Australasian* for many years, under the names 'Biddy Allen' and 'Bicknell Allen'.[12]

Composer Margaret Sutherland was a fellow student with Biddy under pianist Edward Goll at the University Conservatorium. She described the Allen home as a centre for students and visiting intellectuals: 'Visitors enjoyed a relaxing leisureliness and ease . . . Tea was served in fluted flowered cups. Music followed with Biddy Allen singing, and Professor Woodruff's dramatic rendering of [Schumann's] *Three Grenadiers*'.[13] The ground floor of their red brick home contained a book-lined study, with no lack of reading matter.

Author Martin Boyd met the Allens, who had escaped Melbourne's summer heat, in a Tasmanian hotel halfway up Hobart's Mount Wellington. He found the girls remarkably erudite. When Biddy, a few years younger than he, asked him to name his favourite character in French history, Boyd became 'dumb with shame, as I had imagined that all history was English'.[14] Mary was a voracious reader and known for her retentive memory. She later acknowledged the great advantage of her father's library and of discussions with him about what she read.

Mary Cecil Allen, *Lady Allen* c. 1908, pencil on paper, present whereabouts unknown. *From slide in the Frances Derham Papers, University of Melbourne Archive.*

Mary Cecil Allen, *Sir Harry Allen* c. 1908, pencil on paper, present whereabouts unknown. *From slide in the Frances Derham Papers, University of Melbourne Archive.*

In 1909, at the age of sixteen, Mary qualified for entrance to the Faculty of Arts at the university and also gained selection into the prestigious art school of the National Gallery of Victoria. Australia's first public museum specifically devoted to art was established in 1861 and its collection, initially of sculptural casts, occupied a room in Melbourne's Public Library (now the State Library of Victoria). Its art school, founded in 1870, was the only art school attached to an art museum in Australia and gave aspiring artists professional training on the model of the French, German and especially British academies. Instruction at the school was based upon solid draughtsmanship, and entry was gained upon demonstrating drawing ability. Aspiring students were directed to the newsagent's shop across Swanston Street, 'to buy a box of French charcoal, sheets of Michelet paper, and four drawing pins. With these, applicants were asked to draw cast plums and apples in light and shade'.[15] If their drawing was satisfactory, they were accepted into the school, where they spent two years drawing, morning and afternoon, before they could progress to paint or brush. Lectures were given weekly on simple perspective and anatomy.

Mary enrolled there in 1910, perhaps encouraged by May Vale, who had been her private teacher.[16] The Allens' dedication to service and the university environment were early influences upon Mary; so too was Vale, an artist who advocated for recognition of the professional standing of women. She and painter Jane Sutherland were the first women elected to the Council of the Victorian Artists' Society. Vale was also a foundation member in 1898 of the Yarra Sculptors' Society, the first society of sculptors in Australia.

Contemporaneous accounts reveal that Mary was a self-assured and purposeful student. Many remembered her 'fluting voice'. She spoke with 'the rapidity and the clarity of a Gilbert and Sullivan's Major General'.[17] Her speech reflected her lively mind and she was precocious, energetic and undaunted by authority. She also stood out physically, being nearly six feet tall, with a quirky sense of style. 'It was the very white rather prominent teeth, the sparkling blue-eyed gaze, the unruly corn coloured hair that people looked at', said fellow-student Joan à Beckett (later the writer, Joan Lindsay). 'And the expressive gestures of slender hands and high-arched feet . . . [she was] the only person I have ever known who could almost speak with her feet'. Lindsay added:

> She had almost no personal vanity, and I remember her arriving at the Gallery one morning in a deplorable black velvet tam, which she had just bought for half a crown in Carlton on her way from the University. 'Look darlings . . . such beautiful . . . faded colour . . . and it's almost green in the light.' And so it was. Mary could get away with anything.[18]

The school was led by Bernard Hall from 1892 until 1933. He looked upon art with the same rigid, precise approach that characterised his formal dress and manners. To him, the essential quality of a painting rested in its 'decorative beauty and its high technical achievement'.[19] A narrow single-storey addition to the imposing public library building housed the drawing studio, which was filled with plaster copies of antique sculpture. Students drew these under the supervision of the school's long-serving drawing master. Fifty-four-year-old Frederick McCubbin, who had himself been a student at the National Gallery School, was a warm man who was generous to students. Close bonds were formed among his students, whose numbers were small and with women typically outnumbering men. In 1910, thirteen women and eight men were enrolled. In the following year there were seventeen women and thirteen men.[20] Fellow students who became Mary's lifelong friends were Frances Anderson (later 'Frankie' Derham), Mabel Pye and Ethel Spowers.[21]

At the beginning of January 1912 Bernard Hall issued Mary with a certificate of her drawing competency.[22] This noted that she had won first prize for drawing hands and feet and second prize for copying 'figures from the antique'. Yet Mary did not move immediately into the painting school. She interrupted her training to travel to England with her family. There were several purposes to this trip. On behalf of the government, her father was investigating university administration and public health. He also represented the University of Melbourne at the Bicentenary of the Medical School of Trinity College in Dublin. The family then travelled from Ireland to Scotland, where Harry received an honorary degree of Doctor of Law.

For Mary it was a stimulating time to be in London. In 1910 Roger Fry, with the assistance of Clive Bell, had organised his first post-impressionist exhibition entitled *Manet and the Post Impressionists*, showcasing post-impressionist painters like Cézanne, Van Gogh and Gauguin. Fry focused on the formal elements of design, with Cézanne the deity. It had an enormous impact, prompting Virginia Woolf to claim that 'on or about December 1910 human character changed'.[23] For Woolf the show had a significance beyond the merely artistic, pointing to a change in human relations, 'in religion, conduct, politics and literature'.[24] Old standards no longer held sway.

It is not known whether Mary attended Fry's second post-impressionist exhibition in October 1912, where a large selection of paintings by Matisse and Picasso were also displayed. If she did, she would have read in the catalogue that these artists 'do not seek to imitate form, but to create form; not to imitate life, but to find an equivalent for life'. Fry's two exhibitions posed questions about how art was to be judged and the nature of art itself.

It was not only in art that conventions were being challenged. Stella Bowen first arrived in London from Adelaide in the spring of 1914, 'still filled with the naïve self-importance of the small-town dweller'. London unsettled her. She judged the Café Royal, then the meeting place of 'all manner of queer, noisy and exotic folk', to be 'a sink of iniquity', until it dawned on her that the young women she saw breaking conventions 'were quite nice girls and just like anybody else, except that they were rather better educated, and appeared somehow to have disposed of their families'.[25] Now aged nineteen, Mary, like Bowen, had her horizons widened by London encounters.

Six letters written by Mary in 1912 to McCubbin provide clues to the art which impressed her. She was drawn to London's National Gallery, with its superb collection of Old Masters. It was a 'mine of delight', and where she spent her spare time. At the Tate Gallery's Turner rooms she admired the Turner watercolours given by Ruskin to the Fitzwilliam Museum in Cambridge. While in London she also saw exhibitions of the works of Whistler, Burne-Jones and Sargent, the last disappointing her. Her critical eye is apparent in these letters. To her, Whistler's *Harmony in grey and green: Miss Cicely Alexander* (1872–74) resembled 'a bad Velasquez', being 'so colourless and flat'.[26]

Mary also had opportunity to look closely at a number of private collections. She was impressed by works in the collection of Lady Jersey, with whom she stayed as a guest, singling out paintings by Sir Joshua Reynolds and John Hoppner. She spent time with Sir George Clausen, founder of the New English Art Club and from 1906 London advisor to the Felton Bequest on purchases for the National Gallery of Victoria. She was shown sketches by historical genre and portrait painter Sir Francis Dicksee, future President of the Royal Academy. She was a guest of the popular Irish playwright Edward Plunkett, Baron Dunsany, and viewed his eclectic collection of living artists and contemporary craft.[27] She gained a depth and range of knowledge of European and English painting that was generally ahead of her Melbourne contemporaries.

She spent a month in Paris during September 1912, visiting the Louvre to study the Old Masters there. On show at the time was the Salon d'Automne, which that year was remarkable for the cubist work included. It was the heyday of cubism, as Mary noted to McCubbin. Canvases by Picasso illustrating his evolution in the direction of 'a purely abstract art of design' were singled out by the *Times*.[28] Mary reported to McCubbin that these:

> have appalled everybody but even worse than their efforts was a forty foot canvas exhibited by Augustus John at the New Art Club last month – the 'Morning Post' said it was finer than a Michelangelo – but everyone else looked at it in horror – it really was *much* worse than 'Moses' in our gallery!![29]

Mary was unimpressed by Augustus John's *The Mumpers* (1912), 110 inches high and 230 inches long, in her letter comparing it with John Herbert's *Moses bringing down the Tables of the Law* (c. 1872–78). Purchased in 1878, this was the largest painting in Melbourne's National Gallery.

In October 1912 Mary enrolled at London's Slade School. Founded in 1871 with money left by Felix Slade, a wealthy art collector from Yorkshire, it was the first art school in Britain to admit women on equal terms with men. Edward Poynter, the first Slade Professor, had been trained in Paris. He applied the French academic system of teaching, which concentrated on drawing and painting from the living model. In 1912 Frederick Brown headed the school, assisted by Henry Tonks. Training at the Slade at that time, and to become some of Britain's most eminent artists, were Stanley Spencer, Mark Gertler, Christopher Nevinson, Dora Carrington, Edward Wadsworth, William Roberts, Paul Nash and Ben Nicholson.[30] Mary planned to work there for three months and was excited to be working with Tonks, who was known in 1912 as a notable figure painter and a fine colourist.[31] He was a progressive late Victorian artist who exhibited and was closely associated with the New English Art Club. He upheld the Italian system of drawing 'from the inside', which, as the *Times* noted, involved 'constructing the figure in relation to the centre line, though he would allow consideration of the "background spaces" as a useful check upon composition'.[32] This approach contrasted with that taken by Bernard Hall, whose highly structured pictures achieved illusory space by working outwards from a dark background to a middle ground, after which he set silvery lights and reflected highlights at crucial points on featured objects, all props in the composition.[33] Tonks was known for his withering criticism and Mary wrote to McCubbin, hoping he 'won't be even fiercer than Mr Hall!!'[34]

She had intended to spend three months at the Slade but lasted only one. She came away 'sadder and wiser', adding 'they never taught one anything but that one's pencil should be well sharpened and in the Life School the model was to be drawn in outline only!!'[35] Yet, upon returning to Australia in early 1914, it became clear that London had made an impression on her. Mary resumed her studies at the National Gallery School with a confidence that awed fellow students. She was admired by a circle of eager listeners for having knowledge and experience beyond theirs and an independence of mind. Joan Lindsay recalled:

As soon as I entered the shabby common room . . . I could hear Mary's rich plummy voice ringing gaily down the corridors . . . It was an unforgettable voice, well attuned to its owner's gluttonous appetite for good meaty conversation. All her life, art and conversation remained her abiding joys. Like my brother-in-law Lionel Lindsay, she appeared to exist in a practically continuous state of seething ideas awaiting verbal expression. She was never at a loss for subject matter and, like Lionel, tolerated the company of bores with amazing resilience. I remember how we students in the lunch hour used to flock around Mary like hungry sparrows picking up the crumbs of her wit and wisdom . . . Although most of us were too ignorant, or too shy, to hold an intelligent conversation with 'Barney' Hall, the Head of the Art School, Mary had both the courage and the ability to talk to Barney on his own grounds. A shy scholarly man, he must have been astonished at this unusual student's ease of manner and wide knowledge of the Old Masters.[36]

London had left Mary ready to challenge the illusionist orthodoxy of the school. Frances Derham thought her 'the only student of that time to think originally and to innovate'. She was intrigued by the more experimental outlook Mary had to drawing.

> She arrived early one morning and 'snaffled' half a dozen drawing boards and several easels. The boards she placed so that they channelled the light on to the head she was drawing, giving one light only, one beam, as it were. The effect, of course, was to give a dramatic, almost black and white effect, without reflections in the shadows. Almost no half-tones. I watched, fascinated, sitting on my low stool waiting to see the result in her drawing. The lighting arranged to her satisfaction, Mary began to draw . . . Today, or even ten years later, this dramatic black and white effect might have been commonplace but no student at that school had thought of channelling or changing in any way the diffused steady South light which enveloped all our very off-white casts. Then too, it would have been a crime to do other than faithful copying of the model – so that changing the light on it was the only permissible relief to boredom.[37]

McCubbin's departure from the school in 1916 saddened Mary. He was ailing from the heart disease that killed him in December 1917 and it was said that he never fully recovered from the death of his brother at the Dardenelles.[38] On his death, Mary noted how she had found his teaching inspiring:

> he taught no method of painting or drawing but sought to develop in every student an individual point of view . . . he created an atmosphere in the School so singularly unworldly and ideal that we feel we owe him a debt that no words can adequately describe. His whole attitude of mind was so remote from all style and competition that it could not help having a marked influence on those he taught.[39]

McCubbin taught his students to be conscious of what they were seeing: 'He would tell you to look, and see what it was that you took an interest in more than any other thing'.[40] Although Mary's early paintings are stamped

Students from the National Gallery School at the Artists' Ball, Melbourne, c. 1914. *National Art Archives, Art Gallery of New South Wales, Sydney.*

with the realism demanded by Bernard Hall, she responded more to McCubbin's encouragement to develop an individual point of view. Already facing her was the choice between an academic sense of the 'perfectibility' of art, as propounded by Hall, and the 'individual point of view of the artist', as fostered by McCubbin.

Having an opportunity to study overseas and possibly achieve success there was the ambition of most of the students at the school. Mary for her part aimed to win the coveted Travelling Scholarship of the National Gallery School, Australia's richest art prize. Awarded triennially from 1887, from 1917 the scholarship endowed the winner with £450 to study overseas for two years. First won in 1908 by a woman, Constance Jenkins, the 1911 and 1914 scholarships were also won by women.[41]

With her heart set on the award, Mary absorbed herself in the painting studio allotted to competitors for the Travelling Scholarship. Here they painted a figure composition in oils under fixed uniform conditions to ensure that the works were original. Fellow competitor Edith Grieve observed Mary's purposefulness: 'she really became whatever she had in mind'.[42] Joan Lindsay supported Grieve's view when noting Mary's ambition: 'Mary remained virtually in solitary confinement . . . concentrating on her entry for the Travelling Scholarship'.[43]

Students were judged for their paintings of a nude model and for still life, portrait and figure painting. The annual competitive exhibition of work by students of the school was displayed in the antique room at the galleries, where visitors could judge for themselves whether they agreed with critic Alexander Colquhoun's opinion in December 1916 that, among the paintings and drawings exhibited, 'it is to be regretted that there should be so little evidence of individuality or imagination'. Although creative competition was intended to raise the general level of artistic performance, some disquiet existed over how ability, effort and skill were measured. Colquhoun's opinion can be read as evidence of Bernard Hall's hold on the National Gallery School, where 'the teaching at the National Gallery was falling down'.[44] Colquhoun advocated for change. To Mary, it seemed as if her academic training dragged on, with little real focus. 'I could gnash my teeth when I think of the time that was wasted', she later recalled. 'All we learnt of any value could have been given in one third of the time'.[45]

Mary was passed as a Melbourne Gallery diplomatist, but failed to gain the Travelling Scholarship. This was awarded to Bendigo-born Marion Jones, who had been at the school from 1912. Mary's ambitions to return abroad were dashed. Joan Lindsay thought that Mary's maturity enabled her to bear the disappointment, with one particular episode demonstrating this. Lindsay describes how shortly after leaving the gallery Mary painted a small oil of Lindsay in a ballet dress. It was exhibited at Gills, then the most fashionable art dealer in Melbourne, and sold immediately. Mary told Lindsay how Gill had asked her to continue painting similar works of girls in ballet skirts, as he could sell them 'like hot cakes'. 'But Mr Gill', Mary said, ever true to her inner vision, 'I'm afraid I couldn't do that. You see I just wanted to paint this friend of mine in that dress'. Lindsay claimed that to her knowledge Mary never painted a similar canvas. 'For Mary Allen, Truth as she saw it not only in matters of art but in her whole attitude to life, was the golden light by which she lived and worked'.[46]

Developments in art, 1916–1924

In 1914 the Medical School at Melbourne University celebrated its Jubilee.[47] Mary's father had dedicated his life to developing the school. Recently knighted, he was asked to write its history. In it he characterised the past fifty years as a time of unprecedented change, particularly in the sciences. Citing the theory of evolution, the revolutionary practice of antiseptic surgery and the new science of bacteriology, he stressed that the outlook of his generation had been radically transformed: 'all opinion has been in a state of flux and the task of teachers and taught has been correspondingly difficult'.[48] His expansive attitude was one of his legacies to Mary. She shared his vision, welcoming change and being able to recognise the historical and cultural forces that made advances possible. As her father had done for medical students, so Mary would for art. She became an interpreter of the progressive forces in art for her contemporaries, in her books and lectures, making modern art intelligible to both those with an interest in it and those who professed themselves hostile to it.

In the ten years after 1916, when she left the National Gallery School, Mary explored how to express herself artistically and developed her views about art and its purpose. Watercolours made for the Mermaid Play Society indicate the extent of her experimentation with her work. The society was a repertory company of volunteers steered by a committee that included Lady Allen, music patron Louise Dyer and family friends. They included the Solicitor-General, Sir Robert Garran, and the businessman and president of the Victorian Chamber of Manufacturers, Herbert Brookes, who served as the society's patron. Five watercolours illustrating the company's prospectus for the 1919–20 season executed by Mary show that she was tending toward simplified form.[49] Friends witnessed her breaking away from her training, influenced by international poster art and Japanese graphics.[50]

Mary Cecil Allen illustration for *The Winters Tale* 1919 in the programme for the Mermaid Play Society *Season 1919–20: notes on the five plays to be produced, with illustrations by Mary Allen*, Melbourne: Specialty Press, 1919. *State Library of Victoria, Melbourne.*

Also influencing Mary's cosmopolitan outlook was Joseph Biel. Russian-born Biel arrived in Melbourne in 1912, aged twenty-one. Biel operated a buttonhole machine by day; in the evenings, he attended painting classes at the Working Men's College in Latrobe Street, where four-year certificate courses were offered. Alexander Colquhoun taught sketching there in 1912. National Gallery School students viewed the college's recently built art school across the road as the height of modernity, envying its spacious, well-equipped and well-lit facilities. Biel was an activist. Having experienced a Russian pogrom and other social evils in Europe, he believed the artist should use painting as a weapon 'to expose social injustice'.[51] Biel was largely unknown during his nine years in Melbourne, unlike Mary, whose family's standing in Melbourne meant that anonymity was impossible for her. Yet her friendship with Biel made her sensitive to the position of the 'outsider', an empathy which was to further develop when she left Australia.

In 1917 Mary rented a city studio on the third floor of the Dudley Building at 527 Collins Street. She painted landscape and still life subjects but was in demand as a portraitist for 'catching a likeness with sure eye'.[52] Two of her portraits were included in the inaugural Archibald Prize in 1921, which was awarded to W.B. McInnes. He had trained at Melbourne's National Gallery School from 1903 and returned to teach there from 1918. A visitor to Mary's studio noted her early success: commissions absorbed her and 'for a beginner she has had an unusually busy year'.[53] She contributed work to the large and undiscriminating annual exhibitions of local and interstate art societies. At the Victorian Artists' Society Spring exhibition in 1917, one of her four paintings was singled out as the most outstanding of the panels by women artists.[54]

In 1919 during a time of post-war prosperity she held her first solo exhibition – at Melbourne's Fine Arts Society's Gallery.[55] She was aged twenty-six. The reviews were favourable and her skill as a colourist was praised. The *Age* described her as a clever and ambitious painter 'who has not yet realised her full strength' but held 'very definite promise of entire success in the future'.[56] The Melbourne *Punch* likewise saw her as a promising talent, noting that her work was expressive of 'a remarkable personality'.[57] In Sydney, removed as it was from the web of her family connections, criticism was more forthright and pointed to weakness in her handling of shadows. Still, the *Bulletin* echoed Melbourne critics and wrote: 'she has large possibilities as a colorist, and when she fully exerts her talent and imagination she produces canvases of repose and sweetness that the hardest critic would be happy to live with'.[58]

Mary Cecil Allen, c. 1920. *National Library of Australia.*

Mary followed with a second exhibition in 1921 at the same gallery, opened by Dame Nellie Melba (plate 49).[59] Melba was a collector who was attracted to young talent. She understood how vital it was for emerging artists to receive support and declared that Australian talent, in whatever form, deserved the highest encouragement. Melba hoped that Australian artists in all branches of art would seek recognition beyond Australia, such as in Britain, 'where real art is always appreciated and real artists always get fair play'.[60] Melba knew of plans at this time to take Australian art overseas and bring European art to Australia. She was on the committee of the exhibition of Australian art scheduled for the Royal Academy in 1923, a selection of which was subsequently shown at the Empire Exhibition at Wembley in the following year, and with Mary among them.

Melba bought *Tired Dancer*, which the *Argus* singled out for its tonal values.[61] Despite good sales, Mary's second exhibition was not as well received as her first, with the critic for the *Age* judging her landscape paintings 'dull and uninteresting and her figure studies savour too much of the studio exercise'.[62] The *Argus* added her 'paintings are not always strong in drawing or tone and at times the flesh colour is inclined to be a trifle heavy'.[63] The Sydney journal *Triad* summed up the show:

> Miss Mary Allen had the support of the fashionable world at the opening
> of her exhibition at the Fine Arts Society, but even Melba's approval of
> the artist could not be accepted as a diploma of efficiency . . . In effect,
> she remains much of the National Gallery novice, despite all her fervid
> attestations of maturity.[64]

Mary knew this herself and was searching for ways to develop her work (plate 51). From 1915 the Scottish-born painter Max Meldrum ran a school that was the principal alternative in Melbourne to the National Gallery School. A former student of McCubbin and Hall at the National Gallery School, Meldrum gained the prestigious Travelling Scholarship in 1899. This took him to Paris, where he grew to dislike academic conventions. Upon his return to Melbourne in 1911 the diminutive Meldrum, who was an artistic firebrand, gave many lectures in support of his theories, which he propounded with the fervour of an evangelist. Meldrum preached a 'scientific' theory of the painter's craft, now known as tonal realism. He wanted his students to follow the Old Masters in the path of 'the sane, unvarying doctrines of pure art', rather than being duped by the pseudo-theories (as he saw them) of the impressionists and those who came after them.[65] In September 1922 Mary heard Meldrum lecture at the Athenaeum. He made an 'impassioned appeal for a greater truth in art, for a return to the big things in Nature – light, air, and space'.[66]

Mary's studio was in the same building as that of Alexander Colquhoun. As the art critic for the Melbourne *Herald*, he had been the only one to judge her last exhibition an advance on her previous work. He saw her promise – a fluent technique, fine sense of colour, convincing realism, simplicity of execution – and believed that she needed further direction.[67] Alexander and his wife Beatrix, herself an artist, suggested that Mary study under Meldrum. Beatrix had encouraged Meldrum to begin teaching art and their son Archibald was one of his most enthusiastic supporters.[68] Mary's own experiments in the effects of light and shade, as she had demonstrated when manipulating the lighting at the gallery school, made her receptive to Meldrum's approach, which she believed might help her in her search for artistic truth.[69]

Meldrum stressed that a painter's technique was not the result of haphazard inspiration. He believed that nature could be recorded as it first appeared to the 'innocent' eye, teaching students to paint according to the tonal gradations that occur when light strikes objects and to record that image on the canvas quickly and methodically. The artist's eye became an obedient camera. Meldrum's approach differed from Hall's teaching of tonalism. Colquhoun's daughter Elizabeth described Meldrum's technique:

> You went straight on to painting as you saw the object, there was nothing in between . . . Meldrum didn't have any line drawing at all, he drew in mass. When we learnt to draw, we just drew in mass, straight into oil paint . . . He said 'you're not looking at nature and seeing lines, you're seeing mass', and we had to work directly in mass.[70]

In 1924 Mary held her third solo exhibition at the Fine Arts Society's Gallery.[71] By now it was evident how far she had moved from her earlier

style. One reviewer hinted at her growing
distance from naturalistic depiction but
was uneasy about her turn to a more
selective expression: 'her aim is to gain
the effect of light and shade in as simple
a manner as possible, and in this respect
her work often suggests a broad blocking
in, that leaves a little too much to the
imagination'.[72] However, J.S. MacDonald
singled Mary out among Meldrum's
followers: 'Of this group, Mary Allen is the
most distinct; a woman of many gifts, as
well as being a painter of fine abilities'.[73]
Mary's new work demonstrated why
Meldrum's influence upon Melbourne's

David Low, *Max Meldrum*, reproduced
in the *Bulletin*, 9 August 1919.

most promising artists was pronounced. Other 'Meldrumites' – such as Clarice
Beckett, Colin Colahan and Percy Leason – continued to be indebted to his
theories. However, Mary eventually abandoned them and MacDonald saw
why this was necessary: 'His regime admitted of no questioning, no doubts . . .
by acquiescing in its quasi scientific claims, they [Meldrum's followers] denied
and rejected those of imagination . . . Rhythm through arrangement is shut
out and pattern can only be adventitious'.[74]

Yet Meldrum had a lasting effect on Mary's art and thinking. Although he
was scathingly critical of 'the false art of to-day – cubism, post impressionism
and vorticism', he paradoxically made her more receptive to developments then
occurring in art.[75] Meldrum's method, by eschewing fine detail, encouraged
the application of broad areas of paint, a technique resembling the modernist
approach. Mary's painting of *Sorrento Hotel* (c. 1923), faithfully following
Meldrumite principles, appeared more 'modern' than any oil she had painted
so far. This paradox has been noted in connection with the work of a number of
Meldrum's pupils. As early as 1929, Colin Colahan wrote a letter to the *Bulletin*
conceding a resemblance between tonal realism and the 'patterned surfaces'
of modernist canvases.[76]

Beyond her association with Meldrum, Mary exhibited regularly with the Society of Women Painters and Sculptors. Founded in 1901 by women students from the National Gallery School, with Nellie Melba as patron, this was Australia's oldest specialist organisation for women artists. She also showed in 1925 with Twenty Melbourne Painters, another art society coordinated by women painters Alice Bale and Jo Sweatman.

Melbourne was the centre of the nation's art market at this time. A bequest left in 1904 by manufacturing chemist Alfred Felton yielded an annual income of £8000 to be spent on works of art for Melbourne's National Gallery, an endowment that made the gallery one of the richest in the British world. When George Bell returned to Melbourne in 1920 after a long absence, he observed the boom in art. Bell also noted the need for judgement: 'money was plentiful. Business was brisk. So was Art – of a kind. Instead of "art without sales" it was "sales without art". The pot-boiler reigned supreme'.[77]

Alexander Colquhoun thought 'there is so much "art" about at present that a certain amount of confusion is not to be wondered at'. He argued that education was the key: in art, 'Taste is a matter of education'.[78] But disagreement arose about who was qualified to educate the public. Artists blamed the 'lay art critic' for much of the confusion. Bell commented, when looking back in 1959, that such a critic 'has no hope of ever getting the artist's point of view. He remains a layman, with the layman's prerogative of seeing and liking or disliking art as his feelings dictate . . . he is not in a position to speak with authority, gabble as he may'.[79]

Mary, as a practising artist with experience overseas, as well as being the daughter of an esteemed educator, was in a position to speak with authority. It was at this time that she began writing and lecturing on art. William Moore lists her as a critic on the morning daily, *Sun News-Pictorial*, from 1925. A richly illustrated tabloid owned by the *Herald and Weekly Times*, it had an average daily circulation of 170,000, exceeding that of the *Age* and the *Argus*. Mary was one of the first women art critics to write for a major newspaper.[80] Her friendship with art collector Robert Elliott was an advantage. R.D. Elliott, whose wife Mary had painted in 1926, owned a number of regional newspapers and was a trustee of the Public Library, Museums and National

Gallery of Victoria (plate 50).[81] He had initiated and paid for a series of lectures at the gallery in the mid-1920s, some of which Mary gave.

Mary's lectures were exceptionally well attended. They were delivered in the midst of criticism of the National Gallery of Victoria for its failure to buy current Australian art as well as up-to-date examples of international art. Even the collections on which the gallery prided itself, such as those representing the nineteenth century, were disparaged. In her lecture, 'The rise of English art', Mary judged that the works the gallery had acquired in this area were not representative, making this judgement on the basis of what she had seen overseas.[82] Her lecturing required that she develop her own aesthetic position and this gave her experience in arguing and advocating her point of view, becoming the bedrock on which she built her reputation as an art educator. She believed that most people in the West were trained from an early age to respond to words rather than to images and so there was a (regretful) need for a mediator. 'The guide-lecturer has been invented as a medium' because:

> we are trained chiefly in verbal expressions. We unconsciously tend to notice the things that may most readily be translated into words. The lecturer must find something to say about the picture and so he looks up the history of the work and anecdotes about the artist, all of which make very interesting narrative material but only indirectly have to do with painting.[83]

Having given the introduction to the artist and the historical context of the work, the art educator should become redundant, since the aesthetic experience is 'one we must have for ourselves . . . the enjoyment of art is not a vicarious experience'.[84]

Mary gained further prominence in 1925 as an expert witness in a libel case. For the best part of a year attention was focused on the Falcke case, as it was known. It was the most prolonged litigation up to then concerning art in Australia.[85] Falcke, a fortune hunter who came to Australia in August 1923, discovered that money could be made by taking advantage of the credulity of collectors. In Melbourne, he presented an exhibition of Old Masters he had supposedly discovered in Australia. J.S. MacDonald, critic for the *Herald*, disputed the authenticity of the paintings. Falcke sued the *Herald and Weekly Times* for the loss of income resulting from MacDonald's opinion. He claimed that the disputed paintings were worth £20,000 and his commission was now lost to him because of MacDonald's allegedly libellous review. The case was heard in September 1924 and Falcke was awarded £3000. A retrial was ordered. Heard in June 1925, the retrial concluded against Falcke and reversed the earlier decision. Falcke arrogantly asserted that there was 'no person in Australia competent to judge these old masters . . . There is no one in Australia that can compete with my word on art'.[86] MacDonald maintained that Australians such as himself and his panel of expert witnesses, including Mary, Max Meldrum and Bernard Hall, were sufficiently informed to judge on artistic matters. The Falcke case, like the recurrent debates at the time about lay critics, highlighted the question of authority in art, and Mary's expertise.

In 1925 she was made an associate member of the Australian Art Association, a body of prominent artists – founder members included McCubbin and Meldrum – which exhibited annually in Melbourne. Begun as a breakaway group from the Victorian Artists' Society, it was familiarly known as 'The Three A's'. This Melbourne initiative aimed to be a national society and aspired to the position of the Royal Academy of Arts and the Salon of France.[87]

AUSTRALIAN ART ASSOCIATION

ANNUAL EXHIBITION
29th Oct. to 14th Nov., 1930

Cover to the catalogue of the 1930 annual exhibition of the *Australian Art Association*.

Membership was strictly limited to practising artists, who were invited on the basis of merit. Those first invited included George Lambert and Dora Ohlfsen. McInnes presided over the association and was succeeded in 1925 by George Bell. Mary had been invited to exhibit in the association's annual exhibition two years earlier, and was asked to show alongside Thea Proctor and Margaret Preston in the 1924 and 1925 exhibitions.[88]

Around this time, Clive Stephen and his wife Dorothy Hossack became an important part of Mary's life. Completing medicine at the university under Mary's father, Clive had spent a year abroad in 1909. He served in the war with the Royal Army Medical Corps and while abroad saw the London Group exhibition of March 1915 and the Vorticist exhibition of June 1915. On his return to Australia in 1916, via Tahiti and Rarotonga, he took up sculpture – a simplified form of carving – which he pursued for the rest of his life. He worked from 1920 as a general practitioner in Prahran, and his independent means gave him the freedom to be more experimental than many of his fellow Victorian artists.[89] From 1924, Mary worked with the Stephens and George Bell at Bell's Saturday afternoon classes. The Stephens also initiated a 'Thursday Club', whereby life drawing classes were held in their own home, attracting such artists as Will Dyson. Stephen rekindled in Mary an interest in line and expression, which led her, ultimately, to break with Meldrum. He also widened her frame of reference beyond European art. She became interested in tribal and oriental art, as well as child art, which enabled her to make sense of modern trends.

During these busy years, Mary's father suffered a stroke, which left him 'just a shadow', unable to recognise anyone.[90] He died in March 1926. Mary and her family were overwhelmed by the over 1200 letters received from all over the world, reflecting how highly he was regarded. At the memorial service for Allen in a packed St Paul's Cathedral Sir John Monash paid tribute to a man 'who might easily have attained the greatest individual success in his own profession, but preferred to give of his best in helping others'.[91]

Mary had been close to her father and his death sharpened her perspective on work and life. A Sydney critic had judged that she was 'far removed from her future' because she was still 'wrapped up in her past'.[92] Family connections placed her in a privileged position, while social mores demanded a more traditional femininity than professional artistic practice required. By travelling overseas however she could break away from these strictures: her close National Gallery School friend Ethel Spowers had spent between 1921 and 1924 in London and Paris. In 1926 Mary turned thirty-three. Many of her closest friends, like Frances Derham, had married and were raising families. Yet Mary was wedded to her work, as her father had been. She also had a sense that she had exhausted possibilities in Australia. She gave a glimpse of her frustration in Melbourne, when she later said that in New York, 'you never have that feeling of being a little "precious" because you are interested in intellectual things, and there is always the stimulus of meeting someone who knows a little more of this or that than you do'.[93]

When a wealthy American visitor to Melbourne, Florence Gillies, suggested that Mary accompany her to Europe as a personal guide, she jumped at the opportunity. Gillies was from a family who had made its fortune in New York importing coffee.[94] In Australia she was the guest of a number of women's clubs, including the forward-looking Feminist Club, which had been founded in Sydney in 1914 to work for equality of status, opportunity and payment between men and women in all spheres. Leaving Melbourne in January 1927, the couple headed for Europe for eight months, basing themselves in Paris. At the end of this period, Mary sailed to New York.

Living in Areas of Discovery, 1927–1939

Mary arrived in New York when the city was in its fifth consecutive year of boom. It was the time when, as F. Scott Fitzgerald put it, the uncertainties of the 1920s were drowned out in a steady golden roar. English writer Ethel Mannin felt that in New York 'one has somehow arrived at the very heart of the Machine Age'.[95] Mary witnessed the radical reshaping of the midtown skyline. The outline of the Barclay-Vesey Building dominated the horizon from 140 West Street. Hailed as the city's first art deco skyscraper, this brick-clad steel and concrete building towered 152 metres high. 'I shall never forget my first glimpse of New York with the sun gilding the tops of the great buildings that pierced the skyline, like an immense range of icebergs', Mary wrote.

> It reminded me of the old woodcuts of the celestial city in 'Pilgrim's Progress', and I realised that when in those old days the painter or the draughtsman was asked to draw the celestial city he drew New York as it is today, like a giant's castle out of a children's fairy story.[96]

Certain features of the city reminded her of Melbourne. When Rudyard Kipling visited Melbourne in 1891 he thought Collins Street resembled Fifth Avenue.[97] Both cities were laid out in a gridded plan and both were national manufacturing centres. Yet the mix of people and ideas in New York was another thing. During the Jazz Age, New York saw a nineteen per cent increase in its population, from 5.7 million in 1926 to 6.8 million in 1934. It became a melting pot of diverse cultures and languages, possessing, according to Mary, 'the elements of new Europe and a new Asia', the world combined.[98] Although a capricious city that functioned almost in spite of itself – with insufficient housing, inadequate roads and corruption – to Mary, it was unequalled as the place to 'scrap old prejudices and to acquire new sympathies', where 'the only language which was the same to all peoples was the language of art'.[99]

Mary immediately felt at home in this city bursting with creativity and possibility. As a woman she found New York a place where she could 'have a full personal life' in an atmosphere where 'feminine talents were encouraged to flower'.[100] She settled at 225 West 13th street, off 7th Avenue, in the heart of Greenwich Village, America's first genuine bohemia. Her neighbourhood was synonymous with rebellion, the testing ground in the 1920s for cultural experiment and every kind of social and sexual liberation. Four doors up, in the same terrace row, lived critic Edmund Wilson. Across 7th Avenue were the offices of the literary magazine *The Dial*. Under Marianne Moore's editorship, the magazine first published T.S. Eliot's *The Wasteland*. Three blocks east was the New School for Social Research, founded by John Dewey in 1919.

It was reported that Mary was visiting the United States to study schools.[101] She was lecturing within months of her arrival, in March and April 1928. These were part of an experimental programme run by the People's Institute, the adult education division of New York City's Cooper Union for the Advancement of Science and Art, funded by the Carnegie Corporation. Philip Youtz of the institute explained that audiences for the classes consisted 'of every race, religion and social stratum imaginable'.[102] As the only woman lecturing, she was publicised as Cecil Allen. The organisers told her that they had taken this liberty with her name as they did not want her audience to know that she was a woman until she had been given a fair hearing.[103]

In August of that year her lectures were published as *The Mirror of the Passing World* by the five-year-old publishing company begun by William Norton and his wife, translator Mary D. Herter Norton. As well as lectures delivered at the People's Institute, the Nortons published manuscripts by experts in the fields of philosophy, music and psychology, later becoming Sigmund Freud's principal American publisher. *The Mirror of the Passing World* was one of five titles released in a series devoted to aesthetics, the other authors being the philosopher Irwin Edman, the literary critic Henry Wells, the educational psychologist Henry Ladd, and Thomas Munro, who wrote on psychology and aesthetics. Norton followed this series in 1929 with a further five titles, under Youtz's editorship, on 'The New Arts'. Mary's second title in this series was *Painters of the Modern Mind*. Co-contributors to the series were the literary critic John Mason Brown, who wrote on modern theatre, Babette Deutsch on poetry, Joseph Hudnut on sculpture and Russian-born musicologist Alfred J. Swan on the past thirty years of music. All were to play significant roles in the American reception of modernism in the arts. *Stead's Review* considered that Mary's second volume was 'quite novel in art criticism'. Being written with 'a total absence of art jargon', the journal considered that Mary's clarity might be resented in 'high art circles because it has taken many years to build up the imposing edifice of the sanctuary of fine art'.[104] Others, however, criticised her lack of mention of the Mexican muralists and 'the surging of a native mood' in American art in the work of such painters as Thomas Benton.[105]

This criticism was unfair, for *Painters of the Modern Mind* was concerned with developments in Western art since impressionism. American art in the late 1920s, in common with art in Australia, was largely derivative of these developments. Nonetheless, the final chapter of *The Mirror of the Passing World* considered how American art could learn from European movements. It could have its own character without being 'too easily influenced by Europe'.[106] One of the strongest features in Mary's art criticism was her ability to place developments in contemporary art within a wide historical and cultural context. Her interest was never narrowly Eurocentric and her writing is replete with references to the arts of China, Japan, Persia and Africa.

She emphasised that great art was much more than a mere 'mirror of the passing world': 'for the real subject-matter of art is not its raw material – the figures, landscape or flowers which serve to supply a name in a catalogue, but the individual adjustment of the artist to this material, which determines the use which he will make of it'.[107] She admired the way Chinese and Japanese painters avoided the trap of purely descriptive art and believed their structural invention as landscapists 'much more varied than that of European painters'.[108] For Mary all contemporary art was essentially 'expressionist', in that it aimed to convey emotions through imagery.

She was concerned to illustrate, as her title *Painters of the Modern Mind* suggests, the role that the mind and imagination play in contemporary art, challenging the 'tyranny of the eye' with its tendency towards observation and imitation.[109] She believed Western art had historically oscillated between recording what the eye sees and what the artist feels and imagines. For Mary, Cézanne made the eye once more a conscious instrument:

> He does not lend the spectator his eyes – he makes the picture an active instead of a passive thing. This is why his pictures are so irritating, so stimulating. The mind that sees them must act in a similar way to his own or else discern little with the eye but a jumble of forms and colors.[110]

One could not be passive to engage with art.

What is clear from both of her publications is that Mary assumed the role not of an apologist or polemicist for contemporary art but that of an educator. Her prose is remarkably clear – free from jargon as noted by the critics – and she had a great capacity for synthesising complex trends and presenting them in a generally comprehensible manner.[111] Although she saw great beauty and vitality in modern art, she was realistic about the challenges it faced, particularly as 'a new school in which, for the first time in the history of art, the rules will be built, not upon precedent, but upon personality'.[112]

Through her lectures and writings Mary impressed Caroline Hewitt, who was a pioneer of progressive education and who founded a private girl's school in uptown New York, which exists to this day.[113] Future prominent alumni were to include Lord Louis Mountbatten's daughter Patricia, Cornelia Vanderbilt, Christina Onassis, Lee Remick and Barbara Hutton. English-born Hewitt recognised a kindred soul in Mary, whom she invited to head the school's art department in 1931. Here Mary innovatively introduced sketch classes from the live model. Working there forced her to her reconsider the whole field of art education for children. She would share this interest with Frances Derham, who from 1935 taught at Melbourne's Preshil Preparatory School and began building a collection of children's art that was unique for its day.[114] By this time, appreciation was growing for the expressive value of child art, an appreciation that ran parallel to interest in 'primitive' art. Both were valued for what was perceived as their primary interest in expression rather than representation. Mary wrote:

> The ideal of to-day is that each artist should create a new art in his own image, record his own individuality in paint or stone . . . [this] is a return to childhood, a looking within in order to gain a new apprehension of the world outside. For children are all expressionists, which is to say individualists: and the world-wide interest in child-art which characterizes our own time, is a sign of the trend of all modern painting and sculpture.[115]

Mary's position at the school gave her financial security. Miss Hewitt's school was for the daughters of the city's social elite. Mary, however, made her closest friendships outside the establishment. Joseph Biel now lived in New York and was one of a number of politically active Jewish artists. Biel's close friend Louis Lozowick gathered these artists around him. Lozowick became a leader in the radical John Reed Club and joined the editorial boards of illustrated publications like the *New Masses*, while also writing for Yiddish and English-language Jewish publications such as *Der Hamer* and the *Menorah Journal*. These artists drew inspiration from urban New York and from the commonplace, and like them Mary took to capturing the life around her in paint.

She also made friendships at the Art Students League, where the émigré artists Hans Hofmann and George Grosz taught. She attended classes with Lena Gurr, who became a lifelong friend and who eventually married Biel. The league was known for its liberal policies relating to both enrolment and study. With no entrance requirements or any set curriculum, it was a studio-based school in which students enrolled to study with individual instructors.

Teaching was inclusive and students were encouraged to explore a variety of styles, although the school became famed for work depicting American life, in what was known as the American Scene Movement.

Mary adopted the New Yorker's practice of escaping the four summer months by spending them in the country or abroad, often painting in Newfoundland, Nova Scotia or in the artist colonies on the coast, for example, at East Gloucester in Massachusetts. There she attended an artists' school established by Ernest Thurn, whom she probably first met at the Art Students League. Thurn was a pupil and colleague of Hans Hofmann and had organised Hofmann's school on the Isle of Capri in Italy in 1924. By the 1930s Hofmann had made Cape Ann in northeastern Massachusetts his home, with other American Modernists such as Adolf Gottlieb, Mark Rothko, Barnett Newman and Milton Avery. Hofmann taught at the Art Students League from 1932, although by then he was doing figurative work.

Mary's determination to succeed in New York was difficult for her family in Melbourne to appreciate. Perhaps Lady Allen feared that New York would be too much of an adventure in freedom for her daughter. Long-distance communication fostered misunderstandings that were never resolved, to Mary's unhappiness. Curiously, given her sisters' own professional activities, her family seemed to have neither an understanding of the difficulties that Mary faced in New York nor an appreciation of her commitment to achieving self-fulfilment and professional independence abroad.

This became apparent to family friend Herbert Brookes, with whom she shared her frustrations. He was appointed by Stanley Bruce in 1929 as Australia's Commissioner General to the United States, based in New York.[116] In Australia, Brookes was highly regarded as an elder statesman of the establishment. He had served on the Commonwealth Board of Trade and the Tariff Board before going to New York. A man of considerable energy, with wide-ranging interests, he was well suited to the task in New York. His wife Ivy, a gifted violinist, was his match. The eldest daughter of Alfred Deakin, she was active in Deakin's Liberal Party. She also served the National Council of Women of Victoria for fifty years from 1904, being on the Federal Council from 1924 to 1931 and the Press, Arts and Letters Committee from 1927 to 1960.

1. WDB
2. JDB
3. ADB

JDB was never christened   2nd eldest

Mary was godmother to their only daughter Jessie, the eldest of their three children (plate 53).[117]

I remember asking my mother Jessie as a depression she was aware of but it did not affect her or parents much

Herbert and Ivy Brookes arrived in America in late October 1929, only days ahead of the collapse of the stock market. With the crash wiping over $14 billion from the market, Herbert Hoover's assurances of the basic strength of business in the United States rang hollow in New York, where nearly one-third of the city's population lost work. Artists were badly hit, with many forced to give up their studios and accept relief. The charms of the Village palled. Mary found it difficult to see all the to-let signs hanging outside the flats where once her friends had lived so happily. She continued teaching, lecturing and painting, glad at this time to have 'more than one string to her bow', as lecturing gave her a reliable income.[118]

In May 1930 Herbert Brookes opened Mary's first solo exhibition in New York at Contemporary Arts, on East Tenth Street. Despite the depression, she sold six works.[119] Her show caught the attention of the New York Times critic, Edward Jewell, who remained interested in her painting from this time.[120] Wealthy New York broker Louis Horch bought her watercolour Red and Silver for the Roerich Museum, of which he was president. The Russian émigré artist Nicholas Roerich was a charismatic cultural activist; he founded the Master Institute of United Arts (1920) and the International Art Center (1922) in New York, with the aim of fostering understanding and respect through art. He is best known for designing the costumes and sets for Igor Stravinsky's ballet The Rite of Spring. He was also associated with the Eastern philosophy of Agni Yoga, developed by his wife Elena Schaposchnikova, an eminent theosophist. As Roerich led an American artistic–scientific expedition around Central Asia (1924–28), a twenty-nine-storey residential tower and museum was being erected in New York to house his paintings, as well as other collections of European and oriental art, and to provide a venue for the numerous cultural activities he promoted.[121]

The Roerich Museum hosted the first group exhibition of contemporary Australian art to be held in America.[122] A collection of around one hundred paintings, watercolours and etchings was put together by members of the Australian Art Association, the Society of Artists and the Royal Art

Society, with AAA president John Longstaff coordinating the selection from Melbourne. The Australian press correctly reported that 'although several Australian artists have held one-man shows in the city of skyscrapers, this is the first general exhibition to be held there'.[123] Following the First World War, individual artists such as illustrator Frank Nankivell, theatrical designer William Barnes and painters Ambrose Patterson and Hayley Lever had managed to build reputations in the United States.[124] Mary served as the exhibition's organiser in America. It opened to a large crowd on 7 February 1931 in the Riverside Drive International Art Centre of the Roerich Museum, touring to other venues in the United States in the ensuing two years, and with Mary lecturing at some of these.

Jewell again singled out Mary's own work when he reviewed the exhibition. He otherwise found that there was little in the exhibition that could be called remarkable, as Mary did herself. If Americans were expecting to find something of a native tradition giving distinction to Australian art – Brookes reported that he was often asked 'has Australia a native art to build upon like that of the American Indian' – they were disappointed.[125] As the *New York Times* reported, 'Australian artists are simply following continental and British leads', in contrast, the American reports noted, to Canadian art, which had been showcased in the United States the previous year.[126] It was reported that Americans were surprised to find 'not one kangaroo' on display.[127] Mary would have been glad of anything to distinguish the work as Australian. 'When I opened up the work that had been sent from Australia, I could have cried', she said. 'The first was "Landscape in Surrey" and in between were paintings by Australian artists on every subject from primroses to fishing boats at St Ives. If I had come upon as much as a single kangaroo I would have hailed it with delight'.[128] The exhibition was judged derivative and academic, 'with no hint of modernism except for four or five [paintings] by Mary Cecil Allen'.[129]

At this time Mary was exhibiting regularly in group exhibitions, always as an Australian artist (plate 52). This precluded her from membership of such American groups as the National Association of Women Artists. The 1935 Brooklyn Museum Biennial featured an international grouping of artists – four hundred Americans, twenty-eight British and eleven French artists,

— 19 —

Mlle Mary Cecil Allen.

Les dessins et les peintures de Miss Mary Cecil Allen semblent être comme une gageure d'obtenir un maximum de puissance expressive avec un minimum de moyens. Des formes amples, limitées par un trait fortement appuyé et qui pour ne pas rompre l'harmonie d'une belle courbe évite le détail rencontré en chemin, un modelé sommaire et parfois même inexistant, en voilà assez cependant pour que vivent sous nos yeux un beau corps nu, des fleurs, des fruits ou le personnage fortement caractérisé d'une fille de couleur.

Plusieurs des œuvres de Miss Mary Cecil Allen ont été exposées au Brooklyn Museum où l'intérêt que j'ai pris à les regarder pour la puissante originalité qui s'en dégage, m'a incité à faire plus ample connaissance avec un talent que l'on peut diversement apprécier, mais qui ne peut laisser personne indifférent.

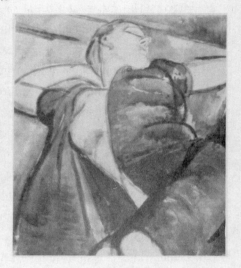

« DORMEUR »

TROIS ŒUVRES DE Mlle MARY CECIL ALLEN. — «NU»

maître français qui sut si bien et de manière si émouvante évoquer la vie paysanne.

Au Salon de Philadelphie (Pennsylvania Academy) Isabelle Duncanson a exposé une toile modeste « La Maison blanche » dont j'apprécie fort la composition et

Née en Australie où elle commença à Melbourne ses études artistiques, Miss Mary Cecil Allen les poursuivit à la Slade School de Londres. Fixée depuis quatre ans à New-York elle a publié deux livres sur l'art : The Mirror ofthe Passing World et Painters of the Modern Mind, qui furent édités en 1929 et 1930 par M. W. Norton. Elle a pris part à diverses manifestations artistiques en Australie, en Amérique et en Angleterre.

Le talent vigoureux et personnel de Miss Mary Cecil Allen serait sans nul doute vivement goûté en France et il est à souhaiter qu'elle veuille bien un jour prochain faire figurer ses œuvres dans l'un de nos grands salons parisiens où l'une quelconque de nos galeries d'art.

Isabelle Duncanson.

Admiratrice de Millet, Isabelle Duncanson s'efforce de traiter le paysage dans l'esprit de simplicité cher au

« JEUNE NÉGRESSE »

Article from *La Revue Moderne* 30 October 1931 illustrating works by Mary Cecil Allen.

among whom was Raoul Dufy. Mary alone represented Australia. She was noticed by the Paris-based journal *La Revue Moderne*, which illustrated three of her works.[130] The journal praised her for creating the maximum amount of expression with the simplest means. By this time she had also expanded the range of her subjects (plate 54). In February of 1932 she held an exhibition of 'impressions of America and Americans' at the Roerich Museum. In 1933 at the gallery, Contemporary Arts, she devoted work to 'negro subjects', reflecting her friendship with the Jewish-American activist Joel Spingarn and the young African-American painter Jacob Lawrence.

The Society of Independent Artists, with which Mary began to exhibit, was open to anyone who wanted to display their work, and shows were held without juries or prizes. Founded in 1916, the society was begun by the collectors Walter Arensberg and Katherine Dreier, along with the artists Marcel Duchamp, Albert Gleizes, Man Ray and Joseph Stella. Its exhibitions were important, if uneven in quality, in that they gave visibility to many experimentalists and public exposure to young untested artists. Artists shared an attitude and purpose rather than a common style. At the nineteenth annual exhibition of the society Mary lectured on the question of 'How modern is modern art?'[131] Earlier, the American *Art Digest* had described her rapid success:

> Since her arrival in New York four years ago, she has lectured on modern painting at the People's Institute, the Metropolitan Museum, the Brooklyn Museum and other institutions throughout the country, and in addition, has written two books on art . . . which give an analysis of the creative principle expressed in the modern movement. In her landscapes and figure pieces America is reflected as seen by Australian eyes.[132]

In March 1933 Mary's mother travelled to London with her sister Biddy. Mary was hoping to meet them on the continent but was dissuaded by Lady Allen, who fell ill while away and died that December. Mary received no mention in her mother's will, which repeatedly made references to 'my daughters Edith Margaret Allen and Beatrice Allen'. Her two sisters were left a Toorak house and £2605 in cash, which set them up for the rest of their lives.[133] It is a testimony to Mary's generosity of spirit that she harboured no resentment about her mother's unjust allocation of the estate, even though a small benefaction would have eased her precarious situation in New York. 'The life of a single woman earning her living in New York', she confided to Frankie Derham, 'is a very strenuous one'.[134]

However, she knew that she must return to Melbourne and reconnect with her sisters. She arrived in July 1935 during turbulent weather – her stay until July 1936 would prove to be as stormy as the gales then tearing across Port Philip Bay. Mary arrived as a celebrity, with the press highlighting the success she had achieved in America. The *Age* said that she had found fame as one of the leading exponents in modern art, besides being recognised as a brilliant lecturer and a talented portrait and landscape painter.[135] The *Argus* described her as 'a woman who has made a name for herself in art'.[136] Her reputation, however, did not impress Victoria's artistic establishment. Brookes had suggested that the Felton Bequest appoint Mary as a selector, but was squarely told to mind his own business.[137]

She held a solo exhibition at the Fine Arts Society's Gallery in August of 1935, exhibiting forty paintings and drawings of New York skyscrapers and cityscapes, African-American portraits and landscapes painted in Newfoundland (plate 55).[138] Works such as the tempera painting *Elevations* 'shocked Melbourne to the core', Frances Derham recalled. 'Nowadays you'd think nothing of it, but it was abstract art and it was different and it was . . . thought disgustingly modern'.[139] No longer the tonal impressionist, as taught by Max Meldrum, seeking to accurately mirror nature, Mary now aimed to reconstruct the world, commenting that 'the picture itself [is] an object'.[140] She was following the path she had traced in *Painters of the Modern Mind*, where painting could no longer be compared with nature: 'the standard of reference is gone, of objectivity . . . it is the idea of an artist, the conception, that now matters'.[141] Unlike most who shied away from her new work, R.D. Elliott bought *Negro girl*, from a series painted in New York of African-American subjects. Her current work appeared immediate, sketch-like and was painted with an intensity of colour and without narrative props.

Meldrum, now aged sixty-one and not long back from a lecture tour of his own in the United States, disapproved of the direction Mary's work had taken. Seeing her coming towards him he crossed the street to avoid her. 'No greeting', Mary remembered, 'I might have been the Devil, with Horns!'[142] He may have been jealous of her success: he had been contracted by Harpers to write two books on art for America but neither eventuated, unlike Mary's two successful publications, which by this time were finding 'a definite place on library shelves all over the United States'.[143] The reception she received from those in George Bell's circle was altogether different. Maisie Drysdale considered 'Mary Cecil was the last word in modern'.[144] It is thought that Mary's influence prompted the dramatic shift in style made at the time by twenty-four-year-old Russell Drysdale.[145]

Derham provides an insight into the hostility Mary encountered in Melbourne. Before returning to New York, Mary asked her to select a work as a gift. Even Derham felt obliged to choose something that would not offend her family. She selected a landscape, because there was 'nothing distorted about it; just done with the utmost economy of strokes'.[146] On one level this climate of hostility is difficult to understand. Mary was not the first artist to exhibit modernist work in Melbourne nor were her abstracted geometrical works particularly radical. Derham's reference to 'nothing distorted' is significant. Throughout the 1920s and 1930s opposition to 'new art' in Australia was galvanised over the question of distortion and the related issues of ugliness and the grotesque (plate 56).[147]

In her Australian lectures Mary defended the role of distortion in modern art, arguing that what 'at first glance appeared grotesque and without meaning' could be beautiful and a reflection of the pulse of the times.[148] Mary had become convinced of this when listening to Gertrude Stein the previous year during Stein's tour of America. The First World War, according to Stein, had forced a radical change in the way people thought and promoted a trend towards what was new and vital, as 'strange things were happening all the time'.[149] For both Mary and Stein this change was positive and had invigorated art. For many Australians, however, the war was seen as a type of madness. Artist Blamire Young thought 'the paroxysm through which Europe has passed will leave a scar behind it . . . an incubus upon our hearts and a shadow upon our brains'. For the art establishment, distorted modern art was a sign of this incubus.[150] Opposing such art was to stand for sanity and order against anarchy.[151] Taking this stand would keep Australian Art pure, uncontaminated.

Resistance to Mary's modernism had a peculiar Melbourne tinge to it. J.S. MacDonald judged Melbourne very 'hard to move to enthusiasm, especially where change is concerned'.[152] Martin Boyd thought that being 'unconventional' was the one unpardonable sin in polite Melbourne society.[153] Coming from the establishment, Mary's views were found to be particularly confronting; so too was her personal style, with her sisters disapproving of her wearing trousers.

Despite Mary's art finding little favour in Melbourne, many were eager to hear her speak. She lectured on modern art to packed audiences, with the newspapers giving extensive coverage to these. Her lectures at the National Gallery were part of a new programme of late-night openings. The staff at the gallery were unsure about the venture, but when Mary gave a lecture entitled 'Photography and modern art' over five hundred people attended, the largest lecture audience the gallery had seen. She illustrated these lectures with slides brought from New York's Metropolitan Museum. By now her extensive experience in America was reflected in her polished performances. She had transformed the lecture into an art form. The dimmed auditorium with projected images, to which she spoke directly, the curtained platform on which she stood, all added to the effect. She appreciated questions from the audience and was compelling in her answers.[154] Arnold Shore, himself a fine speaker, found Mary the greatest orator on art and interpreter who had ever been in Australia.

She also gave what today would be called master classes, working with small groups. These too were an unforgettable experience for participants. The painter and designer Frances Burke first met Mary at one of these, a summer school in Gisborne:

After the first lecture, crayons and paper would quietly appear and Mary Cecil would invite the group to experiment with whatever principle she

Mary Cecil Allen lecturing at the National Gallery of Victoria in 1935.
National Art Archives, Art Gallery of New South Wales, Sydney.

had stressed in her introduction. The reaction was extraordinary. The content of Mary Cecil's lectures in 1936 was as contrary as possible to the conventional ways of teaching to which we had been subjected in Melbourne.[155]

Mary whole-heartedly imparted her American experience to Melbourne: in America artist–teachers such as Walter Gropius, Josef Albers and László Moholy-Nagy were revolutionising the field of art education. Mary was passionate about art teaching, remembering how deficient her own training in Melbourne and London had been. In common with other artists of her generation, she had progressed through a rigid sequence of skill-based teaching, first learning to draw – ornaments, hands and feet, head, antique figure, head from life, figure from life – before progressing to painting. By contrast, she adapted her teaching to the individual skills and vision of each student and her approach privileged expression over technical facility. Instead of making copies of objects, she encouraged her students 'to draw forces . . . show the solidity of nature and not simply its patterns'.[156] She insisted that her students not see with the eye alone, but attempt 'to express on canvas more senses than had ever been attempted before by art'.[157]

She found inspiration for her own art in the Australian landscape and began a series of works which she planned to exhibit in New York (plate 57). Harold Clapp, chairman of the Victorian Railways and the Australian National Travel Association, arranged for her to travel to Central Australia as the association's guest. A railway line linking Alice Springs with Adelaide had been opened in 1929, providing easier access to the remote centre of the continent and opening up interest in Aboriginal culture. Mary shared her enthusiasm 'for everything Central Australian' and encouraged others to appreciate its unique features.[158] Mary no doubt remembered the criticism of the 1931 exhibition of Australian art in New York: that Australia simply followed British leads and lacked interest in its own native tradition.

Her last task in Melbourne was to paint a portrait for the university. Emmanuel Phillips Fox had painted her father for the University of Melbourne's Medical School during the school's jubilee celebrations in 1914. This portrait had hung in the Wilson Hall until destroyed by fire. Despite Mary's early reputation as a portraitist, she was asked to copy the Phillips Fox. She did not sign the copy which she made. She told members of the Melbourne Society of Women Painters at a reception held in her honour that women painters 'must look to the future because women in art have no past'.[159]

Back in New York, Mary experimented with Australian designs and gum-leaf colours, adapting them to fresco work and tiles. She painted a screen of kangaroos outlined in indigo and rust red, executed on five panels, each 72 inches high (and today in the collection of the National Gallery of Australia) (plate 58). By now she was running a private art school for adult students. One student was Maie Casey, whose husband R.G. Casey was establishing the Australian Legation in Washington. Modelling for Mary's students was Australian Pat Jarrett, then the only foreigner to be admitted to the National Women's Press Club in Washington. To Jarrett, Mary 'always lived in areas of discovery', with a passion for absorbing and disseminating new ideas.[160]

During the summer of 1939 Mary was engaged in plans for an exhibition at the New York World Fair, which was to be New York's vision for the future. It attracted more than fifty million visitors. The Australian exhibition formed part of the British Empire Pavilion. Praised for its design, it featured murals by

Douglas Annand and paintings of native flowers by Margaret Preston. The look was slick, showing that 'the days of Wembley's pyramids of oranges and tins of bully beef are gone'.[161] However, it was little more than the same showcasing of industry and trade.

To provide a counterpoint to this display Mary planned an exhibition of Australian art under the auspices of the National Council of Women of America. With the patronage of the council her exhibition could be genuinely representative, free from the self-serving interests of the various artist societies in Australia, which normally organised these international displays. Mary's exhibition was planned for October 1939. She worked with the Melbourne musician Doris Madden, intending to include a supplementary programme of music by Australian composers. Despite her disappointment with the 1931 exhibition of Australian art at the Roerich Museum, she continued to work ahead of official efforts to promote Australian art overseas. The first government-sponsored exhibition of Australian art in America did not take place until 1941. Touring during the Second World War, it was viewed by the Americans as 'part of the good-will program to further relationships with our brother-in-arms from down under'.[162]

The war made it impossible for Mary to proceed with her exhibition. She wrote to Frankie Derham not long after the hostilities began: 'Such a difference to the last one – no boasting or shouting or national anthems or propaganda'. The war ahead was 'a job to be done'.[163]

EPILOGUE

Mary Cecil Allen spent the war years teaching and painting in New York. A small legacy from her uncle in Melbourne enabled her to move to Provincetown, Massachusetts, where for many years she had spent her summers painting the coast of New England. Once she had settled there permanently, she ran painting classes from her studio and lectured across Cape Cod. She was an exhibiting member of the Provincetown Art Association, which she supported in many ways, helping with its annual exhibitions and associated events. She campaigned to ensure that the cape's coastal foreshore was protected, by being designated the Cape Cod National Seashore Park. The seasonal cycles and dramatic weather of the cape inspired her work, as did her close association with fellow Provincetown residents and friends, among them the painters Hans Hofmann and Lena Gurr. She returned twice to Melbourne, in the American winter of 1949–50 and again in 1960. She lectured, exhibited and painted on both visits. She was encouraged to apply for the position of Director of the National Gallery of Victoria, with Professor Joseph Burke, the Herald Chair of Fine Arts at Melbourne University, campaigning for her appointment. She died unexpectedly on 7 April 1962, at the age of sixty-eight, in her Provincetown cottage. Neighbours who had come to take her to church found her seated in an armchair. Lecture series were initiated in her honour, both at Provincetown and in Melbourne, where Sir Herbert Read was the inaugural lecturer. She is buried in Provincetown.

Clarice Zander spent the war years in Sydney. She curated exhibitions, lectured widely and gave radio broadcasts. She returned to England in 1946, finding much of London burnt out, although her Chelsea house had survived the war unscathed. So too had Brook Cottage. War had increased appreciation for the work of public relations. When she began as public relations officer at the Royal Academy, she found herself working in what she termed 'an almost unknown profession'. Propaganda during the war highlighted the strategic importance of public relations. She took up Herbert Read's challenge to 'devise subtler and more suggestive ways of arousing interest in the always apathetic public', and established a business called Tomorrow's News, providing publicity for 'events of artistic, intellectual, social or scientific interest'.[1] During the ensuing decade of post-war recovery, her clients included Salvador Dalí, Jacob Epstein, Alec Guinness and the British designer Zika Asher. The offices of Tomorrow's News in Villiers Street, overlooking London's embankment, became the first stop for many Australian artists newly arrived in London, and she assisted them. Among them were James Gleeson, Sidney Nolan and Peggy Glanville Hicks. Many looked to Clarice in much the same way the artist Ethel Gabain did. Gabain told her, 'I think there are in one's life, events and people who are what Henry James calls "silver nails" – and you have been one of those for me'.[2] She also resumed painting, exhibiting with the London Group and the Women's International Exhibition in 1955. She returned to Australia in poor health in 1956 and died at the age of sixty-three in Sydney on 12 October 1958.

A few months after war was declared, Louise Dyer wrote, 'We must go on and construct to counterbalance all that is being destroyed, making beauty of life in spite of our depressing almost annihilating times'.[3] She had remarried in April 1939. Joseph Birch Hanson, an English-born French scholar who had spent time in Australia during his youth, was twenty-five years her junior. They passed the war years in Oxford, where Joseph was working on his second doctorate. Both were active for the cause of the Free French. Louise was promoted to Officer of the Légion d'honneur for this work, an honour then rarely granted to a woman. The couple was among the first foreigners to return to Paris, where they found that German officers had been quartered in her apartment. She later relocated to Monaco, taking advantage of its mild climate and favourable tax laws. Lyrebird Editions gained in prestige after the war, with her recordings regularly receiving the *Grand Prix du Disque.* Her label was one of the earliest promoters of such artists as Dame Janet Baker and Neville Marriner with the Academy of St Martin's-in-the-Fields. She died in Monaco on 9 November 1962 at the age of seventy-eight and was buried in Melbourne's General Cemetery, according to her wish, next to Jimmy Dyer.

At the outbreak of the Second World War, Dora was aged seventy and Elena ten years younger, though increasingly crippled with arthritis. They felt keenly the escalating curtailments which old age and the war had brought about. In a 1941 survey of monuments, Dora's memorial at Formia was judged 'of great historic and patriotic value, but not of great artistic worth'. The Minister for National Education decided 'for the reason of creating a more pleasing vista' to remove her statue and replace it with a flagpole. Dora and Elena were found dead in their Rome apartment on the morning of the 7 February 1948. The coroner's report found their deaths to be accidental through gas poisoning. Dora and Elena were buried together in Rome's Protestant cemetery. Friends chose her bust of the young Dionysius for their tombstone. Her epitaph reads 'Dora Ohlfsen Bagge, Australian by birth, Italian at heart'. In 2008 her memorial at Formia was restored and rededicated.

ACKNOWLEDGEMENTS

This book was substantially researched during a Creative Arts Fellowship that we jointly received from the State Library of Victoria in 2006. Without the support of this fellowship, its exceptional collections and dedicated staff, particularly the La Trobe Librarian at the time, Dr Diane Reilly, it would not have been written. Eileen Chanin also received the 2006–07 Edmonds Fellowship, Manning Clark House, Canberra, and a Creative Non-Fiction Writing Scholarship at the Norman Mailer Centre and Writers Colony, Provincetown in Massachusetts in 2012. Steven was the recipient of an Australia Council Residency at the B.R. Whiting Library in Rome during 2007, which allowed in-depth study of Dora Ohlfsen's life in Italy.

Numerous colleagues from galleries, libraries and archives in Australia and overseas assisted us with the original research required to reconstruct and contextualise these four lives. In Australia we particularly thank Deborah Edwards from the Art Gallery of New South Wales, who was one of the first curators to take a serious interest in Dora Ohlfsen and who suggested her for inclusion in this book; also Professor Robert Dixon, FAHA, Emeritus Professor Ros Pesman, AM, FAHA, and Associate Professor Richard White from the University of Sydney; Professors Jim Davidson and John Griffiths from the University of Melbourne; Emeritus Professor Jill Roe, AO; Jane Dyer, Archivist at the Presbyterian Ladies College, Melbourne; Associate Professor Joanna Mendelssohn; Leonie Fleiszig, Director of the Makor Jewish Community Library, Caulfield; Pauline Rockman; historians Beverley Kingston and Craig Wilcox; music librarian Evelyn Portek and Jane Eckett from the University of Melbourne; Melissa Campbell, Archivist at Geelong Grammar School; Jacklyn

Mackinnon, Archive Manager, Clyde Old Girls Association; Janda Gooding, senior curator of art at the Australian War Memorial; Jenny McFarlane; Andrew Wager; Diana Hill; Judith White; Tom Foley from the National Library of Australia; Fiona Fraser from the Australian National University; Nicholas Chambers, assistant curator at the Queensland Art Gallery, Robyn Louey, Vivian Huang, Claire Eggleston and Kay Truelove from the Research Library of the Art Gallery of New South Wales; and Joan Patrick and Val Wilson from the Mornington and District Historical Society.

Overseas, we thank Emeritus Professor Sheila Fitzpatrick from the University of Chicago; Jason Steuber, Cofrin Curator of Asian Art at the University of Florida; Julia Fein, Mellon Post-doctoral Fellow and Lecturer, School of Arts and Sciences, Rutgers, State University of New Jersey; Dr Margarita M. Hanson and Kenneth Gilbert, OC, in Paris; Frances Casey, Project Officer, UK National Inventory of War Memorials at the Imperial War Museum, London; Graham Hair, Professor of Music at the University of Glasgow; Dr Jane Mallinson, University of Glasgow Language Centre; Kevin Brown, Trust Archivist and Alexander Fleming Laboratory Museum Curator, St Mary's Hospital, London; Kate Austin at Marlborough Fine Art, London; Jodie Waldron at Lefevre Fine Art, London; staff of the Victoria and Albert Museum, the Victoria and Albert Museum Archives and the National Art Library at the Victoria and Albert Museum; Mark Pomeroy, Archivist for the Royal Academy, London; Dennis Archer and Bernard Coe from Bedales School, Petersfield; Nicholas Martland, Australasian Studies Curator at the British Library, London; Angie Park, Archivist and Manager of Special Library Collections, Brooklyn Museum, New York, and Tara Cuthbert, also at the Brooklyn Museum; Mary Paton, senior archivist at the Noel Butlin Archives Centre; David Langbart from the Textual Archives Services Division of the National Archives of America; Irina Gruzdeva from the Russian State Art Library; James Gaskell from Hanina Fine Arts, London; Douglas Jones from the National Library of Wales; Jonathan Smith from Trinity College Library, Cambridge; Rebecca Wilhelm from the Luton Museum Service; Carol Leadenham from the Hoover Institution Archives; Dr Elena Stolyarik, Collections Manager at the American Numismatic Society; Whitney Hopkins from the American Red

Cross; Bridgette Woodall from the Catholic Archdiocese of Boston; Marissa Bourgoin and Trina Yeckley from the Archives of American Art; Matthew Wiggins from the Chrysler Museum of Art; the librarians of Rome's Biblioteca di Archeologia e Storia dell'Arte and L'Emeroteca Romana; the research staff at the American Academy in Rome and the British School; and, in Provincetown, Stephen Borkowski, chair of the Provincetown Art Commission, Laurel Guadazno, Curator at Pilgrim Monument and Provincetown Museum, David Mayo and Josephine and Salvatore Del Deo.

We are particularly indebted to surviving family members and their friends: to Jocelyn Plate, the daughter of Clarice Zander, and to Cassi Plate, her granddaughter; Ian and Vanessa MacArthur, the great niece and nephew of Dora Ohlfsen; Emeritus Professor John Poynter, AO, OBE, FAHA, and Marion Poynter, Louise Smith from Castlemaine, Norman and Gillian Gengoult Smith in Melbourne; and to Jessie Clarke, Mary Cecil Allen's goddaughter, and Judith Deakin Harley.

Finally, we thank those colleagues and friends who read our manuscript at various stages and made invaluable suggestions: Lesley Brown, Christine Hay, Tony Miller, Adrian Morris, Jock Palmer, Robert Pelletier and Dr Andrew Yip.

NOTES

INTRODUCTION

1 Maie Casey, *An Australian Story 1837–1907*, Michael Joseph, London 1962, pp. 34–5.

2 Germaine Greer, *The Obstacle Race*, Secker and Warburg, London, 1979.

3 'Dora Ohlfsen home', *The Times* (London), 26 September 1920, n.p.

4 William Moore, 'Art and artists. I want to help', *Courier* (Brisbane), 28 February 1931, p. 18.

5 Henry Handel Richardson, *Myself When Young*, Heinemann, London, 1948, p. 74.

6 'International New York: city of many tongues', *Argus* (Melbourne), 10 August 1935, p. 19.

Part 1 – THE ARTIST: DORA OHLFSEN

1 'Opening of the Ballarat East Public Library', *Argus* (Melbourne), 5 January 1868, p. 5.

2 Tom H. Cochran, 'Dora Ohlfsen's work', *Herald* (Melbourne), 7 April 1932, n.p.

3 Grabionne was later Grabionnen, then Kaiserswalde,and is now Grabionna in west Poland, 172 km south of Gdansk and 254 km from Berlin.

4 'Not without work, but with little care – living on his own land, looking down the valleys to his herds – towards the hills to his flocks, amid the humming of bees, which know no winters' (S. Sidney, *The Three Colonies of Australia*, London, 1852, p. 17).

5 Frederick Sinnett, 'The fiction fields of Australia', *Journal of Australasia*, June and December 1856, n.p.

6 'Dora Ohlfsen and her work', *Triad*, 10 September 1921, p. 23.

7 Alfred Frederick Kursteiner (1853–93) is best known for the building which is now the Linden Centre for Contemporary Arts in St Kilda.

8 Henry Handel Richardson, *Australia Felix*, W.W. Norton, New York, 1930, part 2, chapter 4, p. 380.

9   Anthony Trollope, *Australia and New Zealand*, Chapman and Hall, London, 1873, vol. 1, p. 406. The Ballarat School of Mines had been established in the previous year. It quickly became one of the most prestigious institutes of technical training in Australia and by 1875 had Sir Redmond Barry as President, offering courses in mathematics, mining and land surveying, mechanics and natural philosophy, mechanical engineering, mineralogy, geology, metallurgy, chemistry and telegraphy.

10 'Sacrifice', *Sydney Morning Herald*, 6 January 1927, p. 8. Between 1883 and 1896 Christian Ohlfsen appears in the Sydney Sands Directory at 4 Mona Terrace, New South Head Road, Woollahra. He is listed as a 'civil engineer'.

11 Dora remained at the school from 1884 until 1886. She did not get the coveted scholarship, but had to pay. Subjects studied included English and European history, Latin, Greek, French, English and German, geography and geology, algebra, Euclid and plane geometry, perspective and painting, music and biblical studies. Louise Mack, who was there at the same time as Dora, describes the school in her autobiographical novel *Teens*. 'A large, brown, two-storey building, with a wide, wooden staircase, a verandah all round, and an asphalted playground shaded with two huge Moreton Bay fig-trees.' The building was the old St James's School, designed by Francis Greenway, on Elizabeth Street.

12 For an appreciation of the school's progressive stance, see Marjorie Theobald, *Knowing Women: Origins of women's education in nineteenth-century Australia*, Cambridge University Press, Cambridge, 1996, p. 147.

13 'A nation for a continent', *Sydney Morning Herald*, 11 May 1951, p. 2. The origin of the phrase is explained by Sir Robert Garran.

14 See Therese Radic, *Melba: The voice of Australia*, Macmillan, Melbourne, 1986, p. 27; Nellie Melba, *Melodies and Memories*, Dorran Company, New York, 1926, p. 11.

15 Most likely at the school run by the pianist Cecilia Summerhayes, called the Academy of Arts, or the *Conservatoire de Musique*, which French pianist Madame Charbonnet-Kellermann ran at 43 Phillip Street. Kowalski (1841–1916) settled in Sydney in 1885, where he was appointed conductor of the Philharmonic Society, 1886–89. He taught, gave recitals and composed many piano pieces and songs.

16 D.J. Quinn, 'Musicians and musical taste in Australasia', *Review of Reviews*, 20 April 1895, p. 391.

17 'Musical notes: M. Henri Kowalski', *The Cosmos Magazine*, 30 April 1895, p. 436.

18 'The annual audition of musical works', *Maitland Mercury*, 14 May 1889, p. 6.

19 The concert involved Cecilia Summerhayes with her daughters, J.W. Hazlitt (piano) and Gertrude Summerhayes (violin), and artists Henri Kowalski, Horace Poussard, soprano Madame L. Aengenheyster, baritone Mons. Deslouis

and pianists Beatrice Griffiths and Dora Ohlfsen-Bagge, the latter playing Louis Gottschalk's *Tarantella for Two Pianos* (1866).

20 The South Australian pianist and music teacher Immanuel Reimann (1859–1932) also studied at Kullak's Academy from 1880. He returned to Australia to establish the Adelaide College of Music in 1883.

21 'Bound to die', *Los Angeles Herald*, 21 April 1888, p. 10.

22 'Stage and studio', *Sydney Daily Mail*, 10 June 1908, n.p.

23 Amy Fay, *Music Study in Germany from the Home Correspondence of Amy Fay*, Macmillan and Co., London, 1885, p. 246.

24 ibid., p. 11.

25 ibid., p. 89.

26 Freda Sternberg, 'Australian Sculptor: Miss Ohlfsen's studio in Rome', *Herald* (Melbourne), 7 January 1926, n.p.

27 J.D. Fitzgerald, 'The training of a pianist', *Lone Hand*, 1 July 1907, p. 288.

28 Christopher Brennan sailed for Germany on the small NDL steamer *Habsburg* in June 1892

29 Fay, *Music Study in Germany*, p. 82.

30 'An Australian artist. Miss Dora Ohlfsen. Life in Russia. What will-power can achieve', *Sun* (Sydney) 1913, n.p.

31 See 'News', *Launceston Examiner*, 17 January 1894, p. 3.

32 'Australian sculptress', *Register* (Adelaide), 28 December 1926, n.p.

33 Louise Mack, *Girls Together*, Angus and Robertson, Sydney, 1898, p. 38.

34 Fay, *Music study in Germany*, p. 152.

35 Such as, to give two examples, May Vale (1862–1945) and the china painter Blanche Davies (1884–1976), who both turned to teaching.

36 'An Australian artist. Miss Dora Ohlfsen. Life in Russia. What will-power can achieve', n.p.

37 'A Sydney musician', *The Inquirer and Commercial News* (Hobart), 6 November 1896, p. 14.

38 Francesca Wilson, *Muscovy: Russia through foreign eyes 1553–1900*, George Allen & Unwin, London, 1970, p. 214.

39 Elena's uncle, Paul Siegwart Konstantin von Kügelgen (1875–1953), owned the Petersburg *Zietung*. Elena was also related to Werner Zoege von Manteufel (1857–1926), the eminent Estonian surgeon (Professor of Surgery at Dorpat University from 1899), who built the School of Surgery at Tartu University and was life physician to Tzar Nicholas II.

40 Most notable were the twin brothers Carl von Kügelgen (1772–1832) and Franz Gerhard von Kügelgen (1772–1820).

41 'Dora Ohlfsen and her work', p. 23.

42 It is likely that this occurred towards the end of her time in Russia. The Ambassador was probably Robert Sanderson McCormick, son-in-law of the

editor-in-chief of the *Chicago Tribune*. He was the first American ambassador to Austria-Hungary. He then served as ambassador to Russia (1902–05) and to France (1905–07).

43 Carol Sylva, 'Dora Ohlfsen – sculptress', *Woman's World* (Melbourne), vol. 1, no. 3, 1 February 1922, p. 7.

44 'A Sydney musician', *The Inquirer and Commercial News*, 6 November 1896, p. 14.

45 'An Australian artist. Miss Dora Ohlfsen. Life in Russia. What will-power can achieve', n.p.

46 Victor Tissot, quoted in Wilson, *Muscovy*, p. 283.

47 'Miss Dora Ohlfsen's work', *British Australasian*, 20 August 1908, p. 23.

48 'Dora Ohlfsen and her work', p. 23.

49 See A.P. Sinnett, *The Occult World*, 4th edn, Trubner & Co., London, 1884.

50 See, for instance, Judith Kalb, *Russia's Rome: Imperial visions, messianic dreams, 1890–1940*, University of Wisconsin Press, Madison, Wis., 2008, pp. 24ff.

51 She later recommended his book *The Sexual History of the World War* (1930) to Sir Robert Garran: 'You will not be able to get this book in Australia, but it is worth your while to have it out from Vienna . . . it is an amazing revelation' (Dora Ohlfsen to Sir Robert Garran, 26 October 1932, Garran Papers, National Library of Australia, Canberra, MSS 2001 5/54).

52 'Art abroad', *Sydney Morning Herald*, 1 July 1912, p. 8. The press recorded various versions of this story. In some, as in this account, it was the Tzarina herself who purchased Dora's work and encouraged Dora 'to study painting seriously'.

53 'An Australian artist. Miss Dora Ohlfsen. Life in Russia. What will-power can achieve', n.p.

54 'The foreign situation: the chances of peace', *Advertiser* (Adelaide), 18 May 1901, p. 9.

55 Sylva, 'Dora Ohlfsen – sculptress', p. 7.

56 For some time, women artists were well represented among expatriate Australians settling in Italy, beginning with Adelaide Ironside in 1856 and followed by Margaret Thomas (1867) and Theo Cowan (1889).

57 Kalb, *Russia's Rome*, p. 12.

58 Quoted in Kalb, *Russia's Rome*, p. 78.

59 See Rennell Rodd, *Rome of the Renaissance and Today*, Macmillan and Co., London, 1932, introduction. Rodd, who had been part of Oscar Wilde's close circle, returned to a diplomatic post in Rome in 1902, the same year Dora arrived.

60 Sylva, 'Dora Ohlfsen – sculptress', p. 7.

61 Dora Ohlfsen to her sister Kate Ohlfsen, 19 October 1931 (Family correspondence; copies in the collection of the AGNSW Archive, Sydney).

62 MS10808, Louise B Riggall, Diary of Italian tour, State Library of Victoria, Melbourne. This diary entry is dated 8 March 1905. Louise Riggall settled in a pensione at 50 via San Nicola da Tolentino.

63 Franklin Simmons (1838–1913). Dora's building had long been a centre for artists. In 1872, the artists listed as working there included English painters J. Barrett, Walter Crane, W. Lane Connolly and the English sculptor Charles Summers. Summers settled in Australia (1854–67) before his successful career in Rome. He left Australia for 'want of commissions', according to the *Argus* and his bronze group of Bourke and Wills is reputedly the first bronze casting completed in Australia. Also working on the same street were the Italian Symbolist Ettore Ximenes, who in 1902 was commissioned to do the bronze group representing *Law* for the monument to Victor Emanuel II, Ludwig Hasselriis, noted for his sculptures of Hans Christian Anderson and Heinrich Heine, and the German religious painter Hermann Effenberger.

64 From press and other sources we know of at least 121 works. However, the current whereabouts of only 25 of these works is known.

65 The first woman to be admitted to the French Academy in 1911 was the sculptor Lucienne Heuvelmanns (1885–1944), who won the Prix de Rome. The first female painter was not admitted until 1922.

66 *The Lone Hand* more accurately reported that she was invited to work in the studio of artists rather than at the French Academy: 'Alaphillipe, of the French Academy, invited her to work in his studio. Miss Ohlfsen was also fortunate in having another Academician, Dautel, for instructor in the art of engraving in medals and for some time she worked in the studio of Benedito' (2 November 1912, n.p.).

67 *73 Mostra Della Società Amatori e Cultori di Belle Arti*, Palazzo Delle Esposizioni, Rome, 1903. This year the exhibition included national sections for Spain, Austria and Russia. Dora exhibited in the international section: no. 295 *Ritratto del signorina K.*, no. 296 *Studio* and no. 297 *Studio*. She was exhibited in the same room as Franz Ohlsen. Also included in her room was a painting by Basilici. In the sculpture section was work by Hendrik Andersen and medals by Augusto Girardet and Stefano Galletti (see L. Forrer, *Biographical Dictionary of Medallists*, vol. IV, Spink and Son, London, 1909, p. 311).

68 *78 Mostra Della Società Amatori e Cultori di Belle Arti*, Palazzo Delle Esposizioni, Rome, 1908. She is included in the picture, rather than sculpture, section of the exhibition (Sala Z-a) with a work simply listed as no. 668 *Ritratto*.

69 Jahn Arturo Rusconi, 'Un'artista della medaglia', *Rivista di Roma*, anno xii, fascicolo v, 10 marzo 1908, p. 149 (illustrated in black and white).

70 In the *77 Mostra Della Società Amatori e Cultori di Belle Arti*, Palazzo Delle Esposizioni, Rome, 1907, under catalogue no. 670 is listed *Studi di bambini*, or studies of children. This was probably a number of medallions showing children, rather than one medallion depicting a number of children. It was

common to exhibit a group of medallions or plaquettes under one catalogue number. In the previous year, 1906, a group of Dora's 'bas-reliefs in bronze' were exhibited under the one catalogue number (no. 6).

71 'Personal', *Sydney Morning Herald*, 5 September 1905, p. 7.

72 'Mlle Gugelgen, ravissante dans une belle toilette noire', *L'Italie: journal politique quotidian*, 25 February 1908, n.p.

73 'Ateliers-salone', *L'Italie: journal politique quotidian*, 27 February 1908, p. 58.

74 This work has not been found. This quote comes from *Emporium*, vol. 25, no. 150, 1907, p. 420.

75 Rusconi, 'Un'artista della medaglia', *Rivista di Roma*, pp. 148–50.

76 *Journal de Marie Bashkirtseff*, G. Charpentier et cie, Paris, 1890.

77 'An Australian artist. Miss Dora Ohlfsen. Life in Russia. What will-power can achieve', n.p.

78 F.F. Elmes, 'The awakening of Australian art: an interview with Miss Dora Ohlfsen', *Argus* (Melbourne), 18 September 1908, p. 4.

79 A.L. Baldry, *Modern British Sculpture*, Academy of Architecture, London, 1910, p. 4.

80 Elmes, 'The awakening of Australian art', p. 4.

81 Dora Ohlfsen to Gother Mann, 9 January 1917 (BF7/1917, AGNSW Archive, Sydney).

82 Dora Ohlfsen to Sir Robert Garran, 7 January 1932 (Garran Papers, National Library of Australia).

83 National Art Gallery', *Sydney Morning Herald*, 13 April 1910, n.p.

84 Other known nudes include *The Pitcher goes to the Fountain* (c. 1909), *New Zealand Aphrodite* (c. 1918) and *Papuan Daughter* (c. 1927). These have all disappeared.

85 Janet Cumbrae Stewart similarly made the female nude central to her art. She eventually established herself in Italy – like Dora – with her girlfriend, the cross-dresser Billy (Argemone) Bellairs. It is possible that the depiction of the female nude had a political and feminist dimension for Dora, suggesting that 'roles are only as fixed as costume'. (See Erica Rand, *Barbie's Queer Accessories*, Duke University Press, Durham, NC, 1995, p. 2). For a treatment of Janet Cumbrae Stewart see Juliette Peers, 'May I introduce Miss Cumbrae Stewart?' in *Janet Cumbrae Stewart: The perfect touch*, MPRG, Mornington, Vic., 2003). In 1920 the artist John Shirlow thought that Cumbrae Stewart's nudes embodied Australian boldness against 'the average stodgy British mind', which always showed a 'hypocritical aversion to the revealing of any part of the human body (John Shirlow, *The Pastels of Cumbrae Stewart*, Alexander McCubbin, Melbourne, 1920, n.p.).

86 Elmes, 'The awakening of Australian art', p. 4.

87   Deborah Edwards, 'This Vital Flesh': The sculpture of Rayner Hoff and his school, Art Gallery of New South Wales, Sydney, 1999, p. 21.

88   See The British Australasian, 10 August 1908, p. 23. Theodora Cowan (1868–1949) was a gold medallist in this exhibition.

89   Dora replied to the Gallery trustees that the price included copyright. She asked them to reconsider and invited them to make an offer of the original or replica. By July 1909, agreement had been reached on the sale of the medallion for £20.

90   With sculpture, a hierarchy of commissions existed, with the greatest prestige going to free-standing work of monumental size, which Gleichen achieved.

91   At London's Royal Academy School, opened to women in December of 1860, figures show that, among the female students admitted between 1860 and 1914, only 25 were sculpture students.

92   Maud Howe, Roma Beata: Letters from the Eternal City, Little, Brown & Co., Boston, 1909, p. 85.

93   Joseph Collins, My Italian year, Charles Scribner's Sons, New York, 1919, p. 36.

94   Dora Melegari, 'The woman question in Italy', The Contemporary Review, volume LXXVI, 1899, p. 822.

95   Emancipation had been urged by Gualberta Beccari, who founded the influential journal La donna in 1868. She gathered around her kindred spirits, and in 1890 an exhibition of women's work, called after Dante's Beatrice, was held in Florence, with exhibits from writers, painters, sculptors, musicians, lacemakers, embroiderers and others. The exhibition was widely publicised and in the following year small groups sympathetic to feminism were formed in Bologna, Milan, Turin, Venice, Florence and Rome.

96   Elsa Carlyle Smythe, 'A reader studies the women of Italy', Everylady's Journal, 6 July 1925, p. 534.

97   'National Art Gallery', Sydney Morning Herald, 13 April 1910, n.p.

98   'Art abroad', Sydney Morning Herald, 1 July 1912, p. 8; see also Vincenzo Pialorsi & Luciano Faverzani, Gabriele d'Annunzio nelle medaglie, Grafo, Brescia, 2004, p. 127.

99   'On coming back', Sydney Morning Herald, 17 July 1912, p. 5.

100 'Miss Dora Ohlfsen', The Lone Hand, 12 December 1912, p. xl.

101 Ellie Russell, 'Brief impressions of men, women, and events: an Australian sculptress in Rome', Everylady's Journal, 6 June 1913, p. 327.

102 'The Ohlfsen medallions', Sydney Morning Herald, 11 September 1912, p. 20.

103 Russell, 'Brief impressions', p. 327; 'Dora Ohlfsen', The Daily News (Perth), 5 February 1927, p. 10.

104 'National Art Gallery', Sydney Morning Herald, 2 September 1913, p. 148.

105 Including NSW Governor Lord Chelmsford, Attorney-General William Hughes, constitutional lawyer Adrian Knox, physician Dr Alexander Jarvie

Hood, entertainer Nellie Hughes, newspaper proprietor James Fairfax and the Minister for Public Instruction, Campbell Carmichael, who had ministerial responsibility for the National Art Gallery of New South Wales. All these works were made between 1912 and 1913 and show how much she was in demand.

106 This was never completed and the panel remains empty to this day. Swiss-born American Sculptor Rosa Langenegger submitted designs for an 'architect showing the Emperor Titus a model of a triumphal arch', 'Tarquinius and Tullia showing the Works of Rome' and 'Romulus ordering the temple for Jupiter Feretrius'. She was more agreeable to adapting her work at the direction of the trustees than Dora was. On 24 July 1914 Langenegger wrote: 'Should you suggest any modification whatever, I shall only be too pleased to alter any of the sketches accordingly' (CF134/14, CF94/14 AGNSW Archive, Sydney).

107 The sculpture was completed by Bertram Mackennal in 1926 and today stands opposite Sydney's Mitchell Library.

108 Dora Ohlfsen to Gother Mann, 21 October 1913 (CF255/1913 AGNSW Archive, Sydney).

109 'Australian types', *Sydney Morning Herald*, 22 October 1913, p. 7.

110 Dora Ohlfsen to Gother Mann, 6 November 1916 (B&F3/1917 AGNSW Archive, Sydney).

111 'National Art Gallery', p. 148.

112 Dora Ohlfsen to F. Graham Lloyd, London, 25 November 1919 (B&F15/1920, AGNSW Archive, Sydney).

113 A book had also been published with colour illustrations based solely on the chariot race from the silent film, *Ben Hur*, of 1907 (Lewis Wallace, with illustrations by Sigismond Ivanowski, *The Chariot Race from Ben-Hur*, Harper and Brothers, New York, 1908).

114 Gother Mann to Dora Ohlfsen, 22 December 1914 (AGNSW Archive, letter copy book 464c).

115 Dora's work in this exhibition received mention in the journal *La Renaissance*, 9 May 1914 (Dora Ohlfsen to Gother Mann, 24 September 1916, B&F82/1916, AGNSW Archive, Sydney).

116 Dora Ohlfsen to Gother Mann, 6 November 1916 (B&F3/1917, AGNSW Archive, Sydney).

117 The relief *L'artista e la battaglie artistiche* was designed for the Palazzo Bazzani, now Rome's Museum of Modern Art.

118 Dora Ohlfsen to Gother Mann, 9 January 1917 (B&F7/1917, AGNSW Archive, Sydney). After her death Gleichen was made the first woman member of the Royal British Society of Sculptors, established in 1905.

119 *Margaret Baskerville, sculptor*, E.A. Vidler, Melbourne, 1929.

120 Blamire Young, 'Margaret Baskerville', *Herald* (Melbourne), 13 June 1929, n.p.

121 Cochran, 'Dora Ohlfsen's work', n.p.

122 In a letter dated 7 November 1919 to the premier, Gother Mann wrote of Dora's small medallions and noted: 'I consider that Miss Ohlfsen is more successful in the medallions of this size'. (AGNSW Archive, letter copy book, p. 131)

123 Dora Ohlfsen to F. Graham Lloyd, December 1919 (B&F2b/1920, AGNSW Archive, Sydney).

124 'You see every kind of art has been done. Michelangelo was the culmination. After him it is all repetition and imitation. Rodin executed examples of every known form of sculpture, a kind of resume. He left nothing for anyone else to say in plastic art' (Dora Ohlfsen to Kate Ohlfsen, 19 October 1931, Family correspondence, copies in the collection of the AGNSW Archive, Sydney).

125 'Colored spectacles', *Daily Telegraph*, 16 January 1915, n.p.

126 She also nursed in Venice. After the war, Dora reported that she had nursed under the Italian Red Cross as well as possessing her diploma as a British VAD. No records show this and only Italian citizens could complete the Italian Red Cross diploma course. Dora probably took initiative to assist with casualties, as many women did, particularly well-placed women, who found ways around the regulations and protocol.

127 'Dora Ohlfsen Home', *The Times* (London), 26 September 1920, n.p. In 1916 the Gallery paid Bayes £4920 to design two equestrian statues.

128 John Sulman to Gother Mann, 23 January 1920 (CF21/1920, AGNSW Archive, Sydney).

129 Dora Ohlfsen to F. Graham Lloyd, 25 November 1919 (B&F15/1920, AGNSW Archive, Sydney).

130 Dora Ohlfsen to Gother Mann, 9 January 1917 (B&F7/1919, AGNSW Archive, Sydney).

131 'French medal to U.S. Air Force', *Thomasville Daily Times Enterprise*, 28 July 1919, p. 3.

132 Press notices incorrectly said that the silhouette of the slouch-hatted Australian soldier on the obverse was Ohlfsen's brother, 'a lieutenant with the Australian forces in France' (*Sydney Mail*, 25 April 1917, p. 7). This was patriotic propaganda, as she came from a family of girls. However, the soldier may have been a tribute to one of her nephews. The papers reported that Dora's nephew Keith Bayley 'is recovering from wounds received on the Western Front. His brother Olaf was killed on the HMAS *Australia* in 1915' ('Lieutenant K. Bayley', *Sydney Morning Herald*, 28 October 1916, p. 9). Bayley, originally a marine engineer, became a Lieutenant Colonel with the 1st Cavalry Division AASC. Frank (Olaf) Ohlfsen Bayley served as a leading signalman on the HMAS *Melbourne* (not *HMAS Australia* as was reported). He fell ill in England and died of natural causes on 7 March 1916. The Australian War Memorial has a commemorative photograph of him: P02790.028.

133 Art of Dora Ohlfsen', *Sydney Morning Herald*, 9 November 1920, n.p.

134 The Art Gallery', *Sydney Morning Herald*, 24 January 1921, n.p. She made studies of General Monash, Prime Minister Lloyd George and his predecessor Henry Asquith, the Australian Agent-General Sir Charles Wade, the New Zealand High Commissioner, Sir Thomas Mackenzie, and the painters John Longstaff, James Quinn and Solomon J. Solomon.

135 Dora Ohlfsen to Kate Ohlfsen, 9 January 1940 (Family correspondence; copies in the collection of the AGNSW Archive, Sydney).

136 *Miss Dora Ohlfsen Exhibition of Pastels and Bronze Medallions*, Albert Buildings, Sydney, 9–22 November 1920. The press noted that she was also working on bronze medallions of the New South Wales Governor Sir Walter Davidson and his wife Dame Margaret Davidson reputedly for the Australian War Memorial ('Dora Ohlfsen Home', n.p.).

137 Including a large pastel of the Austrian shelling of Venice and a statue of *The Blind Ardito* (c. 1917), both of which are now lost.

138 'The futurist was the pioneer in art; and the term futurism signified the attitude of regarding the past and present with the eyes of the future. It meant freedom for artists as against the slavery of present-day conditions' ('At the Socialist Hall. Art and futurism in Russia and Italy. Instructive lecture by Miss Dora Ohlfsen', *The Socialist* [Melbourne], 20 January 1922).

139 'Art of Dora Ohlfsen', n.p.

140 She initially quoted them a cost of £150.

141 3DRL/3376 Papers of Field Marshal Lord William Birdwood, National Library of Australia, Canberra, 2/12).

142 He sold *The Dutch cap* c. 1917, a bronze sculpture, to the National Art Gallery of New South Wales in June 1921.

143 'Minutes of the First Meeting of the Sub-Committee appointed to consider the questions relating to the appointment of a sculptor to consider matters relating to statuary, 24 July 1928', p. 1 (VPRS2498 General records from the Shrine of Remembrance, Public Records Office of Victoria, Melbourne).

144 Minutes of the Sub-Committee, 28 March 1929 (Public Records Office of Victoria, Melbourne).

145 Rejected were two works by Eva Benson, and others by W. Anderson, Arthur Murch, Daphne Mayo, W.L. Bowles and Montford.

146 Minutes of the Sub-Committee, 17 February 1931 (Public Records Office of Victoria, Melbourne).

147 They also admired *Courage* by Dadswell and *Brotherhood* by Anderson, suggesting that these too might be modified.

148 Cochran, 'Dora Ohlfsen's work', n.p.

149 For example, see Huntly McCrae Cowper, 'The café Cristallini', *Sydney Morning Herald*, 17 October 1935, p. 11.

150 Dora Ohlfsen to Kate Ohlfsen, Ohlfsen, April 1940 (Family correspondence; copies in the AGNSW Archive, Sydney).

151 Dora Ohlfsen to Sir Robert Garran, 8 December 1932 (Garran Papers, National Library of Australia).

152 Disagreements over the statue dragged on until 1937, when it was finally entrusted to William Bowles, only to be cast and installed as late as 1950. The Bowles statue is visible today in the grounds of the Shrine of Remembrance.

153 Dora Ohlfsen to Gother Mann, 5 June 1919 (B&F35/1919, AGNSW Archive, Sydney).

154 See Alastair Hamilton, *The Appeal of Fascism: A study of intellectuals and Fascism 1919–1945*, Anthony Blond, London, 1971, p. xii.

155 Stella Bowen, *Drawn From Life: Reminiscences*, Collins, London, 1941, p. 167.

156 Letter published in *Hawera & Normanby Star*, vol. XLII, 27 January 1923, p. 4.

157 Freda Sternberg, 'Australian sculptor: Miss Ohlfsen's Studio in Rome', *Herald* (Melbourne), 7 January 1926, n.p. On completion, a copy of the work was presented to Mussolini, who expressed his delight at the likeness.

158 'An Australian artist. Miss Dora Ohlfsen. Life in Russia. What will-power can achieve', n.p.

159 Wolfgang Graeser's 1927 publication *Body sense* (*Körpersinn. Gymnastick, Tanz, Sport*) called this interest in body culture 'a movement, a wave, a fashion, a passion, a new feeling for life; this is a reality that has inundated, pursued, inspired, reformed and influenced millions of people'. Elsewhere he wrote 'in all realms and walks of life, blood, new impulses, and intuition are rising up once more against mere reason, will, and the intellect' (quoted in Kenneth E. Silver, *Chaos and Classicism: Art in France, Italy and Germany, 1918–1936*, Guggenheim Museum, New York, 2011, p. 44).

160 'The Art Gallery', n.p. The report gave Barney Gaston as the name of the digger.

161 'The month in Woman's World: A review of women's news throughout the Commonwealth,' *Woman's World*, 1 February 1927, p. 69.

162 Dora Ohlfsen to Sir Robert Garran, 22 July 1932 (Garran Papers, National Library of Australia).

163 'Australian sculptress', n.p.

164 'Sacrifice', *Sydney Morning Herald*, 6 January 1927, n.p.

165 In 1937 the Sydney trustees included her on a list of artists being considered for inclusion in the 150th Anniversary Celebrations exhibition, a surprising decision for such a long-term expatriate. She was eventually not included.

166 'The years, after all, have a kind of emptiness when we spend too many of them on a foreign shore. We defer the reality of life, in such cases, until a future moment, when we shall again breathe our native air; but by and by there are no future moments; or if we do return, we find that the native air has lost its

invigorating quality, and that life has shifted its reality to the post where we have deemed ourselves only temporary residents. Thus between two countries we have none at all, or only that little space of either in which we finally lay down our discontented bones. It is wise therefore to come back betimes, or never' (*The marble faun*, quoted in Ernest Earnest, *Expatriates and Patriots: American artists, scholars and writers in Europe*, Duke University Press, Durham, NC, 1968, p. 171).

167 Dora Ohlfsen to Barbara Ohlfsen, 13 February 1940 (Family correspondence; copies in the AGNSW Archive, Sydney).

168 Dora Ohlfsen to Kate Ohlfsen, 9 January 1940 (Family correspondence; copies in the collection of the AGNSW Archive, Sydney).

169 Dora Ohlfsen to Kate Ohlfsen, April 1940 (Family correspondence; copies in the collection of the AGNSW Archive, Sydney).

170 For instance, she exhibited at the *Seconda Mostra del Sindacato Laziale Fascista di Belle Arti*, Palazzo delle Esposizioni, December 1939 – March 1930, showing her sculpture *Cosacco* (no. 6).

171 Bowen, *Drawn from life: Reminiscences*, p. 167.

172 Quoted in Silver, *Chaos and Classicism*, p. 156.

173 R.R. Garran, 'Letter to the editor ', *Canberra Times*, 16 February 1948 (Garran Papers, National Library of Australia).

174 Dora Ohlfsen to Sir Robert Garran, 7 January 1932 (Garran Papers, National Library of Australia).

175 R.R. Garran, 'Letter to the editor', *Canberra Times*, 21 February 1948, p. 2.

Part 2 – THE PATRON: LOUISE DYER

1 Quoted in Brian Fitzpatrick, *The Australian Commonwealth*, F.W. Cheshire, Melbourne, 1956, p. 22; see also 'The roaring fifties: Victoria's golden epoch', *Sydney Morning Herald*, 18 October 1934, p. 17.

2 His museum displayed items which were considered 'inappropriate' and 'distasteful' and at least on one occasion was closed down by the Muncipal Council, who owned the Town Hall where it was displayed ('Dr L.L. Smith's lectures', *The Cornwall Chronicle* [Launceston, Tasmania], 9 July 1869, p. 2).

3 'Colonial celebrities: Dr L.L. Smith', *South Bourke and Mornington Journal*, 17 March 1880, p. 4.

4 ibid.

5 Collection Mr & Mrs N H Gengoult Smith, Melbourne.

6 Louise Dyer to Anne Fortune Ratho, 1 April 1939 (Letters E6/54, PLC Archives, Melbourne).

7 Kathleen Fitzpatrick, *PLC Melbourne: The first century, 1875–1975*, Presbyterian Ladies College, Burwood, Vic., 1975, p. 112.

8   Maie Casey, *An Australian Story 1837–1907*, Michael Joseph, London, 1962, p. 123. Noted for being a sharp dresser and a man of flair, others described him as the 'thorough bohemian'. He championed local industry, was several times Vice-President of the Chamber of Manufacturers, patron of the Richmond Football Club, owned a large art collection and was known to give freely to charity.

9   See Trollope, *Australia and New Zealand*, p. 60; H. Püttmann, *Pen and pencil in Collins Street by Wayfarer*, Melville, Mullen and Slade, Melbourne, 1891, p. 27.

10   'From colonies to nationhood, an Empire's pride', *Advance Australia*, vol. 4, no. 12, 15 December 1900.

11   Casey, *An Australian Story*, p. 148.

12   ibid.

13   Burkitt taught Grainger until he left for Germany in 1895. He thought none of the tuition he received in Germany matched that which he enjoyed with her. She also taught pianist Fritz Müller (see John Bird, *Percy Grainger*, Sun Books, Melbourne, 1982, pp. 26–32, 252).

14   See 'Musical examinations: successful Victorians', *Argus* (Melbourne), 15 December 1900, p. 18.

15   The situation was similar in Sydney. When Henri Verbrugghen took up the position of first Director of the Sydney Conservatorium in 1915 he interviewed musicians from all over Australia as prospective teachers. He announced to the press that many of the applicants needed, instead, to enrol as students. On the need for standards see 'The Conservatorium', *The Catholic Press*, 26 August 1915, p. 27.

16   Casey, *An Australian Story*, p. 124.

17   Anthea Goddard, 'A lyrebird in Monaco: two Australian music lovers who spend their time reviving ancient classics can't abide those guitar playing minstrels', *Woman*, 13 August 1956.

18   Joan Rimmer, 'Reviewed work(s): *Lyrebird Rising: Louise Hanson-Dyer of Oiseau-Lyre, 1884–1962* by Jim Davidson', *Notes*, 2nd series, vol. 53, no. 2, December 1996, pp. 440–2; *The Times* (London), 17 November 1962.

19   'Carl (Heinrich Carsten) Reinecke', in E. Pauer, *A Dictionary of Pianists and Composers for the Pianoforte*, Novello, Ewer and Co., London, 1895, p. 98.

20   *Athenaeum Diamond Jubilee Souvenir*, Wm Hodge & Co, Glasgow, 1907, p. 2.

21   David Daptie, *Musical Scotland Past and Present*, J. & R. Parlane, Paisley, 1894, p. 73.

22   Considered one of the richest individual collections in Britain, the Euing Library is now housed at the University of Glasgow Library (A. Hyatt King, *Some British Collectors of Music*, Cambridge University Press, Cambridge, 1963, p. 61; see also, Harry Colin Miller, *Introductory Euing Lectures, Musical Bibliography and History*, Bayley & Ferguson, Glasgow, 1914; Glasgow

Athenaeum, *Athenaeum School of Music Prospectus, 26th Session 1915–1916*, Wm Hodge & Co, Glasgow, 1915).

23 Hugh S. Roberton & Kenneth Roberton, *Orpheus with his Lute: A Glasgow Orpheus Choir anthology*, Pergamon Press, Oxford, 1963, p. vii.

24 See Jim Davidson, *Lyrebird rising: Louise Hanson-Dyer of Oiseau Lyre, 1884–1962*, Melbourne University Press at the Miegunyah Press, Carlton, Vic., 1994, p. 40.

25 'When should women marry? The new ideas and the old', *Vanity Fair*, 2 May 1904, p. 7.

26 'Picturesque wedding', *The Weekly Times*, 6 November 1912, p. 13.

27 Grace Evans to Sybil Hewett, 30 August 1971 (MS10770, Box 1536/4 [e], Louise Hanson-Dyer papers, State Library of Victoria, Melbourne).

28 'Not the best word: American artists on Australia. Madame Scotney interviews', *Australian Musical News*, May 1923, vol. 12, no. 10, p. iii. Community singing, despite being maligned on occasions, led to the formation of a Community Singers and Concertgoers Association, which triggered Melbourne's first Music Week, held in November 1921.

29 Captain Louis Lionel Smith was commander of the 51st Battalion. He was killed in action on 2 April 1917.

30 British Music Society, Victoria Branch, *Syllabus for the British Music Society, Victorian Centre*, British Music Society, Victorian Centre, Melbourne, 1931.

31 W.G. Whittaker, 'The B.M.S. in Australia', *Music Bulletin of the British Music Society*, vol. 6, no. 1, p. 18.

32 The International Musicological Society was founded in Basle in 1927, though there had been numerous less formal forums for musicological research before this.

33 From reports, it appears most attending found the experience a novelty. The performers sang to the 'movement and conversation of people who discourteously walked around the gallery while the concert was in progress' (see 'Meldrum on sculpture', *Herald* [Melbourne], 11 July 1925, n.p).

34 'Nationalism in music', *Brisbane Courier*, 11 October 1924, p. 19.

35 Elliston Campbell & Phyllis Campbell, 'Modern music – what it is and what it is not', Lecture at Adyar Hall, 19 November 1926, Campbell Archive, UTS, Sydney.

36 In Melbourne *The Planets* was performed non-orchestrally, arranged for two pianos, British Music Society, Assembly Hall, Melbourne, 19 June 1925. It was first performed privately in September 1918 by the new Queen's Hall Orchestra under Adrian Boult; the London Symphony Orchestra gave the first complete public performance of *The Planets* two years later. Holst first conducted a complete performance in October 1923 with the New Queens Hall Orchestra.

37 Heinze was newly returned to Melbourne after studying in Berlin and Paris with Vincent d'Indy. In Melbourne from 1923, he became a member of the

Melbourne University Conservatorium, of which he was professor from 1925 ('A memorable happening Savitri by BMS', *Table Talk*, 7 October 1926, p. 12).

38 'ibid.

39 Memo from Alberto Zelman, 26 June 1924 (MS9087, Albert Zelman correspondence, State Library of Victoria).

40 Thorold Waters, *Much Besides Music: Memoirs of Thorold Waters*, Georgian House, Melbourne, 1951, pp. 218–9.

41 Therese Radic, *Melba the Voice of Australia*, Macmillan, Melbourne, 1986, p. 37.

42 Undated untitled clipping (MS9807, Alberto Zelman papers, State Library of Victoria, Melbourne).

43 ibid.

44 ibid.

45 Jenny Wren, *Gurglings of an Australian Magpie*, Specialty Press, Melbourne, 1926, p. 18.

46 Undated untitled clipping 'Orchestra for Melbourne, Mr Zelman's appeal, letter to the editor' (MS9807, Alberto Zelman papers, State Library of Victoria, Melbourne). See also the Statement of receipts and expenditure: Melbourne String Quartet 1908–1905, Melbourne Symphony Orchestra, Victorian Orchestral Association, 1911.

47 'Nationalism in music', *Courier* (Brisbane), 27 February 1932, p. 58.

48 See Fiona Fraser, 'Phyllis Campbell and the sounds of colour', *Literature and Aesthetics*, vol. 21, no. 1, June 2011, pp. 213–35.

49 Letter to Louise Dyer (MS10770, Louise Hanson-Dyer papers, box 1536/3 [1] iv, State Library of Victoria, Melbourne).

50 'Mr Alberto Zelman', *Sun* (Melbourne), 5 March 1927, n.p. In 1906 Zelman began the Melbourne Symphony Orchestra. He conducted this as well as the Melbourne Philharmonic Society, besides founding the Orchestral League and the Melbourne String Quartet. He served as President of the Musical Society of Victoria, the Council of Melbourne Musical Societies and the Community Singers Association.

51 'On musical stagnation in Australia', *Australian Musical News*, August 1917, vol. 7, no. 2, p. 47.

52 Louise Dyer, 'Paris', *Herald* (Melbourne), 1 December 1932, n.p.

53 In 1926, English pianist Norman Wilks (1885–1944) inscribed the second page of Louise's visitor book: 'Once upon a time there was a lovely princess. She was called the "princess of wonderful dreams"' (Louise Hanson-Dyer papers, University of Melbourne Archives).

54 See Michael Short, *Gustav Holst The Man and His Music*, Oxford University Press, Oxford, 1990, p. 284. Performed was Gustav Holst, *12 Songs of Humbert Wolfe*, Opus 48 (1929). Present among the guests were James Joyce, Max Ernst,

Marie Laurencin and Albert Roussel, the latter who from 1921 lived reclusively in Varengeville on the Normandy coast.

55   The journal was held in the Public Library of Victoria from 26 May 1921.

56   The *Société Internationale pour le Musique Contemporaine* (SIMC) was begun in Salzburg in 1922. Important premières occurred at these annual meetings (see Louise Dyer, *Herald* [Melbourne], 27 August 1927, p. 27).

57   Hirsch (1881–1951) collected from the age of 18. To commemorate the 150th anniversary of Mozart's birth, Hirsch published a catalogue of his collection (Paul Hirsch, *Katalog einer Mozart-Bibliothek: zu W.A. Mozarts 150. Geburtstag, 27. Januar 1906*, Druck von Wüsten & Schönfeld, Frankfurt, 1906). Hirsch owned many first editions, which subsequently went to Britain (Paul Hirsch, Charles Humphries & Alexander Hyatt King, *Music in the Hirsch Library*, Trustees of the British Museum, London, 1951).

58   She left her collection to the University of Melbourne (Denis Herlin, *Catalogue de la collection musicale Hanson-Dyer, Université de Melbourne*, Lyrebird Press, Melbourne, 2006). She acquired the key item, a collection of Lully's editions, from the Jullien sale in June 1933 (Adolphe Jullien, *Bibliotheque musicale de M. Adolphe Jullien*, Paris, 1933).

59   Louise Dyer, 'Les Polyphonies du Xllle Siecle', articles by Louise Dyer (vol. IX, no. 1, L'Oiseau-Lyre Archive, Louise Hanson-Dyer Music Library, University of Melbourne).

60   Nellie Melba, *Melodies and Memories*, Dorran Company, New York, 1926, p. 9.

61   Her mother had also played the harp. In June 1931 the first permanent recording of the song of the Lyrebird had been made in the Sherbrooke Forest near Melbourne and was broadcast in Australia and then in Britain and America (see R.T. Littlejohns, 'Recording the song of the Lyre Bird', *The Australian Museum Magazine*, 16 July 1932, p. 371).

62   Frontispiece to Dyer's 1932 catalogue for L'Oiseau-Lyre.

63   Louise Dyer, 9 November 1931, secretarial copies (vol. 10, 8–21 November 1932, Secretarial [1914–35] A07, L'Oiseau-Lyre Archive, Louise Hanson-Dyer Music Library, University of Melbourne).

64   Ernest Newman, 'A noble publishing venture: II the result', *The Sunday Times* (London), 25 October 1936, p. 7.

65   Ernest Newman, 'A noble publishing venture', *The Sunday Times* (London), 18 October 1936, p. 7.

66   The 13 books of Attaingnant were priced at £33 15s and the four volumes of the Montpellier Codex at £21 10s. These were the most expensive publications of the press. Editions published by l'Oiseau-Lyre were of two types: the big library editions, limited in number; and editions in sheet music form, published at low prices for students.

67   'Entertainments, medieval music: a famous manuscript transcribed review of polyphonies', *The Times* (London), 6 June 1936, p. 10. Using Australian timber

to encase the edition was a gesture made by Louise to commemorate the Melbourne Centenary.

68 Ernest Newman, music critic for *The Sunday Times*, reported on Louise's success in 1936. He tallied the libraries and collectors who subscribed to her publications. He noted that eight private libraries in Australia were subscribers, the same number as in Germany, and five public libraries. However, this was a much lower number of subscribers than from England and France or America. The Couperin edition was her best selling edition (Newman, 'A noble publishing venture: II The result', p. 7.

69 Professor Anthony Lewis, 'Mrs Louise Hanson Dyer", *The Times* (London), 17 November 1962, p. 10.

70 Keith Murdoch to Louise Dyer, 27 May 1931 (L'Oiseau-Lyre Archive, Louise Hanson-Dyer Music Library, University of Melbourne).

71 MS10770, Louise Hanson-Dyer papers, State Library of Victoria, Melbourne, 1537/2 (b), press cuttings 1931–32.

72 'Air race', *Sun News Pictorial*, (Melbourne) 24 October 1934.

73 'Centenary gala will dazzle Australia', *Australian Women's Weekly*, 20 January 1934, p. 19.

74 'Forest scene for Mayoral Ball', *The Star* (Melbourne) 25 October 1934, Collection Mr & Mrs N Gengoult Smith.

75 *The Age Centenary Supplement*, 6 September 1934.

76 *The Argus* (Melbourne), 16 October 1934, p. 49.

77 Louise Dyer, 'Musical pipes', articles by Louise Dyer (vol. IX, no. 2, L'Oiseau-Lyre Archive, Louise Hanson-Dyer Music Library, University of Melbourne).

78 'Louis Lawrence Smith', in *Men of the Time in Australia: Victorian series*, McCarron, Bird & Co., Melbourne, 1878, pp. 194–5. Smith produced an eponymous medical almanac, among other titles dedicated to health and wellbeing. He owned the *Australian Journal*, subtitled *A Weekly Record of Literature, Science and the Arts*; *A Weekly Record of Amusing and Instructive Literature, Science and the Arts*; and *The Popular Fiction Monthly*. The *Australian Journal* was a successful nineteenth-century Australian magazine with an estimated average circulation of 5500 copies weekly. Dedicated to colonial life or subjects of colonial interest, it was originally published weekly (1865–69) and monthly thereafter.

79 Quoted in Emily Thompson, *The Soundscape of Modernity*, MIT, Cambridge, MA, 1988, p. 320.

80 Louise Dyer to Percy Grainger, 10 May 1938 (Hanson-Dyer correspondence 1936–40, Grainger Museum, University of Melbourne).

81 'Gramophone records duty', *Courier* (Brisbane), 13 February 1931, p. 8.

82 Louise Dyer to H.C. Colless, 2 April 1937 (Louise memorabiliae annees '30, L'Oiseau-Lyre Archive, Louise Hanson-Dyer Music Library, University of Melbourne). H.C. Colless was chief music critic of *The Times* (London) from

1911 to 1943 and also edited the 1927 and 1940 editions of *Groves Dictionary of Music and Musicians.*

83   Professor Anthony Lewis, 'Mrs Louise Hanson Dyer', *The Times* (London), 17 November 1962, p. 10.

84   John Alan Haughton, 'Ancients come to new flower in fine editions. Mrs Dyer, publisher of forgotten classics impressed by music drive in America' *Musical America*, 10 November 1936, n.p.

85   Doyennat of the Consular Corps to Louise Dyer, 4 April 1932 (Archibox 1, Life in Australia, British Music Society, L'Oiseau-Lyre archive, Louise Hanson-Dyer Music Library, University of Melbourne).

86   'Australians work for music: Mrs Dyer and her Lyre Bird Press', undated newspaper clipping, 48, Collection Mr & Mrs N H Gengoult Smith, Melbourne.

87   Ibid.

88   Louise Dyer to Ann Fortune, 16 November 1939 (PLC Archives, Melbourne). Louise promised Jimmy's copy of the twelve volumes of the Couperin edition to PLC. This deluxe edition, one of only five sets on parchment paper, was going to New York for exhibition and then on to the school. Yet it was lost when the ship transporting it caught fire while docked in Le Havre and sank (Sylvie Belin to Ann Fortune, 30 April 1939).

Part 3 – THE PUBLICIST: CLARICE ZANDER

1   Coleraine was known for its scenic views, as pictured by Buvelot in works like *Waterpool* (National Gallery of Victoria). The area featured significant homesteads and was the setting for the Great Western Steeplechase, which was first run in 1857. Noted poet and horseman Adam Lindsay Gordon (1833–1870) rode regularly in the race, which followed a circuit through the town's gardens and over paddock fences. Two of Gordon's poems – *The Fields of Coleraine* and *Bankers Dream* – were based on his experiences there.

2   Anita Selzer, *Educating Women in Australia: From the convict era to the 1920s*, Cambridge University Press, Melbourne, 1994, p. 97.

3   Australian Dorothy Blanchard Jacobson (1899–1987) was the wife of a diamond merchant when she met Roger Hammerstein in 1927 when crossing from New York to London. They married in 1929. She corresponded with Zander into the 1950s. For an introduction to Blanchard see Hugh Fordin, *Getting to know him: A biography of Oscar Hammerstein II*, Random House, New York, 1977, pp. 76–7.

4   School report for 1907. In this year she also won the school prize for scripture (MS1997.10, Clarice Zander papers, AGNSW Archive, Sydney).

5   A. Barker, *What Happened When: A chronology of Australia from 1788*, Allen & Unwin, Sydney, 1996, p. 203.

6   The boat was the HMAT *Wiltshire* (Charles Zander photograph album, Zander papers, AGNSW Archive, Sydney).

7   Dennis Aiken, 'Ever after?', unpublished manuscript (Zander papers, AGNSW Archive, Sydney).

8   Block 427 was secured in the second allocation. On 11 October 1921 he wrote accepting the offer.

9   Copy in Zander papers, AGNSW Archive, Sydney.

10 'Red Cliffs today', *Age* (Melbourne), 9 October 1922, p. 12.

11 Jessie Traill, 'An impression of Red Cliffs, August 1922' (MS7975, Jessie Traill Papers, State Library of Victoria, Melbourne, 795/2[b]).

12 Aiken, 'Ever after?' (Zander papers, AGNSW Archive, Sydney).

13 Mary Gilmore, 'Never admit the pain', in Leonie Kramer (ed.), *My Country: Australian poetry and short stories*, Lansdowne Press, Sydney, 1985, vol. 568.

14 Copy of report in Zander papers, AGNSW Archive, Sydney.

15 J.S. MacDonald, 'The work of Will Dyson', *Art in Australia*, no. 16, June 1926, pp. 45–7.

16 Robert Henderson Croll, *I recall: Collections and recollection*, Robertson and Mullens, Melbourne, 1939, p. 67.

17 Lionel Lindsay, 'Will Dyson', *Art in Australia*, no. 70, March 1938, p. 73.

18 Will Dyson, typescript memoirs (MS11921, Will Dyson papers, State Library of Victoria, Melbourne, box 2440/5). Dyson was critical of the mental timidity and anti-intellectualism he found in Australia (see Ross McMullin, *Will Dyson, Australia's Radical Genius*, Scribe, Melbourne, 2006, pp. 342–5).

19 Both died within a week of each other in 1934. Clarice's mother, Catherine Louise, died on 3 July and her grandmother on 8 July.

20 See Beverley Nichols, *The Sweet and Twenties*, Weidenfeld and Nicolson, London, 1958. Nichols mixed in the circle of intellectuals with whom Dyson was friendly, such as David Low and H.G. Wells. Low, Wells and Nichols were Vice-Presidents of the Federation of Progressive Societies and Individuals, established in 1933 to promote cooperation among those working towards social and economic reconstruction.

21 It took Clarice many years to prove their marriage to the authorities. Once this was verified, she received a pension of £12 a week. This became Charles Zander's legacy, continuing for the rest of Clarice's life.

22 Isabel Fry (1869–1958) was an educationist and social activist. She came from a reforming Quaker background and was the younger sister of the artist and critic Roger Fry (1866–1934). The children of Bloomsbury went to her school.

23 Eric Ambler, *Here Lies: An autobiography*, Weidenfeld and Nicolson, London, 1985, p. 80.

24 Philip Lindsay to Norman Lindsay, no. 31, not dated (6067, Lindsay Family papers, State Library of Queensland, Brisbane). At the age of 21, Betty was commissioned to design the 4000 costumes for the 1934 Pageant of Parliament. She later briefly married Count Yves de Chanteau in 1939; both

were suspected of Nazi sympathies and activities. She died in Jamaica in the mid-1940s.

25   For Dyson's exposition of the Douglas method see Will Dyson, *Artist Among the Bankers*, J.M. Dent, London, 1933.

26   Philip Mairet, *A.R. Orage*, University Books, London, 1966, p. 121.

27   'Epstein', *Evening Standard* (London), 29 September 1932 (From Zander press clipping volumes, Zander Papers, AGNSW Archive, Sydney).

28   'Exhibition of British art: comprehensive collection', *Telegraph*, 5 January 1933, p. 32. Epstein could have influenced Zander's selection; for example, he collected Matthew Smith's paintings (see Ethel Mannin, *Confessions and Impressions*, Hutchinson, London, 1936, p. 158).

29   Mannin, *Confessions and Impressions*, pp. 155, 159; 'Epstein's art: inclusion in Sydney exhibition', *Daily Telegraph* (Sydney), 17 April 1933; undated clipping (Zander press clipping volumes, Zander papers, AGNSW Archive, Sydney); see Frank Rutter, *Art in My Time*, Rich & Cowan, London, 1933, p. 197.

30   Edward Marsh, *A Number of People: A book of reminiscences*, W. Heinemann Ltd., London, 1939, p. 359. On his picture collecting see chapter XV. Courtauld was among England's earliest collectors to buy the work of post-impressionist masters; he did so at the instigation of Roger Fry.

31   Clarice Zander, 'January 1956' (Hospital notebook, p. 36; Zander press clipping volumes, Zander papers, AGNSW Archive, Sydney).

32   *European Art Exhibition for Australia*, Town Hall, Sydney, July 1923. Konody was art critic for the *Observer* and the *Daily Mail* before the First World War and one of three critics to be 'blessed' by Wyndham Lewis (Wyndham Lewis [ed.], *Blast 1*, John Lane, London, 1914, p. 28). See also Lionel Lindsay, 'Australia's achievement in art', in *Art in Australia Commemoration Edition of Australia's 150th Anniversary*, John Fairfax & Sons, Sydney, 1937.

33   'Epstein art to be seen in Melbourne', *Herald* (Melbourne), 20 February 1933, n.p.

34   'British art for Australia', *Evening Standard* (London) 29 September, 1932, n.p.

35   T.H. Cochran, 'This, that and them', *The Home*, 3 January 1933, p. 46.

36   'Mrs Clarice Zander is an enterprising Australian', *Bulletin*, 21 April 1933, n.p.

37   Clive Bell, 'Contemporary art in England', *Burlington Magazine*, May–July 1917; reprinted in Clive Bell, *Potboilers*, London, 1918, pp. 209–30.

38   Basil Burdett, 'Some contemporary Australian artists', in Sydney Ure Smith & Leon Gellert (eds), *A Contemporary Group of Australian Artists*, Art in Australia, Sydney, 1929. This was issued following the group exhibition of *The Contemporary Group* at the Grosvenor Galleries, Sydney, in 1926.

39   'British art: large exhibition in April', *Sydney Morning Herald*, 21 January 1933, p. 8. Zander is referring to the Contemporary Art Society, established in 1910 to develop public collections of contemporary art in Britain. Roger Fry and Clive Bell were among the original committee members. At the time, H.S. Ede

generally ran the CAS, which bought the work of English post-impressionist artists. See Contemporary Art Society, *The First Fifty Years 1910–1960: An exhibition of works given by the Contemporary Art Society to public galleries*, Malvern Press, London, 1960.

40   *Modern Colour Prints and Wood Engravings from the Redfern Gallery, Old Bond Street, London, W.1.* The exhibition was held in Melbourne, 7–23 December 1932. Flight's foreword was reprinted from what is thought to have been a publicity flier for the first exhibition of linocuts held at the Redfern Gallery, London, in July 1929. The Redfern Gallery was at the centre of the modern linocut movement Claude Flight championed (see Stephen Coppel, *Linocuts of the Machine Age: Claude Flight and the Grosvenor School*, Scolar Press, Aldershot, Hants, 1995).

41   George Bell, 'British artists impress', *Sun* (Melbourne), 8 March 1933, n.p.; also see Stephen Coppel, 'Claude Flight and his Australian pupils', *Print Quarterly*, vol. II, 4 December 1985, p. 281.

42   Kenneth Wilkinson, 'Letters. Modern art', *Sydney Morning Herald*, 15 September 1932, p. 4.

43   'Modern art may cause argument. Lieutenant-Governor opens exhibition', *Herald* (Melbourne), 1933, undated clipping (Zander press clipping volumes, Zander papers, AGNSW Archive, Sydney).

44   'Felton Bequest. Etchings', *Argus* (Melbourne), 20 November 1925, p. 10; "The Mountain Road" in National Gallery', *Argus* (Melbourne), 11 December 1928, p. 5.

45   Sydney Long, 'The decay of etching', *Art in Australia*, no. 74, February 1939, p. 13.

46   Margaret Jaye was a pioneer of modern interior decoration in Sydney, selling furniture and *objets d'art* from her Darlinghurst Road shop from 1925. She was the first trader to be listed as an 'interior decorator' in Sydney, when interior decoration was a novel profession worldwide. Some art critics believed that modernist-inspired decoration, which was widespread in Europe by the late 1920s, could be the bridge by which the general public could more closely appreciate art of the day.

47   'British exhibition', *Sydney Morning Herald?*, undated clipping (Zander press clipping volumes, Zander Papers, AGNSW Archive, Sydney).

48   Clarice Zander to J.S. MacDonald, 12 February 1933 (EFO1933, AGNSW Archive, Sydney).

49   As was illustrated in *Art in Australia*, 15 April 1933, p. 38. This display only took place in Melbourne. Fred Ward was a close friend of Melbourne lawyer Allan R. Henderson. Henderson attended to Clarice's affairs in Melbourne and was her lifelong and loyal friend. In 1938 he became a founding member of the Contemporary Art Society in Melbourne along with fellow lawyer John Reed. Reed's sister, Cynthia Reed, actively promoted modern design from her shop,

Modern Furnishings, at 367 Little Collins Street. It was situated near Fred Ward's shop at 52a Collins Street.

50 Allan R. Henderson, 'Art Gallery policy: to the editor', *Herald* (Melbourne), 20 March 1933, n.p.

51 Total sales were £1082 22s 23p; however, Clarice's sales book lists 25 works, titled 'In account with Redfern Gallery', of which eight may be additional sales, not being recorded in the invoices which the sales book contains. They are shown as valued at £642, for which offers of £430 are recorded. Had these offers been received, sales would total £1512 22s 23p.

52 'Modern art is first to sell: judge and professor buy pictures', *Sunday Sun* (Sydney), 23 April 1933, n.p. Anderson bought William Roberts, *The Swimming Lesson*, 1929.

53 The painting is now in The Pier Arts Centre collection of twentieth-century British art, Stromness, Orkney.

54 Paintings by Augustus John included the portrait of the fabled Marchesa Casati (1881–1957). John painted Casati twice in April 1919. His first half-length portrait was left unfinished, presented to Casati, and bought by Lord Alington. Lord Duveen considered the second portrait to be an outstanding masterpiece of the time. It is now in the collection of the Art Gallery of Ontario, Toronto.

55 Clarice Zander, 'To the editor of the Herald', *Sydney Morning Herald*, 25 April 1933, p. 2.

56 Norman MacGeorge, 'Opportunity for gallery: to the editor', *Herald* (Melbourne), 17 March 1933, n.p. The painting is now in the collection of Gallery Oldham, Manchester.

57 These were John Souter's *Portrait Head of William Leask* and William Washington's *St Olaves, Southwark* (1929). Both Souter and Washington were London-based, Souter a portraitist and engraver and Washington, a New English Art Club member, later became principal of the Hammersmith School of Art.

58 Klinghoffer (1900–1970) was a New English Art Club Member from 1933.

59 'British show', *Daily Telegraph* (Sydney), 12 May 1933, n.p.

60 'The right contour – by necessity', *Sunday Sun* (Sydney), 16 April, 1933, n.p.

61 Michael Holroyd, *Augustus John*, Chatto & Windus, London, 1996, p. 457.

62 William Moore, 'Modern art again', *The Brisbane Courier*, 15 October 1932, p. 20.

63 John D. Moore, 'To the editor', *Sydney Morning Herald*, 19 April 1933, p. 6.

64 John Sulman, 'To the editor', *Sydney Morning Herald*, 24 April 1933, p. 6.

65 Clarice Zander, 'To the editor of the Herald', *Sydney Morning Herald*, 25 April 1933, p. 2. Under pressure the Sydney trustees went as a body to Clarice's exhibition in mid-April 1933. They bought nothing. Clarice submitted a number of etchings directly to their Board meeting in May. They purchased Stanley Anderson's line engraving *The reading room* (1930). At the same

meeting they spent 100 guineas on buying *The Cornish Coast* (1932) by Will Ashton. At the same time they also established a credit of £2500 in London for the purchase of works there.

66 *Sydney Morning Herald*, 7 August 1940, n.p. A full account of the Herald exhibition is given in Eileen Chanin & Steven Miller, *Degenerates and Perverts: The 1939 Herald Exhibition of French and British Contemporary Art*, Melbourne University Publishing, Carlton, Vic., 2005.

67 *Sydney Morning Herald*, 4 May 1933. Colin Simpson (1908–1983) became a well-known radio journalist, novelist and contemporary affairs commentator.

68 'The year's art. Violent controversies', *Sydney Morning Herald*, 1 January 1934, p. 6.

69 'New Art Gallery', *Sydney Morning Herald*, 6 December 1933, p. 10; 'Attack on modern art', *Canberra Times*, 2 August 1933, p. 1. Zander wrote that the artist is conditioned by his age (Clarice Zander, 'Modern art: an historical explanation', in H. Tatlock Miller [ed.], *Manuscripts No.4, A Miscellany of Art and Letters*, Geelong, 1932, p. 33).

70 J.S. MacDonald, 'Modern art: Mr J.S. MacDonald's criticism', *Sydney Morning Herald*, 1 May 1933, p. 10. 'Pakie's' operated from 1929 to 1966 on the second floor of 219 Elizabeth Street, Sydney.

71 'Lyceum Club', *Sydney Morning Herald*, 10 May 1933, p. 5.

72 'Social value of the arts, Australia's position', *Labour Daily*, 3 May 1933, n.p.

73 'Mrs Zander's address', *Sydney Morning Herald*, 3 May 1933, p. 10.

74 John D. Moore, 'Letter to the editor', *Sydney Morning Herald*, 21 April 1933, p. 4.

75 'Modern art prints: National Gallery asked to buy', *Sydney Morning Herald*, 6 July 1933, p. 10.

76 'Australian's experience', *Age* (Melbourne), 9 February 1934, p. 12.

77 'New styles for evening. Famous designer confides', *The Star* (Melbourne), 30 October 1933, n.p.

78 'Dancer who developed', *The Star* (Melbourne), 8 January 1934, 11. Bobby (later Sir Robert) Helpmann was at the start of his career when Zander wrote about him. He first came to notice in December 1931 when aged 22, and began dancing in London in 1933 as a member of the *corps de ballet* in the Vic-Wells Ballet. Clarice's promotion of him was typical of her promotion of Australian talent.

79 This was Mr. W.A. Ackland, formerly Chairman of the London District of the Institute of Journalists.

80 In 1934, 43 students were enrolled: 24 studying painting, two sculpture and 17 architecture.

81 Augustus John, *Chiaroscuro, Fragments of Autobiography, First Series*, Jonathan Cape, London, 1952, p. 230.

82 Rutter, *Art in my time*, p. 182.

83 'Art and the Royal Academy', *The Times* (London), 5 May 1934, p. 13.

84 Anthony Trollope, *Australia and New Zealand*, George Robertson, Melbourne, 1873, p. 309. Trollope viewed Australian and American women alike, for their self-dependence and 'bold self-assertion'.

85 R.E.N. Twopenny, *Town Life in Australia*, Elliot Stock, London, 1883, p. 86.

86 Tom Clarke, *Marriage at 6 a.m.*, Gollancz, London, 1934, pp. 96–9. Clarke was managing editor of the *Daily News*. He toured Australia for Lord Northcliffe before he wrote this book.

87 Clarice Zander, 'Memories of my life as a public relations officer', p. 1 (Zander papers, AGNSW Archive, Sydney).

88 Press clipping, source and date unknown (Zander newspaper clippings, Zander papers, AGNSW Archive, Sydney).

89 'How the Royal Academy can make itself more popular', *Daily Sketch*, 12 August 1935, n.p.

90 'The French art exhibition', *The Times* (London), 12 December 1931, p. 13.

91 Zander, 'Memories of my life', p. 1 (Zander papers, AGNSW Archive, Sydney).

92 Ernest Wright (1878–1955) retired in 1948. 'Mr E.E.V. Wright', *The Times* (London), 13 September 1955, p. 11; Clarice arranged an 'In Memoriam' in the *The Times* and used part of the £10,000 windfall to pay for her return to Australia in 1956 (*The Times* [London], 29 August 1956, 13 September 1955).

93 'Chinese Treasures for London' *The Times* (London), 8 April 1935, p. 14.

94 The Amitabha Buddha, 585 AD, now dominates the north staircase of the British Museum. The Chinese Government donated the statue in memory of the Chinese Exhibition. Online at http://www.britishmuseum.org/explore/highlights/highlight_objects/asia/m/marble_figure_of_the_buddha_am.aspx, accessed 14 November 2012.

95 Royal Academy, *Auditors Report 1937*, London, 19 January 1938, p. 60.

96 Clarice Zander, Hospital notebook, 1956, p. 100 (Zander papers, AGNSW Archive, Sydney).

97 Clarice Zander to Basil Burdett, undated postcard (Zander papers, AGNSW Archive, Sydney).

98 'The woman behind the Chinese art exhibition', *The Nottingham Journal*, 30 November 1935, p. 8.

99 Exhibitions of Chinese art from the personal collections of collectors like G.W. Eedy (1920), Professor E.G. Waterhouse (1940), Sydney Cooper (1941) and R.R. McDonnell Parr (1949) were held throughout the first half of the twentieth century. However, the first blockbuster exhibition of Chinese art was *The Chinese Exhibition*, which toured Australia during 1977.

100 Clarice Zander, 'The New Orientation of Australian Art' c. 1942 (Zander papers, AGNSW Archive, Sydney).

101 Jessica Mitford, *Hons and Rebels*, Victor Gollancz Ltd, London, 1960, p. 90. The possibility of a completely Nazified Europe faced Britain in 1938 and Mitford describes the apprehensive mood of the time (pp. 150–3).

102 *Exhibition of British Architecture*, January–March 1937; *17th Century Art in Europe*, January – March 1937.

103 Clarice Zander to Allen Henderson, 26 January 1937 (letter misdated by one year; Zander papers, AGNSW Archive, Sydney).

104 Clarice Zander to Laurence and Eileen Heyworth, 26 January 1938 (Zander papers, AGNSW Archive, Sydney). J.L. Heyworth was for ten years head of the Lever Company in Australia (A.M.K., 'Mr. J.L. Heyworth', *The Times* [London], 6 September 1963, p. 14).

105 The post-mortem portrait shows Dyson lying in his coffin in the funeral parlour, with a bunch of snowdrops that Clarice had left in the coffin (Tom C. Dugdale, *Will Dyson after death*, pencil on cream paper, 1938, State Library of Victoria). Her daughter Jocelyn presented this drawing to the State Library of Victoria.

106 Sir William Lewellyn to Clarice Zander, 31 March 1938 (Zander papers, AGNSW Archive, Sydney).

107 John was reinstated to the Academy early in 1940. Lewis's portrait of Eliot is now in the collection of the Durban Municipal Art Gallery, http://durbanet. co.za/exhib/dag/dageng.htm, accessed 18 November 2012.

108 Burlington Fine Arts Club, *Exhibition of twentieth century German art: July 1938, New Burlington Galleries*, London, 1938. The exhibition included the work of 53 artists who had been exhibited in Hitler's 1937 *Entartete Kunst*. The exhibition included around 400 paintings. In June 1939 it was on display at the Milwaukee Art Institute.

109 Notes, December 1955 (Letters to Zander, Zander papers, AGNSW Archive, Sydney).

110 Sydney Lee to Clarice Zander, 4 November 1937 (Letters to Zander, Box 3, Zander papers, AGNSW Archive, Sydney).

111 Toscanini's first radio broadcast to America was made in 1937, on Christmas night. On his standing see, David Ewen, *Men and Women Who Make Music*, Thomas Y Crowell Company, New York 1939, p. 34. On Toscanini's resistance to Mussolini and Hitler, see Harvey Sachs (comp.), *The Letters of Arturo Toscanini*, Alfred A. Knopf, New York 2002, pp. xvii, 26–7.

Part 4 – THE EDUCATOR: MARY CECIL ALLEN

1 Alexander Colquhoun (ed.), *Year Book of Victorian Art*, Alexander McCubbin, Melbourne, 1923, Introduction.

2 Violet Powell, *Margaret Countess of Jersey*, Heinemann, London, 1978, p. 110.

3 R.J.W. Selleck, *The Shop: The University of Melbourne 1850–1939*, Melbourne University Press, Carlton, Vic., 2003, p. 223. See also Margaret Sutherland

in 'Personal notes on Mary Cecil Allen', unpublished manuscript (Frances Derham papers, 1988.0061, University of Melbourne Archives, box 7).

4   Geoffrey Blainey, *Centenary History of the University of Melbourne*, Melbourne University Press, Carlton, Vic., 1957, pp. 44, 101, 132. Allen was also an active member of the International Association of Medical Museums, membership to which required endorsement by leading world pathologists.

5   Undated obituary (MS9320 Allen Family papers, State Library of Victoria, Melbourne).

6   Frances Derham, 'Recollections of Mary Cecil Allen', unpublished manuscript (Derham papers, University of Melbourne Archives, box 3).

7   Sir Roy Cameron, 'Recollections of Sir Harry Brookes Allen' (MS9320 Allen Family papers, State Library of Victoria, Melbourne, box 2/4).

8   Harry Brookes Allen, 'Australian studies', *The Speculum: Journal of the Melbourne Medical Students' Society*, no. 68, May 1907, pp. 29–35. Also other collections of his poetry, originally published in *The Speculum*, were issued in single volumes, including *Ad lucem* (July 1904) and *Australia's Dead: Alma mater and the war* (July 1915)

9   Vesta (comp.), *Book of Recipes*, The Argus and The Australasian, Melbourne, 1929; Vesta (comp.), *Recipes For All Meals*, The Argus, Melbourne, 1938.

10 Sarah Dunne, *Wartime Cookery*, Edgar H. Baillie for the Herald and Weekly Times, Melbourne, 1945.

11 'An hour of music', *Argus* (Melbourne), 27 March 1926, p. 22; 'An hour with Roussel', *Argus* (Melbourne), 20 April 1926, p. 17; 'British Music Society', *Argus* (Melbourne), 8 June, 1935, p. 11 (performing Max Reger, Arnold Bax, and Sauer's *Frisson de Feuilles*); 'British Music Society', *Argus* (Melbourne), 25 September 1930, p. 13 (performing Arne, Boyce and Purcell).

12 Biddy Allen, 'Bach revival: a musical genius' *Argus* (Melbourne), 30 July 1932, p. 4; Biddy Allen, 'Contemporary music. a festival at Amsterdam', *Argus* (Melbourne), 29 July 1933, p. 9; Biddy Allen, 'Some musical personalities, contrasts in temperament', *Argus* (Melbourne), 16 June 1934, p. 7; Bicknell Allen, 'Modern music, is there any such thing?', *Argus* (Melbourne), 12 August 1939, p. 17. Later criticism includes Biddy Allen, 'The music of Erik Satie', *Meanjin*, vol. 12, no. 2, Winter 1953, pp. 179–85.

13 Sutherland, 'Personal notes', p. 3 (Derham papers, University of Melbourne Archives).

14 Martin Boyd, *Day of My Delight: An Anglo-Australian memoir*, Lansdowne, Melbourne, 1965, p. 17. The Boyds and the Allens were both staying at the same hotel.

15 Derham, 'Recollections of Mary Cecil Allen', p. 3 (Derham papers, University of Melbourne Archives).

16 Caroline Ambrus, *The Ladies' Picture Show: Sources on a century of Australian women artists*, Hale & Iremonger, Sydney, 1984, p. 39. She was enrolled in the

Drawing School, 1910–11 and the School of Painting, 1913–19 'Register of students in Painting and Drawing Schools, National Gallery of Victoria, 1866–1911', in Andrew MacKenzie, *Frederick McCubbin 1855–1917: The Proff, and his art*, Mannagum Press, Lilydale, Vic., 1990, p. 325.

17 Derham, 'Recollections of Mary Cecil Allen', p. 3.

18 Joan Lindsay, 'Personal notes on Mary Cecil Allen', unpublished manuscript (Derham papers, University of Melbourne Archives, box 3).

19 L. Bernard Hall, *Art and Life*, Public Library, Museum and Art Gallery of South Australia, Adelaide, 1918, p. 7.

20 The largest enrolment was in 1892 with 38 students, of whom nine were male and 29 were female (Roll of Art Students [Painting] National Gallery School Melbourne 1886–1967', National Gallery of Victoria AAA file, State Library of Victoria, Melbourne). A list is also available in Helen Topliss, *Modernism and Feminism: Australian women artists, 1900–1940*, Craftsman House, Roseville East, NSW, 1996, p. 204. When Mary was in the Painting Class of the National Gallery School in 1915, seven men and 13 women were enrolled.

21 Derham was enrolled at the Drawing School 1911–13; Mabel Pye, Drawing School 1912–15 and Painting School 1915–19; Ethel Spowers, Drawing School 1911–13, Painting School 1914–17. Also there at the same time was Edith Grieve, Drawing School 1910–12, Painting School 1913–16; Marion Jones, Drawing School 1912, Painting School 1913–17. On Derham's friendship with Allen see Penelope F.B. Alexander, *Frankie Derham: A refuge within*, St Kilda, Vic., Oryx Publishing, 2006, pp. 87, 93.

22 Allen Family papers, box 3, State Library of Victoria, Melbourne. Allen had already won the National Gallery Student's Prize for drawing a hand and foot from the antique cast (*Argus* [Melbourne], 16 December 1910, p. 6).

23 Virginia Woolf, *Mr Bennett and Mrs Brown*, The Hogarth Press, London, 1924, p. 4.

24 Woolf, *Mr Bennett and Mrs Brown*, p. 5.

25 Stella Bowen, *Drawn From Life: Reminiscences*, Collins, London, 1941, p. 36.

26 MS8525, Frederick McCubbin Papers, State Library of Victoria, Melbourne, box 987/2. The painting is in the Tate Collection, N04622.

27 On Dunsany as a collector see Mark Amory, *Biography of Lord Dunsany*, London, Collins, 1972, p. 34.

28 'Post-impressionist exhibition', *The Times* (London), 3 September 1912, p. 7.

29 This was *The Mumpers*, exhibited at the New English Art Club's annual exhibition in 1912 (Mary Allen to Frederick McCubbin, 11 December 1912, McCubbin papers, State Library of Victoria, Melbourne, box 987/2).

30 A number of them were photographed at the Slade School Picnic of 1912 (Richard Cork, *David Bomberg*, Millbank, London, Tate Gallery, 1988, p. 13).

31 'The New English Art Club', *The Times* (London), 24 May 1910, p. 9. The surgeon–artist Tonks could well have been approved of by Harry Allen, who

took interest in art. Harry Allen's own notebooks, filled with drawings of his study of the pathology of disease, at times appear quite abstract.

32 'Professor Tonks', *The Times* (London), 9 January 1937, p. 14. The emphasis that Tonks put on rendering contours of a three-dimensional form in line characterised Slade-trained artists.

33 Ann E. Galbally, 'Lindsay Bernard Hall (1859–1935)', *Australian Dictionary of Biography*, National Centre of Biography, Australian National University, http://adb.anu.edu.au/biography/hall-lindsay-bernard-6528/text11209, accessed 15 October 2012.

34 Mary Allen to Frederick McCubbin (McCubbin papers, State Library of Victoria, Melbourne).

35 ibid.

36 Lindsay, 'Personal notes on Mary Cecil Allen', p. 3.

37 Derham, 'Recollections of Mary Cecil Allen', p. 3.

38 MacKenzie, *Frederick McCubbin*, p. 347.

39 Mary Cecil Allen, three pages of manuscript notes on McCubbin (MS9320 Allen Family papers, State Library of Victoria, Melbourne, box 1/6).

40 Mrs Elizabeth (Bessie) Colquhoun, Recollections, in MacKenzie, *Frederick McCubbin*, p. 350.

41 From 1908, the next nine Travelling Scholarship winners were women (to 1932). For prize winners see MacKenzie, *Frederick McCubbin*, p. 320. As well as being prestigious, winning the scholarship brought commercial benefit. The scholarship was awarded to Marion Jones in 1919, and catalogues to exhibitions held by the Victorian Artists Society show that her paintings, listed for 120 and 150 guineas, were subsequently priced more highly than Bernard Hall's painting *Badinage*, listed at 65 guineas.

42 Edith Grieve, 'Personal notes on Mary Cecil Allen' (unpublished manuscript, Derham papers, University of Melbourne Archives, box 3).

43 Lindsay, 'Personal notes on Mary Cecil Allen', p. 3.

44 Colquhoun, Recollections in MacKenzie, *Frederick McCubbin*, p. 349.

45 Derham, 'Recollections of Mary Cecil Allen', p. 3.

46 Lindsay, 'Personal notes on Mary Cecil Allen', pp. 3–4.

47 The Medical School Building was completed in 1864. The faculty, however, celebrated its foundation in 1862.

48 Harry Allen, *University of Melbourne Medical School Jubilee, 1914*, Ford & Son, Melbourne, 1914, p. 51.

49 The Mermaid Play Society, *Season 1919–20. Notes on the five plays to be produced with illustrations by Mary Allen*, The Specialty Press, Melbourne, 1919.

50 Derham, 'Recollections of Mary Cecil Allen', p. 3.

51 Louis Lozowick, *100 contemporary American Jewish painters and sculptors*, NKUF, New York, 1947, p. xiii.

52 Queen Bee, 'Miss Allen's paintings', *Australasian* (Melbourne), 21 December 1918, n.p.

53 ibid.

54 'Victorian Artists Society. Spring exhibition', *Argus* (Melbourne), 3 September 1917, p. 4. Fifty women artists exhibited in the exhibition of 263 works, including A.M.E. Bale and Adelaide Perry.

55 *Exhibition of Paintings by Mary Cecil Allen*, Fine Arts Society's Gallery, Melbourne, 14–27 September 1919; see also Barbara George, 'Mary Cecil Allen (1893–1962): expatriate Australian and apostle of art', Master of Arts Thesis, University of Adelaide, 2011, p. 52.

56 'Art notes', *Age* (Melbourne), 17 September 1919, p. 8.

57 'Miss Mary Allen's exhibition', *Melbourne Punch*, 25 September 1919, p. 5.

58 'Miss Allen's exhibition', *Bulletin*, 2 October 1919, p. 8.

59 *Mary Allen Exhibition of Oil Paintings*, Fine Arts Society's Gallery, Melbourne, 1–10 September 1921. This was an exhibition of 54 works ranging in price from one to 30 guineas. Twelve works were lent.

60 'Australian art. Melba's advice to artists', *Age* (Melbourne), 3 September 1921, n.p.

61 'Miss Allen's paintings', *Argus* (Melbourne), 2 September 1921, n.p.

62 'Art notes. Miss Mary Allen', *Age* (Melbourne), 2 September 1921, p. 9.

63 'Miss Allen's paintings', *Argus* (Melbourne), 2 September 1921, n.p.

64 'Melbourne art notes', *Triad*, 10 October 1921, p. 8.

65 Colin Colahan, *Max Meldrum: His art and views*, Alexander McCubbin, Melbourne, 1919, p. 9.

66 'Max Meldrum's lecture', *Australasian* (Melbourne), 23 September 1922, n.p.

67 'Oil paintings exhibited', *Herald* (Melbourne), 2 September 1921, n.p. Alexander Colquhoun was art critic for the Melbourne *Herald* (1914–22) and the *Age* (1926–24).

68 MacKenzie, *Frederick McCubbin*, p. 349.

69 Frances Derham, 'Mary Cecil Allen', *Australian Dictionary of Biography*, vol. 7, Melbourne University Press, Melbourne, 1979, p. 46.

70 Elizabeth Colquhoun interviewed by Barbara Blackman, 19 July 1988 (National Library of Australia, Canberra, ORAL TRC460).

71 *Mary Allen*, Fine Arts Society's Gallery, Melbourne, 2–13 December 1924.

72 'Miss Allen's paintings', *Argus* (Melbourne), 1 December 1924, p. 11.

73 J.S. MacDonald , 'Max Meldrum's Art. Exhibition at the Athenaeum', *Herald* (Melbourne), 29 June 1925.

74 J.S. MacDonald, 'Max Meldrum has moulded Australian Art', *Australasian*, 23 November 1940.

75 'Max Meldrum's lecture', n.p.

76 *Bulletin*, 17 July 1929, p. 5.

77 MS6139, George Bell typescript, 'When everybody was poor', c. 1959, p. 1 (State Library of Victoria, MS BOX 299/3). Alexander Colquhoun emphasises the growing interest in art matters (Colquhoun, *Year Book of Victorian Art*, Introduction).

78 Foreword to catalogue for *Exhibition of Paintings by Archibald Douglas Colquhoun*, Athenaeum Gallery, Melbourne, 31 October–12 November 1927.

79 ibid.

80 Along with Ruth Sutherland, who was a member of the Twelve Melbourne Painters and who wrote for the *Age*, and a Miss Carrington, who wrote for the *Australasian* and *Table Talk*. See Murray Goot, 'Newspaper circulation in Australia 1932–1977', *Media Centre Papers*, no. 11, 1979, p. 5, cited in Sybil Nolan, 'Manifest editorial differences: *The Age* and *The Argus* in the 1920s and 30s', in Muriel Porter (ed.), *The Argus: The life and death of a great Melbourne newspaper (1846–1957)*, RMIT Publishing, Melbourne, 2003.

81 He was a trustee from 1924 until 1940. Mary Cecil Allen, *Hilda Elliott with black shawl*, oil on canvas, 122.0 x 152.5 cm, undated, Collection of the Mildura Arts Centre.

82 Draft of lecture, 7 October 1926 (Allen family papers, State Library of Victoria, Melbourne, box 1/6).

83 Mary Cecil Allen, *The Mirror of the Passing World*, W.W. Norton and Company, New York, 1928, pp. 48, xi.

84 ibid., p. xiii.

85 The *Bulletin* reported that public interest in the case was greater than 'Royal Show Week, the Tuckerman murder inquest and a supplementary policy speech by the Premier' ('The Falcke case', *Bulletin*, 23 September 1924, n.p.; the Tuckerman murder inquest concerned the rape and murder of eleven-year-old Melbourne schoolgirl Irene Tuckerman).

86 'Cross-examination in £5000 art libel action', *Herald* (Melbourne), 17 September 1924, n.p.

87 'Australian Art Association', *Argus* (Melbourne), 5 June 1914, p. 5. See also, 'Australian Art Association', *Argus* (Melbourne), 3 October 1919, p. 8.

88 'Art at empire exhibition: Australian works selected', *Argus* (Melbourne), 5 December 1923, p. 24. She exhibited catalogue no. 12 *Vanity*, an oil priced at 20 guineas.

89 See Graeme Sturgeon, *The Development of Australian Sculpture, 1788–1975*, Thames and Hudson, London, 1978), pp. 128–31.

90 Selleck, *The Shop*, p. 619.

91 *Argus* (Melbourne), 30 March 1926, p. 11.

92 'Melbourne art notes', *Triad* (Sydney), 10 October 1921, n.p.

93 'The American scene. Miss Mary Allen returns', *Argus* (Melbourne), 20 July 1935, p. 24.

94 Her father was James Waring Gillies. The company was continued by Florence's brother Edwin J. Gillies and her brother-in-law James H. Schmelzel. For a photograph of Florence see: http://www.flickr.com/photos/12685760@N03/3978090275/in/set-72157622509957034/, accessed 4 April 2014.

95 Ethel Mannin, *Confessions and Impressions*, rev. edn, Hutchinson, London, 1936, p. 75.

96 'The American scene. Miss Mary Allen returns', p. 24.

97 John Oldham & Alfred Stirling, *Victorian: A visitor's book*, The Hawthorn Press, Melbourne, 1969, p. 134.

98 'International New York. City of many tongues', *Argus* (Melbourne), 10 August 1935, p. 19.

99 'The American scene. Miss Mary Allen returns', p. 24.

100 'Australian artists of today: Mary Cecil Allen', *Age* (Melbourne), 6 June 1931, n.p.; 'The American scene. Miss Mary Allen returns', p. 24; 'Art in terms of green apples', *Argus* (Melbourne), 26 July 1935, p. 5; Elizabeth George, 'Australian pictures for New York, Miss Mary Cecil Allen's latest work', *Advertiser* (Adelaide), 17 June 1936, p. 8 (Women's section).

101 *Sunday Times* (Perth), 4 March 1928, p. 2.

102 Philip Youtz to Mary Allen, 1 October 1928 (People's Institute Records 1897–1927, New York Public Library, New York).

103 Youtz to Allen, 1 October 1928.

104 'Mary Allen's book on art', *Stead's Review*, 2 December 1929, n.p.

105 Lawrence Rogin, 'Scanning new books', *The New Leader*, 18 October 1930, p. 20.

106 Allen, *The Mirror of the Passing World*, p. 101. She did, in fact, consider the formal qualities of modern murals, glossing over their political implications, when she wrote 'the ancient formula so pregnant with possible developments in our own day: Let form be three-dimensional and colour two-dimensional' (Mary Cecil Allen, *Painters of the Modern Mind*, W.W. Norton and Company, New York, 1929, p. 75).

107 Allen, *The Mirror of the Passing World*, p. 52.

108 ibid., p. 24.

109 'He is freed from the tyranny of the eye. He no longer merely sees but knows what he sees' (Allen, *Painters of the Modern Mind*, p. 35).

110 ibid., pp. 12–13.

111 This attracted criticism. A review in *Parnassus* criticised Allen for a lack of scholarly rigour, saying that her book resembled 'the wandering discourse of a museum docent on Sunday afternoon, rather than the reflective thoughtful discussion of a mature writer composing written pages for the close attention of adult readers' (A.P. McMahon, 'New books', *Parnassus*, vol. 2, no. 1, 1930, p. 35).

112 Allen, *Painters of the Modern Mind*, p. 81.

113 Miss Hewitt's Classes, begun in 1920, became The Hewitt School in 1955. Its location when Mary taught there was 68 East 79th Street. Today it remains an independent school for girls: http://www.hewittschool.org/.

114 The Preshil Preparatory School began in August 1931. On Preshil see M.D. Lawson & R.C. Petersen, *Progressive Education: An introduction*, Angus and Robertson, Sydney, 1972, p. 120. Derham's collection of child art is now in the collection of the National Gallery of Australia, Canberra. See National Gallery of Australia, *Childhoods Past: Children's art of the twentieth century*, National Gallery of Australia, Canberra, 1999.

115 Allan, *The Mirror of the Passing World*, p. 33.

116 For an outline of family tension see, George, 'Mary Cecil Allen (1893–1962)', pp. 80, 99–104. For background to the appointment of Brookes see Eileen Chanin, 'Pioneering cultural exchange: two international exhibitions 1931–1933, initiated by Mary Cecil Allen and Alleyne Clarice Zander', in Robert Dixon &Veronica Kelly (eds), *Impact of the Modern: Vernacular modernities in Australia 1870s–1960s*, Sydney University Press, Sydney, 2008, pp. 137–8.

117 Jessie Brookes Clarke interviewed by Eileen Chanin, September 2008.

118 'Art colonies in America. Melbourne artist returns', *Sydney Morning Herald*, 16 July 1935, p. 4.

119 Including one to the Cleveland Museum. *Mary Cecil Allen Paintings and Drawings*, Contemporary Arts, 12 East 10th St, New York, 5–17 May 1930. This gallery was founded to aid young and emerging artists

120 . Edward Alden Jewell (1888–1947) began writing on art in 1928, initially as assistant to *Times* art editor Elisabeth Luther Cary (1867–1936). Jewell was appointed to assist Cary review the annually increasing roster of New York's art exhibitions.

121 The museum complex included studios, an international art centre, a theatre, a restaurant, a chapel with a collection of religious art, private apartments available for rent and the Master Institute of United Arts and a museum school.

122 For background on Roerich and the exhibition see Chanin, 'Pioneering cultural exchange', in Dixon & Kelly, pp. 141–3.

123 William Moore, 'Art and artists. Exhibition in America', *Courier* (Brisbane), 28 February 1931, p. 18.

124 William Moore outlines the visibility of Australian art in America, from its first appearance there at the Philadelphia Exhibition in 1876 (William Moore, 'Art and artists. Exhibition in America', *Courier* [Brisbane], 28 February 1931, p. 18).

125 'Australian art. Proposed exhibition in New York', *Argus* (Melbourne), 9 August 1930, p. 8.

126 'Like British', *Courier* (Brisbane), 9 February 1931, p. 10.

127 'Not one kangaroo', *Daily News* (Perth), 9 February 1931, p. 5.

128 George, 'Australian pictures for New York', p. 8.

129 Edward Jewell, 'Australian art shown here', *New York Times*, 8 February 1931, p. 38; 'First show of Australian art ever held in America proves mirror of their spirit', *Bulletin of the Milwaukee Art Insititute*, vol. 5, October 1931, pp. 2–3.

130 Edward Jewell, 'Brooklyn Museum opens 3 art shows', *New York Times*, 2 February 1935, p. 11. See also 'Mlle Mary Cecil Allen' *La Revue Moderne*, no. 20, 3 October 1931, p. 19.

131 'News of art', *New York Times* 18 April 1935, p. 21.

132 'Australian eyes', *Art Digest*, 15 February 1932, p. 18.

133 'Will of Ada Rosalie Elizabeth Allen', 17 July 1930 (Public Records Office of Victoria, Melbourne).

134 Mary Allen to Frances Derham, 10 August 1947 (Derham papers, University of Melbourne Archives).

135 'Art in America as Miss Mary Allen saw it', *Age* (Melbourne), 20 July 1935, p. 24.

136 'Woman's diary in a fishing village', *Argus* (Melbourne), 24 July 1935, p. 16.

137 Rohan Rivett, *Herbert Brookes: Australian citizen*, Melbourne University Press, Melbourne, 1965, p. 207. Rivett (1917–77) was a grandson of Alfred Deakin.

138 *Mary Cecil Allen Paintings and Drawings*, Fine Art Society's Gallery, Melbourne, 2031 August 1935.

139 Alexander, *Frankie Derham*, p. 94; also Barbara Blackman, interview with Frances Derham, 19 March 1984 (National Library of Australia Oral History Project, Canberra). The present whereabouts of this painting is unknown.

140 'Modern painters', *Age* (Melbourne), 20 August 1935, p. 11.

141 Allen, *Painters of the Modern Mind*, p. 7.

142 'Introduction', Frances Derham unpublished manuscript, p. 16 (Derham papers, University of Melbourne Archives).

143 A. Clark, 'Where modern trends in the arts are leading', *New York Times*, 12 January 1930, p. 64. In *The Mirror of the Passing World* Mary also offered a critique of the Meldrum's tonal approach in the light of the influence of contemporary photography and familiarity with Japanese printmaking (Allen, *The Mirror of the Passing World*, pp. 76–7).

144 George Bell was abroad when Allen lectured students at the school. She was invited by do so by Arnold Shore (Felicity St John Moore, *Classical Modernism: The George Bell Circle*, National Gallery of Victoria, Melbourne, 1992, pp. 3, 24, 29).

145 Mary Eagle & Jan Minchin, *The George Bell School: Students, friends, influences*, Deutscher Art Publications, Melbourne, 1981, p. 92.

146 This work was probably *Folly Cove*, now in the Cruthers Collection of Women's Art, University of Western Australia. The work is believed to have been painted as a demonstration work during one of Mary's classes at the Bell-Shore School.

147   In 1931 J.S. MacDonald, then Director of the National Art Gallery of NSW, was invited to give a lecture on modern art at the Melbourne state gallery. He commenced with the observation: 'I do not know what modern art is; I do not understand it . . . but it is bad art. It is only distortion that the man in the street cannot appreciate' (Sali Herman, 'In defense of modern art', *Daily Telegraph* [Sydney], 7 April 1939, n.p.).

148   'Modern art. Distortion defended', *Argus* (Melbourne), 27 August 1935, p. 10. Chapter 2 of Allen's *Painters of the Modern Mind* was entirely devoted to 'The use of distortion'.

149   'The American scene. Miss Mary Allen returns', p. 24.

150   Mary elaborated on 'The New Grotesque': 'Invention and distortion are no new things in art: they lie at the very root of all emotional and dramatic statement. The real error that stands in the way of appreciation of the unfamiliar and the apparently grotesque in art, is the deeply rooted idea of chronology as leading to perfection . . . Distortion of some kind is a necessity if we are to express what we are thinking about when we look at the world around us' (*Countertide*, eds Alastair Crombie & Eric Wilson, May 1936, pp. 6–7. This was a single issue 'journal' released from Trinity College, University of Melbourne).

151   'Sanity in art. Fight against anarchy. Mr Syd Long's return', *Sydney Morning Herald*, 21 June 1921, n.p.

152   J.S. MacDonald & Harold Herbert, 'Melbourne, special number of Art in Australia', *Art in Australia*, Sydney, 1928, p. 4.

153   Boyd, *Day of my Delight*, p. 238. Australian intolerance of non-conformists and the gifted is also noted by Beverley Kingston, *My Wife, My Daughter and Poor Mary Ann: Women and work in Australia*, Thomas Nelson Australia, Melbourne, 1975, p. 116.

154   Norman Macgeorge, 'The lecture as an art form', in *The Arts in Australia*, F.W. Cheshire, Melbourne, 1948, p. 56.

155   Frances Burke, 'Personal notes on Mary Cecil Allen', unpublished manuscript (Derham papers, University of Melbourne Archives, box 3).

156   'Miss Mary Allen talks on art', *Argus* (Melbourne), 13 August 1935, p. 10.

157   'Modern painters', *Age* (Melbourne), 20 August 1935, p. 11.

158   *Argus* (Melbourne), 30 May 1936, p. 19.

159   'Women painters entertain Miss Allen', *Argus* (Melbourne), 10 October 1935, p. 15.

160   Pat Jarrett, 'Personal notes on Mary Cecil Allen', unpublished manuscript, p. 7 (Derham papers, University of Melbourne Archives).

161   'New York Fair', *Art in Australia*, 15 August 1939, p. 76.

162   'Australian exhibition', *Los Angeles County Museum Newsletter*, 15 July 1942, n.p.

163   Mary Allen to Frances Derham, undated postcard (Derham papers, University of Melbourne Archives).

EPILOGUE

1   Quoted by Clarice Zander in her article 'Two modern groups', *Art in Australia*, 3rd series, no. 56, August 1934, p. 56.

2   Ethel Gabain (Mrs John Copley, President of the Royal Society of British Artists) to Clarice Zander, 28 November 1949 (Letters to Zander, Zander papers, AGNSW Archive, Sydney, Box 3).

3   Louise Hanson-Dyer to Sibyl Hewett, 16 November 1939, Louise Hanson-Dyer Papers 1926–1971 (Manuscript), State Library of Victoria, 1536/1

SELECT BIBLIOGRAPHY

PRIMARY SOURCES

Victoria

MS10808 Louise B Riggall, *Diary of Italian Tour*, State Library of Victoria, Melbourne

MS10770 Louise Hanson-Dyer Papers, State Library of Victoria, Melbourne

MS9807 Alberto Zelman Papers, State Library of Victoria, Melbourne

MS11921 Will Dyson Papers, State Library of Victoria, Melbourne

MS7975 Jessie Traill Papers, State Library of Victoria, Melbourne

MS9320 Allen Family Papers, State Library of Victoria, Melbourne

MS8525 Frederick McCubbin Papers, State Library of Victoria, Melbourne

MS8647 Una Mabel Bourne Papers, State Library of Victoria, Melbourne

MS9267 Daryl Lindsay Correspondence, State Library of Victoria, Melbourne

MS9203/MSB24 Dora Wilson Notebooks, State Library of Victoria, Melbourne

MS 9377 Women's International League for Peace and Freedom Papers, State Library of Victoria, Melbourne

MS13111 Sybil Craig Scrapbook, State Library of Victoria, Melbourne

MS11675 Dr Samuel Arthur Ewing Papers, State Library of Victoria, Melbourne

MS12443 Alan Fraser, *Some Memories of the Working Men's College 1910–1913*, State Library of Victoria, Melbourne

MS12951 William Lucas, *The National War Memorial for Victoria. A Review of the Competition 1924*, State Library of Victoria, Melbourne

MS11524 Gustav Kruger, *A Few lines of my voyage from Hamburg to Melbourne 1879–1880 in the 'La Rochelle', 738 tons, 24th October 1879 – 24th January 1880*, State Library of Victoria, Melbourne

MS11356 Material relating to soldier settlement in Victoria c. 1925–27, State Library of Victoria, Melbourne

MS1988.0061 Frances Derham Papers, University of Melbourne Archives, Melbourne

MS1976.0006 Sir Harry Brookes Allen Papers, University of Melbourne Archives, Melbourne

MS1963.0003 Sir Harry Brookes Allen Correspondence, University of Melbourne Archives, Melbourne

MS6139 George Bell typescript 'When everybody was poor' c. 1959, State Library of Victoria, Melbourne

VPRS2498 General records from the Shrine of Remembrance, Melbourne, including minutes of the Executive Committee, Public Records Office of Victoria, Melbourne

Australian Capital Territory

MS2001 Sir Robert Garran Papers, National Library of Australia, Canberra

3DRL/3376 Field Marshal Lord William Birdwood Papers, National Library of Australia,

MS8396 Lucy Bellew Papers, National Library of Australia, Canberra

MS2862 L.A. Garvan Papers, National Library of Australia, Canberra

MS7647 William Moore Papers, National Library of Australia, Canberra

AWM92 Dora Ohlfsen Anzac Medal Fund 1919, Australian War Memorial, Canberra Australian War Memorial Correspondence files

New South Wales

MS 13286 Cecilia Summerhayes Papers, Mitchell Library, Sydney

MS1997.10 Clarice Zander Papers, AGNSW Archive, Sydney

MS2000.8 Ethel Stephens Scrapbook, AGNSW Archive, Sydney

EFO1933 Exhibition file, AGNSW Archive, Sydney

Dora Ohlfsen family correspondence; copies in the collection of the AGNSW Archive, Sydney

Queensland

6067 Lindsay Family Papers, State Library of Queensland, Brisbane

Overseas

People's Institute Records 1897–1927, New York Public Library, New York

THESES AND REPORTS

Royal Commission on Soldier Settlement 1925, *Report*, Government Printer, Melbourne,

George, Barbara 2011, 'Mary Cecil Allen (1893–1962): Expatriate Australian and apostle of art', Master of Arts, University of Adelaide.

SELECT SECONDARY SOURCES

Alexander, Penelope F.B. 2006, *Frankie Derham: A refuge within*, Oryx Publishing, St Kilda, Vic.

Allen, Harry 1907, 'Australian studies', *The Speculum: Journal of the Melbourne Medical Students' Society*, no. 68, May, pp. 29–35.

Allen, Harry 1914, *University of Melbourne Medical School Jubilee, 1914*, Ford & Son, Melbourne.

Allen, Mary Cecil 1928, *The Mirror of the Passing World*, W.W. Norton and Company, New York.

——1929, *Painters of the Modern Mind*, W.W. Norton and Company, New York.

——1935, 'Craft work of today', *Argus*, 17 October, p. 12.

Ambler, Eric 1985, *Here Lies: An autobiography*, Weidenfeld and Nicolson, London.

Ambrus, Caroline 1984, *The Ladies' Picture Show: Sources on a century of Australian women artists*, Hale & Iremonger, Sydney.

Bailey, K.H. 1957, 'Sir Robert Garran', *The Australian Quarterly*, vol. 29, March, pp. 9–15.

Basler, Adolphe 1928, *La Sculpture Moderne en France*, Les Editions G. Cres & Cie., Paris.

Besant, Annie 1927, *The New Civilisation*: four lectures delivered at the Queen's hall, London in June 1927, Theosophical Publishing House Limited, London.

——1896, *The Future that Awaits Us*, Theosophical Society, London.

Besterman, Theodore 1934, 'Mrs Annie Besant: Being the substance of an address delivered at a meeting of the London Lodge on the 25th November 1895 by Mrs. Besant', Kegan, Paul, Trench, Trubner & Co., London.

Borg, Alan 1991, *War Memorials*, Leo Cooper, London.

Borzello, Frances 2000, *A World of Our Own: Women as artists*, Thames and Hudson, London.

Bowen, Stella 1941, *Drawn From Life: Reminiscences*, Collins, London.

Boyd, Martin 1965, *Day of My Delight: An Anglo-Australian Memoir*, Lansdowne, Melbourne.

Burke, Janine 1980, *Australian Women Artists 1840–1940*, Greenhouse Publications, Collingwood, Vic.

Burton , John Hill 1851, *Emigrant's Manual Australia, New Zealand, America, South Africa*, William and Robert Chambers, Edinburgh.

Butler, Nicholas Murray 1939, *Across the Busy Years: Recollections and reflections*, Charles Scribner's Sons New York, London.

Butler, Rex & Donaldson, Andrew 2010, 'The complex issue of expatriate artists: "Trans Pacifica and moderns on the move"', Art Association of Australia and New Zealand Conference, Adelaide, 1–4 December.

Campbell, F.A. 1925, *The Working Men's College in the Making 1887–1913*, Working Men's College, Melbourne.

Casey, Maie 1962, *An Australian Story 1837–1907*, Michael Joseph, London.

Casey, Maie 1966, *Tides and Eddies*, Michael Joseph, London.

Chavchavadze, David 1990, *The Grand Dukes*, Atlantic International Publications, New York.

Clarke, Clarke 1934, *Marriage at 6 a.m*, Gollancz, London.

Cockfield, Jamie H 2002, *White Crow: The life and times of the Grand Duke Nicholas Mikhailovich Romanov, 1859–1919*, Praeger, Westport, CT.

Colahan, Colin 1919, *Max Meldrum, His Art and Views*, Alexander McCubbin, Melbourne.

Collins, Diane 2009, 'Henri Vergrugghen's auditory Utopianism: sound, reform, modernity and nation in Australia, 1915–1922', *History Australia*, vol. 6, no. 2, pp. 36.1–36.18.

Collins, Joseph 1919, *My Italian Year*, Charles Scribner's Sons, New York.

Colquhoun, Alexander (ed.) 1923, *Year Book of Victorian Art*, A. McCubbin, Melbourne.

Coppel, Stephen 1995, *Linocuts of the Machine Age: Claude Flight and the Grosvenor School*, Scolar Press, Aldershot Hants.

Cork, Richard 1994, *A Bitter Truth: Avant-garde art and the Great War*, Yale University Press in association with Barbican Art Gallery, New Haven, CT.

Croll, Robert Henderson 1939, *I Recall: Collections and recollection*, Robertson and Mullens, Melbourne.

Damousi, Joy et al. 2007, *Talking and Listening in the Age of Modernity*, Australian National University Press, Canberra.

Davidson, Jim 1994, *Lyrebird Rising: Louise Hanson-Dyer of Oiseau Lyre, 1884–1962*, Melbourne University Press at the Miegunyah Press, Carlton, Vic.

Dennie, John 1909, *Rome of Today and Yesterday: The pagan city*, G.P. Putnam's Sons, New York.

Derham, Enid 1912, *Empire: A morality play for children*, Victorian League of Victoria, Melbourne.

Derham, Frances 1995, 'Mary Cecil Allen', in Joan Kerr (ed.), *Heritage: The national women's art book*, Craftsman House, Roseville East, NSW, pp. 302–3.

Dixon, Robert & Veronica Kelly (eds) 2008, *Impact of the Modern: Vernacular modernities in Australia 1870s–1960s*, Sydney University Press, Sydney.

Drayer, R.A. 2005, *Nicholas and Helena Roerich: The spiritual journey of two great artists and peacemakers*, Quest Books, Wheaton, Ill.

Dyson, Will 1933, *Artist Among the Bankers*, J.M. Dent, London.

Eagle, Mary & Jan Minchin 1981, *The George Bell School: Students, friends, influences*, Resolution Press, Sydney.

Earnest, Ernest 1968, *Expatriates and Patriots: American artists, scholars and writers in Europe*, Duke University Press, Durham, NC.

Edwards, Deborah 1995, 'Dora Ohlfsen' in Joan Kerr (ed.), *Heritage: The national women's art book*, Craftsman House, Roseville East, NSW, p. 251.

Edwards, Deborah 1995, 'Dorothea Ohlfsen Bagge', in Joan Kerr (ed.), *Heritage: The national women's art book*, Craftsman House, Roseville East, NSW, pp. 420–21.

Edwards, Deborah 1999, *'This Vital Flesh: The sculpture of Rayner Hoff and his school*, Art Gallery of New South Wales, Sydney.

Eldredge, Charles C. 1982, *Charles Walter Stetson: Color and fantasy*, Spencer Museum of Art, Lawrence, Kansas.

Fay, Amy 1885, *Music Study in Germany from the Home Correspondence of Amy Fay*, Macmillan and Co, London.

Featherstone, Guy 1976, 'Louis Lawrence Smith (1830–1910)', *Australian Dictionary Biography*, vol. 6: 1851–1890, Melbourne University Press, Victoria, pp. 151–2.

Fenton, James 2006, *School of Genius: A history of the Royal Academy of Arts*, Royal Academy, London.

Fitzpatrick, Brian 1956, *The Australian Commonwealth*, F.W. Cheshire, Melbourne.

Fitzpatrick, Kathleen 1975, *PLC Melbourne: The first century, 1875–1975*, Presbyterian Ladies College, Burwood, Victoria.

Forrer, L. 1909, *Biographical Dictionary of Medallists*, Spink and Son, London.

France, Christine 1995, 'Exhibition of British contemporary art' in Joan Kerr (ed.), *Heritage: The national women's art book*, Craftsman House, Roseville East, NSW, pp. 24–5.

France, Christine 1995, 'Alleyne Clarice Zander', in Joan Kerr (ed.), *Heritage: The national women's art book*, Craftsman House, Roseville East, NSW, pp. 479–80

Fry, Roger 1926, *Art and Commerce*, The Hogarth Press, London.

Gabin, Jane S. 2006, *American Women in Gilded Age London: Expatriates rediscovered*, University Press of Florida, Florida.

Gaze, Delia 1997, *Dictionary of Women Artists*, Fitzroy Dearborn Publishers, Chicago.

Grant, Frances R. et al. 1926, *Himalaya: Banners of the East*, Brentano, New York.

Graves, W. Brooke 1928, *Readings in Public Opinion*, D. Appleton-Century Company, New York.

Greer, Germaine 1979, *The Obstacle Race*, Secker and Warburg, London.

Herlin, Denis 2006, *Catalogue of the Hanson-Dyer Music Collection, The University of Melbourne*, Lyrebird Press, Melbourne.

Hirschfeld, Magnus 1934, *The Sexual History of the World War*, The Panurge Press, New York.

Holroyd, Michael 1996, *Augustus John*, Chatto & Windus, London.

Howe, Maud 1909, *Roma Beata: Letters from the Eternal City*, Little, Brown & Co., Boston.

Hudnut, Joseph 1929, *Modern Sculpture*, WW Norton & Company, New York.

Hudson, Philip B. 1933, *Thesis on the Shrine of Remembrance*, Shrine of Remembrance, Melbourne.

Hull, Robert H. 1927, *Contemporary Music*, The Hogarth Press, London.

Kalb, Judith E. 2008, *Russia's Rome: Imperial visions, messianic dreams, 1890–1940*, University of Wisconsin Press, Madison, Wisconsin.

Kingston, Beverley 1975, *My Wife, My Daughter and Poor Mary Ann: Women and work in Australia*, Thomas Nelson Australia, Melbourne.

Norman, Lilith 1983, *The Brown and Yellow, Sydney Girls High School 1883–1983*, Oxford University Press, Melbourne,

Lloyd, Andrea 1996, 'The Mary Cecil Allen Story', *Meanjin*, vol. 55, no. 3, pp. 480–6.

Locke, Ralph P. 1997, *Cultivating Music in America: Women patrons and activists since 1860*, University of California Press, Berkeley.

Lozowick, Louis 1947, *100 Contemporary American Jewish Painters and Sculptors*, NKUF, New York.

Lucas, E.V. 1926, *A Wanderer in Rome*, Methuen & Co. Ltd, London.

Lukacs, John 1998, *A Thread of Years*, Yale University Press, New Haven, CT.

McCredie, A.D. 1979, *Musicological Studies in Australia from the Beginnings to the Present*, Sydney University Press, Sydney.

Mack, Louise 1898, *Girls Together*, Angus and Robertson, Sydney.

Mack, Louise 1915, *A Woman's Experiences in the Great War*, T. Fisher Unwin Ltd, London.

MacKenzie, Andrew 1990, *Frederick McCubbin 1855–1917: The Proff, and his art*, Mannagum Press, Lilydale, Vic.

Macleod, Diane 2008, *Enchanted Lives, Enchanted Objects: American women collectors and the making of culture 1800–1940*, University of California Press, Berkeley, CA.

Mairet, Philip 1966, *A.R. Orage*, University Books, London.

Mannin, Ethel 1936, *Confessions and Impressions*, Hutchinson, London.

Marsh, Edward 1939, *A Number of People: A book of reminiscences*, W. Heinemann Ltd, London.

McCarthy, Kathleen D. 1991, *Women's Culture: American philanthropy and art, 1830–1930*, University of Chicago Press, Chicago, Ill.

McCarthy, Kathleen D. 2001, *Women, Philanthropy and Civil Society*, Indiana University Press, Bloomington, Ind.

McMullin, Ross 2006, *Will Dyson: Australia's radical genius*, Scribe, Melbourne.

Melba, Nellie 1926, *Melodies and Memories*, Dorran Company, New York.

Mermaid Play Society 1920? 'Notes on the five plays to be produced, season 1919–20', with Illustrations by Mary Allen, The Specialty Press, Melbourne.

Moore, William 1906, *Studio Sketches: A Jubilee volume, glimpses of Melbourne studio life*, William Moore, Melbourne.

Negri, Antonello 2012, *The Thirties: The arts in Italy beyond fascism*, Palazzo Strozzi, Florence.

Nichols, Beverley 1958, *The Sweet and Twenties*, Weidenfeld and Nicolson, London.

Nicolson, Harold 1939, *Why Britain is at War*, Penguin, Harmondsworth, Eng.

Oliphant, Mrs 1895, *The Makers of Modern Rome*, Macmillan and Co, London.

Peers, Juliette 1992, 'A rare and difficult art', *The Medal*, no. 21.

Peers, Juliette 2003, 'May I introduce Miss Cumbrae Stewart?', in *Janet Cumbrae Stewart: The perfect touch*, Mornington Peninsula Regional Gallery, Mornington, Vic.

Pesman, Ros 1991, 'Australian images of Rome', in *Bolletino del C.I.R.V.I*, no. 23, January–June, pp. 49–68.

Pesman, Ros 1994, 'Some Australian Italies', *Westerly*, no. 4, Summer, pp. 95–104.

Pesman, Ros 1995, *Duty Free: Australian women abroad*, Oxford University Press, Melbourne.

Pesman, Ros 1996, 'The Italian Renaissance in Australia', *Parergon*, no. 14.1, July, pp. 223–39.

Petrov, Vsevolod Nikolayevich 1997, *Russian Art Nouveau: The world of art and Diaghilev's painters*, Parkstone, Bournemouth.

Pierpont, Claudie Roth 2000, *Passionate Minds: Women rewriting the world*, Alfred A. Knopf, New York.

Pigot, John 2001, *Norman Macgeorge: Man of art*, Ian Potter Museum, Melbourne.

Pillsbury, W.B. 1919, *The Psychology of Nationality and Internationalism*, D. Appleton and Company, New York.

Porter, Muriel (ed.) 2003, *The Argus: The life and death of a great Melbourne newspaper (1846–1957)*, RMIT Publishing, Melbourne.

Powell, Violet 1978, *Margaret Countess of Jersey: A biography*, Heinemann, London.

Prampolini, Gaetano & Marie-Christine Hubert (eds) 1993, *An Antipodean Connection: Australian writers, artists and travellers in Tuscany*, Slatkine, Geneva.

Pratt, Ambrose 1934, *The Centenary History of Victoria*, Robertson & Mullens, Melbourne.

Pratt, Ambrose 1936, *The National War Memorial of Victoria: The Shrine of Remembrance*, W.D. Joynt, Melbourne.

Radic, Therese 1986, *Melba: The voice of Australia*, Macmillan, Melbourne.

Rees, A. 2010, 'Mary Cecil Allen: modernism and modernity in Melbourne 1935–1960', *electronic Melbourne Art Journal*, no. 5.

Rivett, Rohan 1965, *Herbert Brookes, Australian Citizen*, Melbourne University Press, Melbourne.

Rodd, Sir Rennell 1932, *Rome of the Renaissance and To-day*, Macmillan and Co, London.

Roe, Jill 1986, *Beyond Belief: Theosophy in Australia 1879–1939*, University of New South Wales Press, Sydney.

Royal Academy 1978, *A Dictionary of Artists and Their Work in the Summer Exhibitions of the Royal Academy of Arts, Royal Academy Exhibitors 1905–1970*, EP Publishing Limited, Wakefield, Yorkshire.

Rutter, Frank 1924, *The Little Book of the Royal Academy of Nineteen Twenty-four: Being a rapid guide to the more important features*, G.T. Foulis & Company Ltd, London.

Rutter, Frank 1933, *Art in My Time*, Rich & Cowan, London.

St John Moore, Felicity 1995, 'Mary Cecil Allen', in Joan Kerr (ed.), *Heritage: The national women's art book*, Craftsman House, Roseville East, NSW, p. 291.

Selinvanova, Nina 1924, *World of Roerich*, Corona Mundi, International Art Centre, New York.

Selzer, Anita 1994, *Educating Women in Australia: From the Convict Era to the 1920s*, Cambridge University Press, Cambridge.

Silver, Kenneth E. 2011, *Chaos and Classicism: Art in France, Italy and Germany, 1918–1936*, Guggenheim Museum, New York.

Speck, Catherine 2004, *Painting Ghosts: Australian women artists in wartime*, Craftsman House, Melbourne.

Speck, Catherine & Downey, G 2008, 'Cosmopolitanism and modernism: on writing a new Australian art history', *Australian and New Zealand Journal of Art*, vol. 9, no. 1/2, pp. 101–117.

Sturgeon, Graeme 1978, *The Development of Australian Sculpture, 1788–1975*, Thames and Hudson, London.

Swann, Herbert 1968, *Home on the Neva: A life of a British family in Tsarist St Petersburg – and after the Revolution*, Victor Gollancz Ltd, London.

Theobald, Marjorie 1996, *Knowing Women: Origins of women's education in Nineteenth-Century Australia*, Cambridge University Press, Cambridge.

Topliss, Helen 1996, *Modernism and Feminism: Australian women artists, 1900–1940*, Craftsman House, Roseville East, NSW.

Waters, Thorold 1951, *Much Besides Music: Memoirs of Thorold Waters*, Georgian House, Melbourne.

Willis, Anne-Mariel 1993, *Illusions of Identity: The art of nation*, Hale & Iremonger, Sydney.

Wilson, Francesca 1970, *Muscovy: Russia through foreign eyes 1553–1900*, George Allen & Unwin, London.

Vsevolod, Petrov 1997, *Russian Art Nouveau: The world of art and Diaghilev's painters*, Parkstone Press, Bournemouth, England.

Wren, Jenny 1926, *Gurglings of an Australian Magpie*, The Specialty Press, Melbourne.

Zander, Alleyne Clarice 1934, 'Two modern groups', *Art in Australia*, 3rd series, no. 56, August, pp. 56–61.

Zander, Alleyne Clarice 1934, 'Individualists', *Art in Australia*, 3rd series, no. 57, November, pp. 54–6.

Zander, Alleyne Clarice 1935, 'The exhibition of British Art in Industry Exhibition', *Art in Australia*, 3rd series, no. 59, May, pp. 41–3.

Zander, Alleyne Clarice 1935, 'Negro art, Vlaminck and Epstein's religious carvings', *Art in Australia*, 3rd series, no. 60, August, pp. 52–4.

Zander, Alleyne Clarice 1935, 'Impressionism and the English painter', *Art in Australia*, 3rd series, no. 61, November, pp. 65–8.

Zander, Alleyne Clarice 1936, 'International exhibition of Chinese art in London', *Art in Australia*, 3rd series, no. 62, February, pp. 51–4.

INDEX